KT-454-837

The

Red

Flannel

Rag

Memories of An
Appalachian Childhood

Peggy Ann Shifflett

Peggy Ann Shifflett

The Red Flannel Rag: Memories of an Appalachian Childhood, by Peggy Ann Shifflett.

The Red Flannel Rag: *Memories of an Appalachian Childhood* © Peggy Ann Shifflett, 2004

Published by Brightside Press, Radford, Virginia 2004
540-633-6747; brightside@nrvdc.org;
www.brightsidepress.com

ISBN: 1-888813-11-3

Photos courtesy of: Shirley and Ethel Morris; Joyce Crawford; Ethel Knight Wilfong; Brenda Shifflett Rhodes; Myrtle Shifflett; National Geographic Society; The Author

The people, places and events described in this book are factual. However, out of respect for family members, in some instances fictional names of people have been used in place of their real names.

References can be found on page 335.

CONTENTS

Peggy Ann Shifflett

ACKNOWLEDGEMENTS

Thank you Mom for sharing with me, in your beautiful, honest language, all the community secrets, family secrets, and your secrets. Thank you for your little push and your support as I drifted away from the mountain tradition, and thanks for holding me back just enough to give me time to appreciate it.

Thank you Dad for your incredible memory and your devotion to sharing Hopkins Gap history with your children. Thank you for passing on to me your curiosity and intellect.

Thank you Uncle Shirley, Uncle Jim, and Aunt Goldie for choosing and trusting me as the depository of Hopkins Gap history and stories. Thank you Uncle Shirley and Aunt Ethel for permission to use your pictures to illustrate my memories. Thank you Dr. Elmer Smith for offering me the opportunity to appreciate my rich heritage.

Thank you Dr. Dorothy Rowe for naming this book and for your editorial work and encouragement in the early stages of the writing. Thank you for offering me a pillow and good food on my trips back home to fill in the blanks in my memory.

Thank you Virginia Balzerak, Katrina Mabery, Angelika Kaite, Evelyn Jordan, Audrey Boggs for your persistent encouragement and unwarranted exclamations of the value of earlier drafts that kept me working on the manuscript.

Thank you to my colleagues at Radford University: Dr. Grace Edwards, Dr. Melinda Wagner, Dr. Stevan Jackson, Dr. Nelda Pearson, Dr. Mary Lalone for reading early versions and offering comments and encouragement. Thanks to all my students who listened to various sections of this book as they related to class material.

Thank you Scottie and Bucky Pritchard for your encouragement and for use of your peaceful home on Elk Creek where I could plug in my computer and ignore you on many occasions as I was inspired to work on this book in the midst of your great company.

Peggy Ann Shifflett

Thank you for the wonderful food, hikes, sights, and inspiring conversations.

Thanks to all my relatives in Hopkins Gap, present and past, who live and lived lives worthy of committing to permanent record. I have changed some of your names so as to make your stories less personal.

Thanks to Hilda May Woolwine of Brightside Press for editorial comments and suggestions for the final product.

**DEDICATED TO THE MEMORY OF TWO
HARD-WORKING, HONEST PEOPLE**

Norman C. Shifflett and
Myrtle Morris Shifflett,
Dad and Mom,

and to their descendants

Peggy Ann Shifflett

PROLOGUE

My phone rang at 7:15 in the morning on December 10, 2001. When I answered it was my sister, Brenda. I braced myself for the onslaught of her voice yelling about Mom being home from the hospital when she really needed to be in a nursing home. I knew Brenda and Hilda were very tired and stressed after five years of twenty-four hour care giving. Brenda gave up her job so she could spend the daylight hours with Mom. Hilda gave up her nights with her family. But this time Brenda's voice was quiet and calm, "Peg, I believe this is the day that Mom is going to die." "What are you saying?" I answered, trying not to panic. "She can't die today. It's her birthday." My sister was silent on the other end of the line as I considered the possibility that Mom would die on her birthday. She was turning eighty-one today.

I concluded, after what seemed like an hour, that to choose to die on her birthday would be classic Myrtle Shifflett. She had continued to make all choices related to her life up until this day. She had just insisted on returning home from the hospital two days before her birthday although her doctors had recommended recovery and rehabilitation in a nursing home. I immediately knew that Mom was still in charge of her life and was choosing her birthday to die so her life would have no frayed edges such as eighty-one years and one month. She was choosing for her life to be exactly eighty-one years. I said to my sister, "She just got well enough to come home to die. I will be there in two hours."

The drive seemed to last forever as my mind considered what I would face when I got there. If in fact she was dying, would she struggle and cling? Would she know me? She had been so sick so many times before, and she hadn't died. Was this just another false alarm? What would life be like without Mom? I didn't bring any clothes to wear to her funeral. I'm glad I didn't bring clothes, what would people think if I arrived with clothes to wear to a funeral and she didn't die? She couldn't be dying because she had just gotten well enough to be released from the hospital. She must be stronger than I thought. She had just gone through major surgery. She was home now, and she always improved when she came home after each crisis. How would I be able to be with her and let her go if she was dying? Could this be the moment I had been dreading for my entire life?

Finally, the trip ended with me pulling up in front of Mom's house. There was only one car there — Brenda's. Maybe Mom had rallied? I expected more cars when I drove up. I walked in the house. My sister was in the kitchen washing dishes. Everything seemed normal — this was another false alarm.

I knew that Mom was in a hospital bed in the living room, so I walked slowly to the door. Her eyes immediately met mine, and she said my name, "Peggy." I walked to her bed and took her hand. I said, "Happy birthday, Mom. Are you feeling bad today?" She shook her head yes, and a faint smile came to her lips. She looked deeply into my eyes and said, "Help me, I'm afraid."

I knew then she was really dying, so I told her, "Mom, close your pretty eyes and rest." She closed her eyes and her breathing became slower and very calm. I told my sister that she was really dying this time. We called my brothers and as many of her grandchildren as we could find.

All my brothers came home and each had a few minutes alone with Mom. As each one approached her bed and held her hand, she opened her eyes and acknowledged that she knew him. She did the same with the grandchildren as they arrived.

With each new visitor to her bedside, she asked for Hilda who had been her daily companion for nearly forty years. Hilda had gone away that morning to take her own father to the hospital for a blood transfusion — a regular routine for him now. Warnie's wife, Dianne, is a nurse. She arrived and began to monitor Mom's heart rate and blood pressure. Both were slowly dropping.

After Mom had said goodbye to everyone except Hilda, she slipped into a mild coma. She was very calm and appeared to be resting. An hour later, Hilda returned. She walked behind Mom's bed and took her hand. Mom awakened from her coma and acknowledged Hilda's presence. Then she immediately began the final stages of the dying process—her breathing changed, and her skin became cold. She slipped back into a deeper coma.

For a period of time, while she was in the coma, Mom was talking as if she was carrying on a conversation with someone. We couldn't understand what she was saying or to whom she was talking. I wondered if she was talking to God. Mom had never returned to church after I refused to be confirmed at age twelve. She remained half mad at the Mennonites for the rest of her life.

About two years ago, a Mennonite preacher had visited her in the hospital during a crisis. He stayed in the room with her for about fifteen minutes. When he walked out, he looked at Brenda and me and said, "That's the hardest woman I have ever tried to talk to." Fortunately for him he was striding down the hospital hall as he made the remark. We were both shocked and appalled.

When we went back in the room with Mom, I asked her what had happened. She said, "He wanted me to renew my membership in the church and accept Jesus Christ as my savior. I didn't like his attitude. I am not ready to die yet. I told him to leave and not come back." I forgave the preacher a little after that remark, but still think his comment was unnecessary.

Hilda stayed by Mom's side and caressed her cheeks and forehead, telling her to relax. Suddenly, Hilda looked at me and said, "Mary Kirkpatrick's picture fell off the wall in the dining room this morning at 4:00 a.m." I had no doubt then that Mom was leaving us on her birthday. My mind went back to a discussion she had with me within the last year. She told me about the Vienna sausages that she and Bonny Crawford had stolen from Mary Kirkpatrick's store many years before. Mom was concerned at the time that stealing those sausages might keep her out of heaven.

I wondered if Mary was sending a message of forgiveness to Mom when her picture fell off the wall. The picture had been hanging in the same place since 1961. Why did it fall on this day? I

11

walked into the dining room. Hilda had picked the picture off the floor. It was lying on the table. I picked it up and looked at the back.

"Did the nail hole tear?" I wondered to myself as I studied the back of the picture. "The nail hole didn't tear," I said to Hilda. I checked the nail in the wall. It was still there and had not slipped. There was no identifiable reason for the picture suddenly falling off the wall.

I went back to Mom's bedside. She had slipped deeper into the coma. Her breathing was more shallow and not as frequent, but very peaceful. Hilda was still holding her hand and caressing her forehead. Dianna told us the end was very near. We gathered around the bed.

Just as we all settled around Mom's bed, she opened her eyes and looked up. Her eyes were focused and staring. We knew she was seeing something the rest of us could not see. Hilda asked her, "What do you see, Mom? Do you see Pap up there with a big birthday cake? Are all your friends waitin' for you to come to your birthday party." Mom's mouth opened in a huge smile, as she continued to stare at the ceiling. At that moment, her head rolled to the left, and she died.

Hilda, with tears rolling down her checks and an angelic glow on her face, looked up at all of us standing around the bed and said, "Now she's up there telling them they didn't bake the birthday cake right. I can hear her now, 'What did y'all put in this icing?'"

The comment was so appropriate. The same image came into everyone's head. Mom was now judging the talents of the cooks in heaven. We all broke into laughter and began our own comments. My sister said with a smile between sobs, "Now she's looking around for the lemon meringue pie." One of the granddaughters quipped, "Now she's asking who made the coconut cream pie because it doesn't taste right." At the very end of her life, Mom was still taking care of her family. Her final smile and Hilda's comment softened the fact that this was our last moment with her.

Shortly after she died we realized we needed to make funeral arrangements. Who would preach her funeral? She had never let us talk to her about whom she might want to preach or what kind of funeral she wanted. I asked, "Has any preacher been to visit her lately? Larry said, "Wendell Henkel has been in the hospital to see her. He was just in there last Thursday—the day before she came home."

Suddenly I knew what kind of funeral she would want. It was so appropriate. Wendell's daddy had hauled her cow's milk to the processing plant for years. After Charlie Henkel died, Wendell took over his business for some years, and he hauled her milk to the dairy. She had a life-long connection to Wendell Henkel who was now a lay Presbyterian minister. I suggested that we call him, and everybody agreed that he was the only one she would want to preach her funeral.

Sometime after her last breath, the undertaker arrived to remove her body. This was a very difficult moment for me. She had always loved her home, and I knew this was the last time she would go out the door as she started her journey to the cemetery to sleep next to Dad forever.

I walked to the back yard as far as I could get from the hearse so I didn't have to watch her body leave the house. Just at the moment her body was carried across the front yard, someone called my name. I looked up as the undertakers walked past the lilac bush and started to put Mom's body in the hearse. At that very moment, a few drops of rain began to fall. My mind immediately returned to when I was five years old and the day of Uncle Rob's funeral, when I had heard Mom's voice say, "Happy is the corpse that the rain falls on."

13

Peggy Ann Shifflett

INTRODUCTION

*"Let us be intimate with ancestral ghosts
And music of the undead."*
Alice Walker (1)

I always thought of graveyards as silent, sad, and desolate places, and in fact they are for those who are buried there. However, when I visit Mom and Dad's grave in the cemetery at Gospel Hill Mennonite Church, my memory comes alive. Memories of growing up in my small Appalachian Mountain community, and my experiences with all the people buried here, begin to flow into my mind.

In plain view of Mom and Dad's headstone is the grave of Tom Crawford, shot in the back and killed by revenue agents while he was making moonshine. Just up the hill to the right is Jesse Craig's headstone. I remember him as a tall, skinny man filled with stories of witches. Uncle Shirley bragged about the varieties of wine produced by Jesse Craig. Tomato and potato wine, rhubarb and cucumber wine are a few that come to mind as I look at his headstone. Every time I visit the cemetery, I cannot help but smile as I remember my favorite Jesse Craig story. The revenue agents came to his house in disguise to catch him selling his homemade wine. They asked him to buy some wine, but he refused to sell to them. Instead, he offered them a glass or two. By the time they left, they were so drunk he had to lead them to their car.

The cemetery lies across a low ridge on either side of the small white, clapboard church. Thick, dark woods surround the cemetery on two sides. The boundary on one side is a little stream called Mash Run, named for the amount of moonshine made there during the 1930s and 1940s. On the other side is Long Run Road where Uncle Shirley drove the truck to take the Sunday school kids on picnics after church.

The burial pattern reflects the eternal connection to family and the man as the head of the household. My daddy is buried in the Shifflett row along with his brothers and sisters. Grandpa Austin and Grandma Molly are buried at the beginning of the Shifflett row. There is space in the Shifflett row for my final resting place since I never married and cannot be buried beside my husband in his or her family burial row.

Just behind the Shifflett row is the Morris row. Grandpa John and Grandma Mary were the first buried in that row. Just up the hill is the crude river-rock headstone of Great Grandpa Banks Shifflett. The midwives, who helped bring into the world most of the people born in the community and buried here, were laid to rest just behind the Morris row.

The way we lived and died and buried the dead seemed very normal to me when I was a young child. I never questioned how we lived in my mountain community.

The Red Flannel Rag Gives Me Away

It was the first cold day in October, 1947, when I learned that I was different from the other kids in first grade. My cousin Virgil stepped off the school bus with a red flannel rag tied around his neck. Our classmates and the teacher responded to the rag with curiosity at first, and then they asked Virgil why he was wearing the rag. He answered, "Mama put it on me because it's cold outside today. She said if I wear it, I won't get a sore throat or a cold."

Virgil, wearing the red flannel rag, was the laughing stock of the whole school. The children in first grade laughed at him. When he went to the lunchroom other kids laughed, and when he went to recess after lunch, even more children joined in to point and laugh.

I knew exactly why Virgil was wearing the rag. It could as easily have been my neck. Mom was just a little late with the red flannel rag preventative that particular fall. I felt lucky she hadn't tied one on me that morning.

16

The teacher, Miss Arlene, was curious as to why the children were laughing. She asked what was so funny and they said, "That thing around Virgil's neck." She looked at Virgil and walked over to his desk as all the children turned their heads and watched. She touched the rag and asked him what it was. Virgil sheepishly explained the reason he was wearing it.

Miss Arlene chuckled along with Virgil's classmates. She told him, "Colds and sore throats are caused by germs that travel through the air. They go up your nose or down your throat when you breathe. Once you have the germs you have to treat them on the inside of your body. Wearing a rag around your neck won't keep you from getting a cold or sore throat."

Virgil was silenced and humiliated, but he continued to wear his red flannel rag day after day because he trusted his mother's opinion over the teacher's opinion. He continued to tell the truth when his way of life was questioned. He dropped out of school in the third grade.

Virgil's experience effectively changed my behavior and made me begin to question my community's way of living. There was no way I was going to school with a red flannel rag around my neck. Although I resisted having it tied on my neck, my mother insisted that I wear it. I just made sure I took it off on the school bus before I arrived at school.

The other children in my first grade were bussed in from Dayton or Bridgewater or lived in the Mt. Clinton area. They made up the vast majority of the students at Mt. Clinton Elementary School. Two busses brought the mountain children to school. The red flannel rag incident was only the first sign that I was not like the other kids in our school who didn't ride across Little North Mountain on my school bus. As each incident occurred, I realized more and more that to avoid humiliation for being different, I needed to watch and listen before I wore something to school that my mother wanted me to wear.

I grew up living in two very different worlds separated by a narrow range of the Allegheny Mountains called Little North

Mountain. I was born and raised in an Appalachian community, but I went to school with mainstream American children just a few miles outside that community. I often picture myself straddling Little North Mountain with one foot in my small Appalachian community and the other foot in the Shenandoah Valley of Virginia. I am facing westward in my picture, so my right foot is in Appalachia, and my left foot in the Shenandoah Valley–a very different, mainstream American world. Many times during recent years I have brought this picture to mind when I needed to understand my responses to everyday situations and challenges.

All of my life I have felt the effects of living with my feet separated by a mountain. My right foot was embedded in traditional Appalachian Mountain culture. Here I identified with family and community commitment foremost. My left foot led me, sometimes reluctantly, into mainstream American culture where I identified with competition, achievement, and individuality.

There was another dimension to my divided identities. My Appalachian community was not highly regarded in the outside world just a short distance away. So when I was outside my community, I heard Shenandoah Valley folks talk about my people in very negative ways. But when I was in my mountain community watching the events at a hog killing or an apple butter boiling, I felt very comfortable. I felt a sense of connectedness and continuity. I knew I was going to enjoy that apple butter with a nice, big slice of Dad's home-cured ham in the winter months to come. I safely anticipated these mouth-watering treats because I had enjoyed them the year before and the year before that.

I loved my community, but I also felt ashamed of it when I heard outsiders discuss the latest news-making events. People talked for a long time about how one community member stood on his porch with his twelve-gauge shotgun and blew large holes in a father and son also from the community. I heard folks say the fight started over a gallon of moonshine. Judgments were made about the worth of a gallon of moonshine compared to two lives, and they commented about how the people in my community didn't know or didn't care about the difference.   At the same time, I was never totally comfortable in the Shenandoah Valley community.   As anyone can imagine, this was not a pleasant position from which to face each morning of my early life.

Even to this day, sixty years later, I frequently feel the contradictions that growing up and living in two different cultures inevitably brings. Most of my life now is spent in the mainstream American culture; however, my heart remains, at times, deeply embedded in the early tradition of my Appalachian community. When spring comes every year, I yearn to make a vegetable garden; and, as strawberry, cherry, and blackberry season roll around, I long to go pick, process, and prepare for winter pies and biscuits and jam. Vegetable canning season is difficult for me to pass through without "puttin' up" some tomatoes and green beans. A year ago, I bought pork tenderloin from the grocery store, borrowed a pressure canner, and   "put it up" for the cold winter months ahead.   As I went through the process of canning the pork, I thought about opening a can of tenderloin on Sunday mornings and making a pan of gravy to eat over homemade biscuits. On the practical level, I know I don't need to hunt and gather to survive, but gathering and preserving for the cold weather months is still a part of who I am today.

My connection to Appalachian tradition shocks me at other times. Not long ago my brother, Warnie, told me a story about one of my uncles. Dad had shared the story with him when they were in the mountains cutting wood one day. It so happens that my uncle avenged the death of Tom Crawford, who, as I said before, was shot by a revenue agent while he was making moonshine.

It was always a mystery to me why my uncle left our community and moved to Ohio where he lived the remainder of his life. All eleven of his brothers and sisters lived out their lives in our home community.

When my brother told me about my uncle shooting the revenuer to avenge Tom's death, I felt tremendous pride — the same pride that my other uncles must have felt when they packed his clothes and fixed him some sandwiches for his escape to Ohio.

Then, I suddenly caught my breath as I found myself thinking of one of my uncles taking another person's life. Not only were his actions illegal, but, by my values today, they were immoral and intolerable. Also, he was one of my favorite uncles, the most gentle of all. I looked forward to his occasional visits to our house. He caught me smoking my very first pack of cigarettes when I was about eight years old. Instead of whipping me, he put me on his knee and gave me a gentle talking to about how bad cigarettes were for me—how they would turn my new teeth brown and make it hard for me to breathe.

So growing up in Appalachian tradition and eventually leaving to make my way in a different culture resulted in my becoming a person with two identities. Once I embraced the values of the world outside my community, I no longer belonged totally in the mountains. Because Appalachian tradition was so deeply instilled in me, I have never been totally comfortable in the world outside the mountains. Yet I have also, at times, felt ashamed of the way my people lived. So I was destined, by circumstances, as thousands before me, to "straddle" two different cultures separated by a small mountain range. Never fully fitting in either world filled me with conflict that only those who have experienced divided identities can understand.

As with all of life's events, the experience of growing up in two cultures is not all about discomfort. I think others who have had the same experience would agree that to survive one must become more attentive and mindful of the events of everyday life. The result for most folks is a deeper involvement in life.

As I gather my memories for this book, I realize that the most painful aspects of my growing up were the times when my mountain culture clashed with mainstream American culture. It first happened in school when Cousin Virgil wore "the red flannel rag" around his neck to prevent sore throat; it happened in church when the Mennonites, at times not so subtly, let us know we were not "born Mennonites" and would have to work especially hard to enter the kingdom of heaven; it happened when I spoke our language, filled with colorful metaphors, outside our community. Over time, the clashes became fewer and farther apart for me, but even today, as with the story of my uncle, I still experience an occasional incident of conflicting values.

After I graduated from high school, I worked for a short time in a women's lingerie factory. Cousin Ruby had worked there for years. In keeping with our community tradition, she had gotten her sister, Joyce, a job there and also found jobs for several other female cousins of ours. While I worked in the factory, Mom insisted I continue to watch the want ads in the newspaper and send applications to organizations that were advertising for secretarial help.

One day I got home from work and Mom told me I had gotten a phone call from Dr. Elmer L. Smith. He was a Professor of Anthropology at Madison College now James Madison University. He needed a secretary. He invited me for an interview. My world was still very small and therefore my radius of comfort was limited. This interview was going to be the first time I had interacted in the everyday world with a person who wasn't somehow connected to my community.

As the time for the interview grew near, I got more and more scared. Mom wanted me to have a job as a secretary so finally she said she would go with me to the interview. I assumed she meant she would actually sit with me while I was meeting with Dr. Smith, so I said I would go. When we arrived on campus and parked the car near his office, Mom said, "You go on in and talk to him I'll wait in the car." I told her she had tricked me. She argued, "He's not going to hire somebody who has to bring their mother with them. Now you go on." I was so scared. He would figure out I was from the mountains and never hire me. I wanted to run back to the lingerie factory and work with Cousin Ruby, but there was Mom sitting in the car watching me. For some reason, she didn't want me to work in a factory for the rest of my life. I shivered in my shoes as I slowly walked to Dr. Smith's office and knocked on the door. Dr. Smith interviewed me and had me type for him. A few days later he called and offered me the job.

I worked six hours a day for Dr. Smith and two hours for Dr. Dorothy Rowe. She was a nutritionist and headed the Home Economics Department. Both of these people immediately became very important influences in my life. Dr. Rowe went to Ohio State University to do some additional graduate work, and she invited me to ride the train to Columbus and spend the weekend with her. It was the first time I had been away from home overnight and definitely the first time I had left my community. That trip gave me the urge to travel and see more of the country someday.

Dr. Smith became fascinated with the people living in the isolated mountain communities west of Harrisonburg, Virginia, after he discovered an article in the *National Geographic*. The article emphasized the extensive isolation of these mountain hollows that had resulted in the maintenance of a very traditional way of life. The article reported that a long time ago, Pennsylvania Dutch culture and Scots-Irish culture had met in these mountains. Long-term isolation had resulted in some people still speaking Pennsylvania Dutch in their homes.

Dr. Smith showed me the article and pictures and, to my surprise, I recognized my daddy's sister, Aunt Vernie! There was a full-page picture of her standing in her kitchen stirring an iron skillet of fried potatoes on her wood-burning stove. She was dressed in her homemade bonnet, apron, and dress. The drinking-water bucket sat on a bench in the background with the dipper handle sticking up. Two cats stood behind Aunt Vernie enjoying the warmth of the wood stove.

Aunt Vernie, my Daddy's Sister, frying potatoes in 1949.
Printed with permission of the National Geographic Society.

I looked at the picture and realized that I had eaten many potatoes fried in that pan on that very stove. I had put wood in that stove, had taken many drinks of water from that very dipper, and had petted the offspring of the cat curled on the rug in front of the stove. I wanted to tell Dr. Smith that was my Aunt Vernie, but I couldn't tell him then.

I had looked at pictures in the *National Geographic* many times in school. Now here was my own Aunt Vernie. I never thought anybody from my family would be worthy of a picture in *National Geographic*, but there she stood stirring her fried potatoes.

23

I found myself in a bind. If I told Dr. Smith the woman in the picture was Aunt Vernie, then he would want to know more about my family and me. He might want me to take him to Aunt Vernie's house. At the same time, I felt very proud that somebody in my family had gotten their picture in a magazine. The people in the *National Geographic* were from faraway, exotic places so there must be something special about Aunt Vernie and the way she lived. Suddenly my mind was overwhelmed with the memories of Virgil's humiliation in the first grade and my own fear of humiliation. I still couldn't tell Dr. Smith that this woman was my daddy's sister.

Dr. Smith, inspired by the *National Geographic* article, started a massive research project with the mountain people, including the people of my community. He interviewed them as they talked about the red flannel rag and thousands of similar beliefs and practices. My job as his secretary included helping him collect his data and transcribe the interview tapes for him. He was overwhelmed by what we were finding and constantly talked about the beauty of this way of life and how it should be recorded. As time went by, I trusted Dr. Smith enough to talk about a few of my own experiences. One day he recognized that my silence had prevented me from being one of his first interviewees. He lectured me for hiding and denying my rich cultural heritage.

After I had worked for Dr. Smith for five years, he told me I should go to college. He insisted that I was too bright to be a secretary for the rest of my life. I didn't believe him, of course, but he continued to suggest I sign up for a college course during my lunch hour. A year later I got enough nerve to sign up for an introductory English composition class. I fell in love with reading and writing essays. Dr. Smith said he would help me get Office of Economic Opportunity grants and teaching loans if I wanted to go to college full time.

I began to talk to Mom about resigning my job and going to college. I told her I was thinking about selling my new car I had just bought and buy a cheaper car so I wouldn't have a car payment.

Mom said, "No, you are not selling your car and buy one that will break down with you."

I was really scared to let go of my job so I talked the situation over with Uncle Shirley. I always had a lot of respect for him. He advised me to not quit my job and go to college. He calculated how much money I would lose during the four years I would be in college and said, "You got a sure thing now, and it's not worth the risk." At about the same time, my cousin, Randy—my fishing and hunting partner—located a tract of land on top of Little North Mountain. He wanted me to buy it with him so we would always have a place to hunt squirrels.

Meanwhile, Mom, without discussing it with me, went to a bank in Harrisonburg and applied for student loans to pay off my car debt and reduce the payment to fifty-five dollars a month. While she was there, she made the first payment.

It was a difficult decision because the three people I respected most—Mom, Uncle Shirley, and Randy—were giving me opposing opinions, I was in a lot of conflict. It took a bizarre prediction from another cousin to make up my mind for me. He told me, "Your head won't be able to hold all the stuff you have to learn in college. You'll end up killing yourself." That was all I needed to hear. I was angered by his ignorance and lack of respect for me. I resigned my secretarial job and enrolled full time in college.

Learning was such fun for me. When I received my Bachelors degree, I enrolled in the Masters program in sociology. I taught four years at Madison College, resigned, and went to Texas to earn my Doctor of Philosophy Degree. I am now a Professor of Sociology.

This book is reclamation! Finally, forty years later, I have come to recognize the rich, beautiful heritage given to me by my ancestors and my community of birth. My purpose in this writing is to share my memories of my grandparents, aunts, and uncles. In my mountain community, life was enriched by colorful characters and great storytellers with memories sharpened by oral tradition. My generation, before television, was entertained with stories of witches, ghosts, and hoop snakes. We were made to feel a part of our community by participating in survival rituals such as hog-killing day and apple butter boilings. The memories I report here belong to me and only me. Others who grew up with me may have somewhat different memories or perceptions of events.

Why am I writing this now and not ten or twenty years ago? The time is right for several reasons. First, I have recently been challenged by Chellis Glendinning in her book titled *My Name is Chellis, and I'm in Recovery from Western Civilization*. She offers a personal challenge ". . . to embark upon the process of recovery from western civilization, by beginning to claim those parts of yourself and the earth that have been lost." Her book is about individual recovery from addictions and cultural recovery from ecological crisis using the wisdom of native cultures. Glendinning does not suggest, nor will I suggest, that we all wear red flannel rags but that we reclaim the "connectedness" that native peoples had to the universe, the earth, the community, and to each other.

Another reason I am telling my story at this time is that many people who have written about Appalachia have recognized that the traditional culture was founded on an unwavering respect for the earth. This has been referred to as a connection to "the land." It is my purpose to demonstrate that "connectedness" extended to all aspects of the universe including plants and animals, the solar system, and the weather. The same sense of "connectedness" was revealed in responsibilities to family and the community as a whole. Although specific beliefs and practices from traditional Appalachian culture have been recorded and reported, the simple logic that held "connectedness" in place has rarely been revealed in the context of reporting the beliefs and practices. Defining a logical context for my community will be a daunting task, and perhaps difficult for those born into mainstream America to grasp even if I successfully achieve this purpose.

A third reason for writing this book now is that I finally understand the discomfort I have always felt when exposed to folk festivals and academic conferences on Appalachian culture.

Participants at these events report Appalachian beliefs and practices in the fragmented, objective, and unfeeling way demanded by scientific investigation. Some have claimed pieces of Appalachian culture as their own and act them out for sale. The story of Appalachian culture is greater than the red flannel rag and its uses that can so readily be demonstrated in a classroom, at a folk festival, or at an academic conference.

Very few people who actually lived Appalachian culture have been able to claim it because they have been silenced from early childhood by being shamed at school and church and by invasion upon invasion of the "do-gooders," the academics, and the industrial robbers.

Some readers will want to think about what they read here, and they may want to be more reflective than the local colorists and less academic than the sociologists and anthropologists. Some readers will find only entertainment and amusement in this life of the not so distant past, and that is as it should be. But some readers, as they reflect on the life of these out-of-date Appalachian Mountain people, may be moved to only smile at its superficial crudities and to incorporate some of its fundamental values into their own lives.

Peggy Ann Shifflett

Part One

THE SETTING

Always a silence and content
Or evening bronze shadows
And blue fog beyond fathoming
Goes with the unforgotten.
Carl Sandburg (2)

The earliest days of my childhood began with familiar sounds and smells of morning. I awakened to Mom calling her cows to the barn for the morning milking and the sound of Dad stirring the slop bucket as he prepared to feed the fattening hogs. He carried the five-gallon bucket of table scraps mixed with bran and a little corn meal up the path to the hog pen located far from the house so the smell of pig manure wouldn't drift too close.

The roosters crowed at least an hour before to announce the sunrise. Other sounds that drifted into my upstairs bedroom window depended on the season of the year. In the early spring, the lambs on the hillside cried until they found the ewe's full teat. In the summer, free-ranging chicken hens followed by as many as a dozen baby chicks wandered around the yard clucking and singing while they scratched in the dirt for a breakfast of insects. The proud rooster father, with his head held high and his tail feather plumes giving off a rainbow of colors in the morning sun, stood guard near his hens and babies. In the fall the sound of rustling leaves dominated and winter often brought the cracking of icy limbs and the drip, drip, drip of snow melting and dripping from the house roof onto the front porch roof.

No matter what season, the smells from the kitchen were the same. The whiff of wood smoke announced a new fire in the

29

kitchen stove. Then there was the smell of sausage made from the hogs--raised, fattened, and butchered the year before. Mom always fried the sausage before she milked the cows. The aroma of fresh perked coffee would slowly waft its way to the bedroom I shared with my sister.

When Mom returned to the kitchen with the morning milk, she strained it through a clean cotton cloth into a glass pitcher. She reheated the iron skillet where she had fried the sausage, mixed in some flour, and browned it. Then she poured in a portion of the morning milk to make a huge skillet of milk gravy to eat with fresh, homemade biscuits. While her gravy was boiling, she completed our breakfast with fried eggs, gathered from the hen house the day before. A pot of oatmeal with raisins simmered on the back of the stove. Each day began with a comforting sense of predictability, a sense of routine that started with the sounds and smells from the kitchen and ended with Mom, Dad, my brothers and sister and me gathering around the table to partake of this early morning feast.

I was the oldest of five children, so I was twenty-one years old, working as a secretary while living at home, when this daily routine suddenly changed. My brother Larry decided to take a wife.

Most men in my mountain community had married girls in their teens and the couple lived with the male's parents for a period of time, mostly until the first baby was born. I know that Uncle Shirley married Aunt Ethel when she was fifteen, and Aunt Goldie became a wife at age twelve. I often heard it said that a man wanted his own mother to train his new wife to cook, clean, and take care of babies.

This pattern of starting new families was the source of resent-ment for the daughters in the family until they understood that their own husband's mother was supposed to take over their raising and train them to be good wives to her son. The mothers seemed to accept these arrangements as a matter of routine. Until I under-stood the situation, I thought that mothers cared more about their sons than they did their daughters. In my community, the strong connection between a mother and her son continued after his marriage. The new couple often spent the first years of their marriage under the groom's mother's roof.

I didn't really think much about this arrangement until it happened to my family. Larry married a girl in the mountain tradition. Her name was Hilda Dove. He chose her from a mountain community further back in the Alleghenies called Fulks Run. He was twenty years old, and she was fourteen. He had just received his draft notice. A man could avoid the army and perhaps avoid going to Vietnam if he got married. When he asked for Hilda's hand, her parents freely signed the documents to allow him to marry her. Hilda was not pregnant so it was not a "shotgun" wedding.

Once they were married, Larry brought Hilda home to live with Mom and Dad and my younger brothers and sister. Mom finished raising Hilda and taught her how to cook, clean, preserve food, bake bread, and do all the things a mountain wife did for her family.

My sister and I were jealous of Hilda and Mom because their relationship was different from our relationship with our mother. They had a unique connection as mother-in-law and daughter-in-law and also as mother and child without the complications that real daughters sometimes have with their mothers. Mom wanted the life she had provided for her son to continue in his marriage. She patiently taught Hilda how to cook the way she did using her methods and recipes.

When I wasn't being jealous of her relationship with Mom, I felt sorry for Hilda. Many times I watched her walk out the back porch door and head for the pasture. She would find a cow lying down chewing her cud. Hilda would sit down beside the cow, lay her head over on the cow's belly, and cry for long periods of time. I assumed she was crying for her lost youth and because she was afraid of her new role as a mountain man's wife.

One day, I followed Hilda to the pasture and waited until she settled her head on the cow's belly. I tiptoed up to where I could

31

hear her sobbing. The old cow, named Betsy, turned her head and looked at Hilda. Even the cow had a big wet blob below her eyes, as if she were crying too. I walked up and touched Hilda's shoulder and asked her, "What's wrong, Hilda?" She looked up and smiled through her tears and said, "Oh, I am just a little homesick today." She promptly got up and went into the garden to hoe the cabbage.

Over the years, Mom and Hilda shared their roles as mountain wives. Hilda had her first baby when she was sixteen and the second when she was seventeen. Larry continued to live in my parents' home. I eventually got over my jealousy of Mom and Hilda after I left home. Hilda became a sister to me. I am not sure my sister ever became comfortable with their relationship, even after her own marriage, possibly because she never lived more than a quarter of a mile from the house where we grew up.

Hilda was Mom's constant companion because she had dropped out of school and was too young, even if Larry had allowed it, to get a job. After the babies started coming, she was busy with them while continuing to learn her role as a mountain housewife. Mom and Hilda got up early in the morning to get their husbands off to work and then get the rest of the kids off to school. Hilda told me recently, "After we got everybody out of the house, we hurried up and washed the dishes, swept the house, grabbed our baskets and back over the hill we went. In the spring we went to hunt toadstools [morels] and in the fall we gathered apples that had fallen on the ground in Dean's orchard." She added, "By dinner time, we were back in the house planning our supper. We would make a big family pie with the apples we picked up."

Hilda's coming to live with us was a mixed blessing. Her presence took a lot of pressure off my sister and me to help with chores around the house, but her presence also brought a bit of the reality of growing up in an Appalachian community, especially for girls.

Hopkins Gap

The official name of my Appalachian community was Palos, Virginia, but only a few folks remember the community as Palos. The common name came from a gap in the mountains called Hopkins Gap. This name is as old as slavery because the gap was once part of a large plantation owned by the Hopkins family. The original plantation home still stands as a historical site, near Muddy Creek, west of Harrisonburg, between Mt. Clinton and Singers Glen, in the Shenandoah Valley of Virginia.

Hopkins Gap is located in the upper left corner of this map, about 15 miles NW of Harrisonburg. Harrisonburg lies in the center of the Shenandoah Valley of Virginia, between the Allegheny Mountains and the Blue Ridge Mountains.

Hopkins Gap is nestled among the Allegheny Mountains on the eastern edge of the area known as Appalachia and in the western section of the Shenandoah Valley of Virginia. Hopkins Gap was forged into the mountains by the Shoemaker River that now divides the eastern side of the Allegheny Mountains from the western side of Little North Mountain, a smaller range of the Alleghenies. The Shoemaker River still cools the Gap as it carries away the rain that falls on the mountainsides and dumps it into the larger Shenandoah River far away. As the river carries the rain away, it replenishes the rich soil that once nourished small fields of corn, rye, and wheat of the highest quality. The best potatoes east of Idaho were grown in vegetable gardens near the river's edge.

If you walk north or west from any point in Hopkins Gap, in a short while you will find yourself on top of the Allegheny Mountain range of the Appalachians and in the state of West Virginia. If you walk east or south, you will soon be in the Shenandoah Valley of Virginia facing the Blue Ridge range of the Appalachian Mountains.

Hopkins Gap is approximately five miles long and varies from one mile to three miles wide. Smaller ridges flow into the gap from the mountainsides creating a succession of deep dark hollows with the narrow Hopkins Gap running through the center. The hollows all had streams running through them. Rainfall kept most of the streams flowing, but some were fed by cold springs that dripped through the rocks from beneath the mountains.

There was an abundance of resources available in Hopkins Gap for subsistence living. The ridges that angled into the Gap were rich with wild fruit of all kinds — blackberries, strawberries, raspberries, and huckleberries. The huckleberry crop was periodically guaranteed. When the old huckleberry bushes stopped bearing, people would set fire to a mountain ridge. The following year, new huckleberry bushes replaced the burned trees and underbrush. On top of the ridges, local people cleared patches of land and planted communal orchards of cherry, apple, peach, and pear trees.

The mountains provided abundant wild game that was harvested for meat and skins — deer, bear, squirrels, raccoon, skunks, and bobcats. Muskrats were trapped along the streams for their skins that brought a good price from the fur buyers.

In the early days, the mountains were covered with soft wood and hardwood trees. White pines, spruces, bull pines, and poplars blended with white oaks, red oaks, chestnuts, hickory, walnuts, and maples of all varieties. Each type of tree had a different quality that made it useful for the folks in Hopkins Gap. White oaks provided "splits" for chair bottoms and baskets and wood for furniture.

In the hands of a good craftsman with a shaving bridge and a sharp froe, red oak wood split into thin slabs that were used as roofing shingles. In the dry, hot summer months, the shingles shrank and allowed air to flow in and out of the house. When a thunderstorm came over the mountain or a spell of rain began to move into the Gap, the humidity preceding the rain swelled the red oak shingles and closed the air holes. Not one drop of rain fell into a Hopkins Gap house with a good red oak shingle roof.

Hickory trees provided nuts for the squirrels, a major source of meat in the diet of Gap folks. Mom boiled the squirrel meat until it was tender, then she rolled the pieces in salt and pepper seasoned flour and fried them until they were crisp. She made thick white gravy from the squirrel broth. We ate the meat and gravy with warm bread — biscuit dough baked in a family-size oval chunk.

Hickory wood was used to make rocking chairs because it could be bent and shaped when green. It held its shape after it dried. American chestnut trees provided huge logs for cabins. Some of the old cabins are still standing. The hand-hewn chestnut logs were as much as three feet thick. Thin rails of chestnut were used for fences. The wood became harder with age.

Chestnuts were gathered in the fall for roasting and making flour before the great chestnut blight in the early 1900s. Even after the blight killed all the chestnut trees, the dead logs provided "wormy" wood for handcrafted furniture that is now nearly price-less. Walnut trees, much like the chestnut, provided both nuts for food and wood for sturdy furniture made to survive many genera-tions. Pie safes, tables, and chairs, with white-oak split bottoms, were made with walnut. My Grandma Molly's pie safe was made with softer poplar wood combined with walnut.

Maple trees provided wood for furniture; and one variety, the sugar maple, provided sap for syrup. The most important and enduring contribution of the maples was the variety of foliage colors in the fall. The oranges, yellows, and reds blended ascetically with the maroon red oak leaves, green pines boughs, and yellow poplar leaves as each October rolled around.

Let's not forget the lowly pine. These trees provided many products including pine knots. Pine knots were split into slivers of rich, oily kindling to start fires quickly on cold winter mornings. Early in my life, Mom gave me, and my brother, Larry, the job of using the axe to split pine knots and keep her kindling box filled. I liked this job because the kindling box sat by the kitchen stove and as the hard, oily slivers were warmed, a slight aroma of pine filled the house.

Large pine trees were harvested for two reasons. The outer layers of the trees made good "slab" wood for quick fires because it was softer. The inner layers or the "heart" pine was a much harder wood and was used for flooring in the homes, for doors and trim wood, and for furniture, and I will never forget the sweet whisper-ing music made by the breezes blowing through a white pine tree.

Pine trees provided the best hiding places when the children played in the woods and many out of season hunters escaped the game warden by ducking under the protective boughs of a white pine tree. Pine tree boughs saved me once when I was hunting for squirrels out of season. I was having a good day. I had six squirrels hanging on my belt. I had shot each one in the head with Dad's .22 caliber single-shot rifle, so the meat wasn't damaged.

I was thinking about fried squirrel, gravy and warm bread, as I sneaked up on squirrel number seven who was noisily chewing on a tender hickory nut. I was waiting for him to finish and jump out on a limb for another nut so I could determine his location.

Suddenly the breeze picked up slightly and carried the sound of men's voices to me. I dashed under the boughs of a large white pine and snuggled up as close as I could get to the trunk. In just a few minutes, two game wardens walked so close to the tree that I could read their badge numbers. They were saying, "The shots sounded like there were coming from around here, but there's no sign of anybody." I could barely hear them over my heartbeat. They stood by my hiding place for what seemed like a week, and then they moved on. I dashed into Lloyd Myers' cornfield and made my way to his barn, where I borrowed a sack and put my squirrels in it. I nonchalantly walked on home with the sack across my shoulder, the squirrel bodies looking like vegetables in the sack.

Each hollow in Hopkins Gap has a name. There is Shaving Bridge Hollow, Ground Squirrel Bridge Hollow, Cry Baby Lane, Cold Spring Hollow, Mine Hollow, Mash Run, Hog Pen Run, Little Hog Pens, Big Hog Pens, Slate Lick Run, and many others. Hearing the names of all these places always reminds me of different events in local history. The stories behind the names were told to me so often and with such detail that the pictures I developed in my mind have remained consistent and permanently imprinted in my memory.

Shaving Bridge Hollow is where Joe Crawford made his living. He peeled bark, split shingles from the red oak trees, made white oak splits for split-bottom chairs, and built furniture from the variety of oak trees that were abundant in that one hollow. When he grew too old to work anymore, he walked away and left his shaving bridge set under a tree until time and the weather returned it to the earth. That hollow is known to this day as Shaving Bridge Hollow and anybody who was born in Hopkins Gap, young and old, knows exactly where the hollow is located.

Ground Squirrel Bridge Hollow acquired its name because a large tree fell across the creek and was used as a bridge to cross from one side to the other by a family of ground squirrels. To this day, those hollows still carry those names long after their namesakes have rotted and disappeared from sight.

Cold Spring Hollow was named for a very cold spring that ran full of water all the time. It was well known as the place where a man could produce a week's amount of moonshine in half the time because the water in the "cooling tub" stayed cold twice as long. Mom told me that women in Hopkins Gap liked to wash their clothes in this water because it was "soft," meaning there were fewer minerals.

There were three locations named Big Hog Pen Ridge, Little Hog Pen Ridge, and Hog Pen Run. These areas served as community hog pens where families would let their hogs run wild to eat chestnuts and acorns in order to fatten them up for the fall butchering. Each family marked their hogs in some way that was recognized by the whole community so there was no question about who owned the hogs when it was time for the fall roundup. Uncle Shirley told me, "The Morrises always notched each hog's ear in a certain place. Everybody knew and respected each family's mark."

Many babies were stillborn in Hopkins Gap. They were left unnamed and immediately buried. The midwife or the father buried the babies near the homes where they were born. There are several locations where folks still report hearing the late night crying of babies. One location has carried the name "Cry Baby Lane." It was told to me that one mother, who lived at the end of this winding mountain road, birthed at least eight stillborn children. To this day, young and old people in the Gap claim that if you go up Cry Baby Lane late at night and say, "Cry baby, cry baby, cry baby, cry," you can still hear the ghostly cries of the unnamed babies.

Mash Run was given its name because it is often said that so much moonshine was made on this little creek that the water smelled sour like mash. When cattle drank this water, depending on how much mash had been dumped in it, they got drunk. Mine Hollow was named because it was thought that a man had discovered a mine there. After he discovered the mine, he went home for

38

tools. When he came back he could never locate the mine, so he spent the remainder of his days wandering around looking for the lost mine. After he died hunters reported seeing his ghost in Mine Hollow still searching for the lost mine.

The people in Hopkins Gap carry a colorful map in their heads and hearts handed down to them by the storytellers. So if a stranger asks for directions, he or she will likely be given directions along with a tale of local history.

I dare say that no person who grew up in or near Hopkins Gap ever needed a compass to find his or her way. When the sun slid down behind Second Mountain, we knew that was the West. The other three directions were easy to determine. Each person knew that spot on Second Mountain where the sun went down, so we never lost our way even on a cloudy day. I felt very comfortable and protected by the mountains. I was in their embrace at all times without realizing it until I left home.

When I moved to Lubbock, Texas in 1975 to work on my doctor's degree, I made every effort to take some of the mountains with me, not realizing I would be leaving behind my sense of direction. I packed my belongings in the back of my Ford pickup. My inventory included many cans of sauerkraut, green beans, tomatoes, hog sausage, tenderloin, and pork ribs from Mom's cellar. I had a half-bushel of new potatoes from Dad's garden.

I traveled along Interstate 81 to the southwestern end of Virginia. I stopped to rest in Hungry Mother State Park just before entering Tennessee to make the long drive across the state to Arkansas then on to Texas. When I got back in my truck to leave Virginia, I broke into uncontrollable sobs. It was as if my heart was being torn from my chest. I was thirty-four years old and had never lived anywhere except near Hopkins Gap. The most unsettling realization was yet to come.

When I arrived in Lubbock, I found the land is very flat, like a tabletop, and the extreme opposite of the land in the Appalachian Mountains. I couldn't find my way around Lubbock for the first six months. I felt so lost, vulnerable, and cold under the big sky.

I suffered severely from homesickness. When October came, I missed the smell of falling leaves, so I wrote to a friend back home and asked her to send me some leaves. She mailed a shoebox full of fallen leaves to me. It helped some; but nearly every day, I lay on the couch and cried while I listened to Dolly Parton's song, "My Tennessee Mountain Home."

I never adjusted to the flat land. I was always searching for a landmark that would guide me. There was one tall, square building on the Texas Tech University campus. I immediately latched onto that landmark only to realize after I lost my way several times that all four sides of the building were the same. There were no special ridges or hollows to guide me.

Early Settlers and Blended Cultures

Germans from Pennsylvania first settled Hopkins Gap in the late 1700's, followed by the Scots-Irish in the early 1800's. These two groups settled at opposite ends of the five-mile-long gap in the mountains. By the mid to late 1800's, two or three families lived at opposite ends of Hopkins Gap—the Lams, the Kirkpatricks, and the Carrs. Other family names distributed throughout the Gap included the Reedys, the Shoemakers, the Finks, and the Rigglemans.

Between 1890 and 1900 four other families migrated west from Greene County located in the Blue Ridge Mountains. They crossed the Shenandoah Valley and settled in the Hopkins Gap area. The migration was slow with the men coming first and making many trips back to Greene County before bringing their families and settling permanently.

There were many stories as to why this wave of settlers migrated to Hopkins Gap from Greene County in the Blue Ridge Mountains on the eastern side of the Shenandoah Valley. My daddy and others claimed that Greene County was becoming too crowded and that the men came to homestead land that was available in the

Hopkins Gap area. Another story was that three of the migrants were running away from Greene County because they were wanted for crimes they committed there.

According to Grandma Molly, the first Shifflett settled the area during the Civil War. She told me that my great-grandfather, Banks Shifflett, was a deserter from the Battle of Bull Run. She told the story many times. "He was fighting for the confederate army, and when he saw the water in Bull Run flowing red with blood, he ran to the west and ended up in Hopkins Gap. He had a wife and many kids in Greene County; but he never went back to see them."

This picture was taken shortly before Banks Shifflett died in 1921. He is holding Vernie Shifflett, his granddaughter --the oldest child of John Austin and Molly Crawford Shifflett.

41

On Sunday afternoons in the summer months, Dad would load us into the car and cross Little North Mountain to pick up Grandma Molly. We would ride down through Hopkins Gap and stop at Gert Shoemaker's general store at the lower end. Dad would buy a hunk of strong cheese, a dozen slices of bologna, bread, crackers, and a little bottle of coke for each person. With our picnic in hand, he drove us through the Allegheny Mountains to Feedstone Mountain. These were great times for store bought treats but also for memorable history lessons.

Matilda (Tildy) Crawford holding Aunt Pauline on her lap. Pauline was one of the deaf mute daughters of John Austin and Molly Crawford Shifflett.

Grandma Molly always pointed out the foundation of Banks Shifflett's and Ellen Crawford's house on Feedstone Mountain. It was located at least twenty miles from Hopkins Gap hidden deep in the mountains near the West Virginia border. There were a few of the old logs left, but the foundation of mountain boulders was intact. She said, "Banks took up with a local woman, Ellen Crawford, and lived here to hide from the army. He had three daughters by her—Vic Knight and Laura Fulk and one who died named Becky. He had two sons by Frances Crawford while he still lived in Greene County—Austin and Warnie. I married Austin. He is your Grandpa Austin. Frances Crawford and my mother, Tildy, were sisters. That made me and Austin first cousins. My daddy's name was Ang Shifflett, and I think he was pretty close kin to Banks. So me and Austin might be even closer than first cousins."

From my own research in the U.S. Census, I discovered that Grandma Molly had confused some of the details of Banks' life. I found that Banks Shifflett left Greene County between 1880 and 1890. He had left his wife, Elizabeth Collier Shifflett and their ten children to live with the Simean Crawford family in Greene County. Banks took up with their daughter, Frances Crawford, and had two children with her. John Austin, my paternal grandfather, was one year old in 1880. Soon thereafter, another son, Warnie, was born to Banks Shifflett and Frances Crawford. By the 1900 census, Banks Shifflett was living at Feedstone Mountain in Hopkins Gap with a third woman, Ellen Crawford. He had three daughters by Ellen—Victoria, Rebecca and Laura. Simean Crawford had also migrated to Hopkins Gap before 1900 and Frances and her children, John Austin and Warnie Shifflett were again living with Frances' father, Simean, in Hopkins Gap.

As I grew older and put two and two together, I realized that Grandpa Austin was not legally a Shifflett. His legal name was Crawford. This was quite a shock to me, so I asked my daddy, and he verified the story and the legal name. It was then that I began paying attention to my history and taking notes when Grandma Molly and Dad started talking about my roots.

Eventually Banks Shifflett abandoned his remote homestead at Feedstone deep in the Allegheny Mountains and moved into Hopkins Gap with his former neighbors from Greene County so that by the early 1900's, four families originally from Greene County—the Shifflett's, the Crawfords, the Morrises, and the Conleys—had made permanent settlements in Hopkins Gap. They established homesteads in the hollows and lowlands along the winding Shoemaker River and among the earlier Gap settlers.

The original settlement pattern of the families from Green County was unique with the Morris family settling near the mouth of the gap next to the Carrs. Then the Conleys, the Shiffletts, and the Crawfords settled next to the Morris family as they moved into the gap. To the present day, remnants of this early settlement pattern are distinguishable although there has been some blending of the boundaries through marriage and land trade.

Isolation and the existence of a limited number of surnames created problems with naming children. Numerous times young women married and didn't have to change their maiden names. My closest cousins, Ruby and Joyce, married two brothers with the same last name as theirs. At one time there were four men with the same given name and surname. As a way of avoiding duplication of names, a habit of giving as many as three first names to children developed for a period of time. One example of this was Joseph Crawford. His full name was Joseph Robert Jackson Crawford.

Isolation from the Outside World

Hopkins Gap was both physically and socially isolated, by choice and reputation, from the rest of the world. The physical isolation began to end in the 1930's when a road was built into the area. Until then, transportation in and out of Hopkins Gap was limited to walking, horseback riding, or buggy riding. The new road was very narrow with room for one car, so passing an on-coming car was often a challenge. The road wound around the ridges and crossed Shoemaker River at several points. There were no bridges, so cars had to drive through the river. The road was predictably passable only during the dry summer months because any extra rain would flood the river making it impossible to cross. During the winter there was often a sheet of ice and packed snow that made driving very treacherous.

Even after the road was built, very few people owned cars. Uncle Shirley described the road through Hopkins Gap, "It was just a dirt road filled with ruts. In the summer, you could get stuck in a mud puddle. That same mud puddle froze in the winter with ruts as deep as two feet. Slipping into one of them with your car got you a broken axle."

One of the first persons to own a car was Oscar Crawford. Oscar was a round-headed man with a few hairs left on top of his head. He was known for spitting a lot as he talked. Uncle Shirley tells a story about the time he was walking home to the Gap from Harrisonburg and Oscar offered him a ride. "Oscar was driving along through Mennonite town and came up on me walking home to the Gap. He offered to take me home, and I got in with him. We hadn't gone a quarter of a mile, until he had a flat tire. He got out, jacked the car up, took the tire off the rim, patched the tube, and put the tire back on. He lowered the jack and when the weight of the car hit the tire the air spewed out. Oscar cussed a while and spit a few times, then fixed the tire again. To make a long story short, he had seven flat tires, and we hadn't made it through Mennonite town. Finally, I thanked Oscar for the ride and told him I would just go on and walk home."

Uncle Shirley walked all the way to Hopkins Gap, about twelve miles, ate his dinner and was sitting on the porch when Oscar drove down the road. Uncle Shirley later asked Oscar what took him so long to get home. Oscar cussed and spit and said, "I had twenty-three flat tires." After that, Oscar tied at least half dozen spare tires across the top of his car when he left the Gap for Harrisonburg.

In the early years of my childhood, most people still walked wherever they wanted to go. One of my earliest memories is of Joe Crawford stopping at our house to rest as he made his frequent thirty-five mile walking trips to Greene County. He was a small man with white hair and a white beard and warm blue eyes that danced when he smiled. He always wore bib overalls and a hat. Mom fed him pie and coffee when he arrived at our house. My brother John crawled on his lap, and Uncle Joe sang to him. He sang an old song called "John Boo." One line that I remember from the song was "A rat chased the cat around my granddaddy's hat." When Joe sang that line, John would run his finger around the brim of Uncle Joe's hat as he acted out the path of the rat chasing the cat.

By 1943, my daddy had a car. Occasionally, he was so determined to get to Grandma Molly's house for Sunday dinner that he drove us to the edge of the flooding Shoemaker River and parked the car. Then we crossed the river on a footbridge and walked the rest of the way to her house. This footbridge was particularly high and scary, and I always got nauseated and dizzy when I crossed a footbridge. It consisted of a long log that spanned the width of the river. A narrow flat board was nailed along the top of the log for safer walking, but the log bounced up and down with each step. A rope tied to upright sticks of wood provided a very flimsy handrail. Once when I was about seven years old, I was walking across the footbridge in front of my daddy. He kept telling me not to look down at the water flowing ferociously, far below my feet. Of course, you don't tell a kid not to look down. I looked down at the rushing water and suddenly it seemed as if the water was standing still and the footbridge was moving rapidly up the river. My immediate impulse was to jump into the river. I let loose of the rope and started to jump off the "moving" bridge. Dad reached out and grabbed me. After he nearly lost me to the rushing river, he picked up each of us, one by one, and carried us across the river.

Even when the Shoemaker River was at its normal depth after a flood, Dad would sometimes drive through and damage the oil pan under the car by hitting rocks that had washed into the road

46

and lay hidden under the water. The brakes on the car always got wet, and Dad had to use the emergency brake. We all held our breath as we watched him pull the handle as needed to slow the car as we lurched our way literally "over the river and through the woods" to Grandma Molly's house for Sunday dinner.

In the winter months, the car would slip and slide across the ice and occasionally plunge into a ditch. One time Dad wanted to get to Grandma Molly's house so much that he decided it best that we drive in the opposite direction and enter the upper end of the Peak. That way he wouldn't have to cross Little North Mountain. The Peak road came out at the foot of the mountain on the Hopkins Gap side. Just like the Gap road, the Peak road was covered with gravel and extremely icy this particular Sunday. We weren't halfway through the Peak until the car slid into a ditch. Dad got out, jacked up the car, and started putting on the chains. My mother sat in the car with us kids. She kept saying, "I've never seen anybody like your daddy. There's no reason we have to go to the Gap today. The car is going to fall off the jack and kill him."

I often had nightmares about falling off a footbridge into a flooding river, careening down a steep mountain road in a car with no brakes, and watching my daddy's last gasps as he lay under the weight of his fallen car. The United States Postal Service took their motto from my Dad. Neither wind, nor rain, nor snow and ice would keep him from going to Grandma Molly's house in Hopkins Gap for Sunday dinner.

It was not until 1955 that the road was improved and bridges built so that automobile travel was possible throughout the year. The folks in my family called the new road the "BIG" road. It was paved and had enough space for two cars to pass without a problem.

When I was born and for the first five or so years of my life, there were no telephones. The first telephone was put into Mr. John I. Myers' house. When newsworthy events happened he would receive a call. He rode his horse to deliver the news to the people involved. Then in 1948, the telephone company put a central phone in our next-door neighbor's house. Rawley "Pop" May and his wife served as the operators for the neighborhood, and people began to join their party line.

It was good to have a phone, but that was the end of family privacy. Because all the phones on the party line rang when a call came through, a few of the neighbors picked up their phones and listened to private conversations. When we finally got a phone, Mom got so mad at the "nosey" neighbors, she started making up news for them to spread. This got them in trouble because they couldn't tell where they heard the "false" news, as they knew they would be giving away their habit of listening in on private conversations. Folks already knew they were nosey anyway.

Since I was born in 1941, I grew up during the time that Hopkins Gap was changing from a very isolated mountain community to a more open, accessible area. My generation was the first to have the opportunity for a high school education. The children of Mom and Dad's generation attended White Hall, a one-room school in the middle of Hopkins Gap. One teacher taught grades one through seven. All the children walked to school because the one-lane gravel road was not wide enough for a school bus

.   My mother dropped out of school at the beginning of fifth grade because she didn't have shoes to wear. It was after 1947 when Hopkins Gap children started riding the bus to school.

Grades one through seven, Hopkins Gap White Hall School, circa 1928

Mom and Dad Moved Away, But Not Too Far

For different reasons, Mom and Dad moved out of Hopkins Gap when they were in their late teens. At age nine, Mom had moved in with her sister Goldie's family who raised her after her parents died. Goldie and her husband, Rob, bought a small farm with a sawmill about a mile from the Little North Mountain entrance to Hopkins Gap in the Shenandoah Valley. So Mom left Hopkins Gap with Goldie's family.

Dad left the Gap when he was eighteen after spending two prison terms for making moonshine. He moved in with his brother,

Uncle Lurty, about four miles from Little North Mountain. When families moved out of the Gap, they didn't move far, and they spent as much time as possible in Hopkins Gap or with Gap folks even outside the area.

Uncle Rob Crawford sitting on a huge log at his saw mill. Circa 1942

After Mom and Dad got married, they never lived more than a mile from Hopkins Gap, and they always considered the Gap their home. They maintained their connections by attending church and visiting their relatives every Sunday. All of their spare time was spent in Hopkins Gap or with Hopkins Gap folks. Gap folks stuck together wherever and whenever possible.

On Saturdays when the Gap adults went to Harrisonburg to buy their staples, there were three places they congregated to spend the afternoon. Two places were located side by side on Liberty Street-- Layman's Restaurant and Hobe's Restaurant. The third place was the Daily Lunch on Water Street.

They met at these places to eat hamburgers and hotdogs and drink coke and a beer or two. If there was a conflict going on at home, it was often brought to the restaurants on Saturday. The first time I was hit in the jaw by a large fist was in Layman's Restaurant. Two men from the Gap were having a few beers at the bar when their conversation turned to a sore subject. They started to fight, rolled off the barstools, and a misguided blow landed on my young jaw. It was sore for a couple of days.

The first time I fainted was in Hobe's Restaurant when two of my male cousins got into a fistfight in the poolroom in the back. They had been peacefully playing pool together when all of a sudden they were hitting each other in the face with their fists. There was a lot of bloodshed in that fight. I always had a problem with seeing blood, so I just rolled off the barstool in a dead faint. Mom gathered me up and left the restaurant. It was a long while before she let me go to Harrisonburg with her again, because she got really scared when I fainted.

These two incidents were not typical of Saturday afternoon gatherings of the Gap folks at the Liberty Street restaurants. Most gatherings were happy and fun with the exchange of information such as which couples were expecting a new baby, who was getting married, and who was courting. These were fun times, and I usually looked forward to my turn to go to Harrisonburg with Mom and Aunt Goldie on their weekly trips to buy groceries.

The Liberty Street restaurants served as the central location for courtship among Hopkins Gap teenagers. Many future Hopkins Gap marriages and families got their start on Liberty Street. Young boys and girls would individually arrive with their fathers or older brothers or sisters. A courting couple would get together on Liberty Street and spend the afternoon at a movie or shopping; when the day was over, they returned to their separate homes with their family members. Mom and Dad were among the many couples that started their courtship this way. They courted for a year or more by meeting and going to Saturday afternoon movies.

Life Begins to be Different in Hopkins Gap, But Not Too Different

During my lifetime, I observed and experienced three changes in the way my relatives in Hopkins Gap made a living, healed their illnesses, birthed their babies, entertained their children, and solved their disputes. I was told by the older members of the community that in the early years after Hopkins Gap was settled and remained isolated from the outside world, people survived by hunting, gathering, and subsistence farming. The families cooperated through mutual aid and community food preservation events such as berry pickings, hog killings, apple butter boilings.

When the road to the outside world opened, the isolation of Hopkins Gap came to an end. Two changes came together to make life different. The road to the outside world opened making it easier to travel in and out of the Gap. At about the same time, there was a demand for illegal whiskey due to Prohibition. There had always been some whiskey made in the Gap for personal consumption and medicinal purposes. But suddenly, the dark hollows, streams, and springs, with their dark wood surroundings, made perfect spots for the new economic enterprise — moonshining.

Little Hog Pen Ridge and Big Hog Pen Ridge kept their names, but their original use changed. Families started making moonshine as their main financial endeavor. The demand for illegal whiskey soared and the people of Hopkins Gap seized the opportunity to get a greater return on their labor investment. Without moonshining, many families in the Gap would not have survived the Great Depression. However, the introduction of moonshining was not without consequences for the people of Hopkins Gap.

The early years of my life coincided with the time that the people of Hopkins Gap were experiencing the consequences of the moonshining years. While they needed to make moonshine to survive, they also experienced, for the first time, the ravages of competition. Hopkins Gap families began to compete with each other in the enterprise of producing illegal whiskey and selling it to people outside the community. Uncle Shirley explained the change to me. He said, "Before everybody started tryin' to outdo each other in the moonshine business, we shared and shared alike. If a man came to my house and wanted rye whiskey and I only had corn whiskey, I would send him up the road to another man who had rye whiskey. The man did the same for me. We kinda kept each other informed as to what we had, and everybody got along good."

Moonshining ultimately destroyed the spirit of the community that had developed out of survival by subsistence and mutual aid. Although people continued to hold community events such as apple-butter boilings and hog-killings, a heavy cloud of distrust was obvious from things unsaid and small groups of men quietly talking to each other out of hearing distance of the community group. When caught by government agents, young men and women were sent to faraway prisons. People who had never left the community were suddenly exposed to different people and places. A few people in the Gap responded to these changes with self-destructive alcohol abuse and violent explosions occasionally resulting in murder.

The production of moonshine gave Hopkins Gap a reputation as a dangerous place in the communities just across Little North Mountain. I heard it said many times by Shenandoah Valley people that they were afraid to drive their cars through the Gap. They were afraid of being mistakenly identified as a revenue agent and shot before any questions were asked.

The practice of moonshining further isolated Hopkins Gap from the outside world in a different way. Outsiders began to drive into the isolated gap in the mountains. They came to buy the cleanest and best tasting moonshine to be found anywhere; however, it was an illegal product. As is typical of folks who enjoy the benefits of illegal activity, those who purchased moonshine from Hopkins Gap were the worst gossipers. As they returned to their homes, they covered their own illegal actions by telling stories about the wild people who lived in Hopkins Gap. In their stories, we became known as the "Gappers."

You Can Take the People Out of the Gap, but They'll Always be "Gappers"

Although Mom and Dad had moved across Little North Mountain and out of the Gap, they were never referred to as anything other than "Gappers." My first contact with the name was when I was six years old and entered first grade. The school bus came out of Hopkins Gap, crossed Little North Mountain into the Shenandoah Valley, and stopped at our house. Thus, arriving at school on that bus made me a "Gapper." To this day, the term "Gapper" carries an exaggerated image of drinking and fighting, of thievery and "good for nothing" people.

Later, when I was twelve years old, Mom and Dad bought the little farm. It was less than a quarter mile from our original house and still on the "Gap" bus route. After we moved to the farm, Lloyd and Fannie Jane Myers were our closest neighbors and were always kind to us but kept their distance. We also kept our distance from our valley neighbors because our connections were to our relatives in Hopkins Gap. We looked forward to the weekends when we went back to the Gap to church and to visit our relatives.

Lloyd Myers recently told me, "When y'all moved in up on the hill, me and Fanny Jane figured our house would become a free grocery store. But y'all didn't bother us. In fact, I'll never forget the

54

time you saved one of my cows from dying from the bloat. You saw her down and ran to get me. Your folks were hard workers and raised a bunch of good children." In time, some of our other neighbors told us that Lloyd and Fannie Jane bragged that we were pretty good people to be "Gappers."

After we had lived on the farm for a while, our valley neighbors began to walk or drive by slowly to check out what we were doing. One family was named Showalter. Sadie, their oldest daughter, was the local spinster and was known as a gossip. She came to visit occasionally to stare at us "Gappers" and see what we were doing. Long before she ever entered our house, she would just walk by on the far edge of the road and stare at the house and all the kids in the yard. Mom made extra money by babysitting my cousins' children, so there were often as many as ten kids in the yard. I am sure all the kids convinced her that we were truly "Gappers," because part of the "Gapper" list of characteristics was that each family had many, many children. Sadie always carried a big stick with her as she walked by the house.

During my school years, not all my teachers treated the Hopkins Gap kids differently; however, there were a few who judged us by the reputation of Hopkins Gap and considered us to be a waste of their time. When I was in the seventh grade at Mt. Clinton High School, I had a teacher named Mrs. Moomaw. One of her relatives, Elbert Stultz, was dating my widowed Aunt Goldie. Mrs. Moomaw was a Stultz before she married, and the Stultzs did not like the "Gappers." She somehow knew that I was Goldie's niece; therefore, I was a "Gapper." She was openly hostile to me by refusing to acknowledge my hand if I raised it to answer a question. I got just enough "Ds" in her class to pass. After that I went back to earning average grades as I always had before. That experience left a lasting scar on my self-confidence.

There were two families nearby that immediately befriended the "Gappers" after Mom and Dad got married and set up their first household just outside Hopkins Gap. John I. and Ada Myers owned a big farm that joined our little farm. Mr. Myers let

Dad drive Mom's cows to his farm when it was time to breed them; he never charged them a breeding fee. Dad always took me with him when he herded a cow to the Myers farm for breeding. I helped him keep the cow going in the right direction until she got to the barn door to meet the bull.

On one of these trips, I stepped in soggy cow manure and sunk in to my knees. Mr. Myers sent me to the house so Mrs. Myers could wash the manure off my legs. I went up to the yard and opened the wooden gate. There was a concrete walk running from the gate to the back door of the house. For the first time in my life I walked over concrete walkways. I immediately saw the concrete walkway as a solution to my mother's constant complaining about us dragging mud into the house. We just had a dirt path that ran from the road to the back door of our house, so when it rained we had to walk in the mud. I made a note in my mind to discuss these walkways with Mom when I got home.

As I walked along the walk, the manure dropped onto the concrete. Mrs. Myers kindly reprimanded me for messing up her walk and asked me to stand in the grass while she washed the manure off my legs. I was very embarrassed that I didn't think to walk in the grass in the first place and told Mrs. Myers that I was sorry. I went home and asked Mom if we could get rid of the dirt path that led from the road to our back door and build a concrete walkway to our kitchen door. She said, "We can't afford it." I told her then, "When I grow up and get a job, I'll have concrete walks put in for you." I also decided that my future home would have concrete walkways instead of dirt paths. It is perhaps at that moment that I was motivated to finish school, get a job, and earn my own money. My first goal when I got some money was to put in concrete sidewalks for Mom.

While I was still in high school, Mrs. John I. Myers hired me to paint the inside of her house. She bragged about my work and paid me an unheard of high wage of seventy-five cents an hour. In one summer, I earned seventy-six dollars. That was more than enough money to pay for my high school ring and buy the necessary things for my graduation.

Mr. Myers owned a large amount of land west of and adjoining Hopkins Gap. He was a fine neighbor to all the folks in Hopkins Gap. Everyone held him in the highest regard. Since he had the only telephone in the area, he knew everybody for miles around. Another neighbor, "Pop" and Minnie May helped my mother survive after my dad was drafted into World War II, leaving her with two small children and my tiny baby sister, Brenda.

With the exception of these two kind neighbors, the people that I knew in the world outside Hopkins Gap thought of us mainly as "Gappers" who made moonshine, drank, fought, and killed each other. Most people had very low expectations for our success in their world, and they were not always wrong. My own memories of growing up in Hopkins Gap include exposure to occasional violent incidents and alcohol abuse. These were very scary times for me, and it was these rare events that made the front page of the *Harrisonburg Daily News Record.* As rare as these events were, they were used to classify all the "Gappers."

Over time as I continued to experience humiliation at school, I began to think of myself and my family in the way the term "Gappers" portrayed us. This was a dark time in my life, when I was ashamed of my people. As stated before, my work with Dr. Elmer Smith was a catalyst for reclaiming my culture. Also, the "back to earth" movement, when people became scared of how our environment was being destroyed, helped me regain respect for my heritage. People started paying attention to the simpler life of the past. The Harrisonburg newspaper then began to publish pictures of my relatives as they taught my students how to split shingles, make apple butter, and butcher hogs.

I now realize that in spite of our reputation as "Gappers," and my occasional exposure to violent events, the majority of my life was filled with joy, security, and trust. Most of my childhood was spent watching the people of Hopkins Gap help each other survive poverty, isolation, sudden change, and a reputation as a backward, violent, drunken hoard of people.

Like Produces Like and Other Beliefs

In the times of subsistence survival and communal sharing in Hopkins Gap, a simple belief system shaped everyday events. The belief system was shaped from two cultures. Over the years, the Pennsylvania German and Scots-Irish cultures blended in Hopkins Gap so that one could find practices traceable to the Celtic tradition, but the language used in the practices was Pennsylvania Dutch. For example, *abneme*, a Pennsylvania Dutch word for "undergrowth" in children, was treated with Celtic sympathetic magic rituals described in Sir James Frazier's, *The Golden Bough*, a thirteen-volume collection that serves as a behavioral bridge from the past to the present. Frazier traced the evolution of human behavior through his studies of magic, taboos, sexual practices, medicinal practices, superstition, and wizardry. Frazier pointed out that in an effort to comprehend an unpredictable world; isolated people around the world transferred the practical aspects of their everyday world to their supernatural world. He wrote, "Because it is possible to shift a load of wood, stones, or what not from our own back to the back of another, the primitive fancies that it is equally possible to shift the burden of his pains and sorrows to another, who will suffer them in his stead."

Pain and suffering could be transferred to another person or to an object. The object could then be destroyed by fire or other means thus destroying the affliction.

The logic underlying the belief system in Hopkins Gap was basically the same as that reported by Sir James Frazier. It was simple and comprehensive. The purpose of the belief system was to coordinate the phenomena of the outside world according to cause and effect. Two basic principles were followed. The first principle was that of contagion; that is, the belief that a relationship exists

58

between two objects that are joined and when the two objects are physically separated, the relationship continues to exist. A person's shadow, footprint, name, dress, body waste, or portrait remained connected to his or her body and could be used to affect him or her when not present or unaware.

The second principle is that of homeopathy based on the belief that similar items are related in cause and effect. It includes the belief that nature provides clues such as shape, color, odor and taste so humans will know which plant or herb to use to cure certain illnesses. Understanding homeopathy is essential in understanding the red flannel rag around the throat to prevent sore throats and colds. The rag had to be red to prevent an "inflamed" throat. A child had to be measured for undergrowth in the "new" moon because, as the moon grows larger in its cycle, the child would grow larger.

Grandma Molly, a Granny Woman with special powers, made tiny biscuits from yellow corn meal and placed them in the diaper of a baby suffering from yellow jaundice. Once the baby urinated on the biscuits, she assumed the yellow jaundice had transferred from the baby through the yellow urine to the yellow cornmeal biscuits. She threw the diaper and the biscuits into the fire and destroyed the jaundice by burning it.

Homeopathy also served as a preventative; that is, a pregnant woman was warned about stooping to go under a horse's neck, a wagon tongue, or a fence, or she would twist the umbilical cord around her unborn baby's neck and choke it to death. Most activities related to healing, planting, and preserving were based on the principles of contagion or homeopathy or a combination of the two.

These principles abounded in every day life and framed all activities, from combing hair and cutting fingernails to planting a garden and butchering hogs. When my mother combed her hair, she was careful to clean all the hair from her comb when she finished. She wound the hair around her finger into a ball and burned it in the kitchen stove. Many times she handed me a ball of her hair and told me to put it in the stove so it would burn. The hair ignited and the smell of burning hair permeated the house for a few minutes. She told me if I just threw her hair into the yard, a bird might use it to build a nest, and she would have a headache until the nest was found and destroyed.

I watched my mother cut my brother's fingernails when he was a baby. She carefully saved all the tiny clippings and burned them in the fire. As she clipped, she told me the story of a witch getting a baby's fingernail clippings and using them to make the baby have colic. A ritual had to be performed by Grandma Molly to bring the witch to the house to try to borrow something that belonged to the family. The family would refuse the witch's request, and the baby would get well.

We planted our vegetable gardens and killed our hogs by the signs of the moon. When Grandma Molly gathered the leaves of herbs to make teas and poultices, she noted the sign of the moon. If the moon was increasing in size, she pulled the leaves upward as she took them from the stalk; and if the moon was decreasing in size, she pulled the leaves downward.

Another principle guided life in Hopkins Gap. It was a pattern of taking the good or useful elements of all things when they were needed and offered. No person, plant, or animal was considered totally useless.

In Hopkins Gap every person had a place and a purpose. The deaf mute, as he was called in my early days, appeared on Sundays after church and stopped at each house to open the trunk of his car and give children candy from a large supply. This same man was known to be mean to children if he caught them away from their moms and dads. Moms and dads watched their little children carefully when he was around but allowed them to accept his gifts of candy.

My Uncle Jake was generally known as a mean person. He killed kittens and puppies and some believe he cut pigs' tails off and let them bleed to death. He was definitely a thief because he was caught, found guilty and spent time in prison for robbing an elderly couple of their life savings of one thousand dollars. My dad and mom went to visit him in prison on several occasions. These were my first car trips out of the Hopkins Gap area. Mom packed huge picnic lunches, Dad piled us in the car, and off we went to Richmond to visit Uncle Jake in prison. I was barely four years old and found those trips long and boring. I was never able to understand why Mom fixed all the food and went along with Dad to the prison because she complained the whole week before about Uncle Jake being "good for nothing."

On the other hand, when people had too many puppies or kittens, Uncle Jake was a good man to have around. Many Sundays when we arrived at Grandma Molly's house, there would be four or five dead kittens or puppies on the chicken house roof waiting to be picked up by hawks or buzzards. I asked Mom, "Why are those puppies on the chicken house roof?" Mom would say, "Jake killed them because there were too many to take care of."

One day a year, butchering day, Uncle Jake made an important contribution to the community. He was the only person in Hopkins Gap who could clean hogs' heads. He had his own tools with his own special "head" table. I watched in awe as he cracked open the hogs' skulls and removed the brains. I always kept my distance because he would throw unmentionable parts of the head and hit me in the face or smear blood on my clothes. He carefully trimmed every sliver of meat from the skull. Butchering day was the one day each year when Uncle Jake was held in high regard and was very much an esteemed member of the community because of his head-cleaning talents.

The head butcher, who directed all the butchering activities and carved out the shapely hams and pork shoulders, was also very important. He traveled with the butchering equipment from house to house until every family in Hopkins Gap had their meat in the meat house curing for the winter.

The woman of the house where a butchering occurred was, on that day, also very highly regarded. She made all the decisions about how the butchering day meal was to be cooked and which foods were to be cooked. She guarded the finer cuts of meat such as the tenderloin and the very tender strip of meat called the "fish" that came from along the backbone of the hog. The butcher's helpers would steal this meat and boil it in the lard kettle for their own consumption if the woman of the house didn't watch them. She wanted these special pieces for Sunday morning breakfasts in the coming months.

The Granny Woman who healed all ailments was always important, but she was very highly regarded when there was a baby sick with "undergrowth" or there were warts to be removed from the hands of a child. The midwife birthed most of the babies born in Hopkins Gap. In her everyday life, she drank a lot of moonshine and was openly promiscuous, but was very highly regarded when labor pains indicated it was time for a new baby to be born.

The evil witches who lived in Hopkins Gap and cast spells on babies, pigs, cows, and cars were important too. They provided explanations for unexplainable events. The community historian, the community drunk, the storytellers, the musicians, the dancers, each had a place and each made a contribution to the wholeness of the community. There was a sense of ease with whom each person was and a sense of fulfillment with what each person contributed. The attitude of Hopkins Gap people was openness to differences, including the good and the bad, in people.

From infancy, each person growing up in Hopkins Gap was encouraged to have empathetic concern, compassion, reverence, and fear toward nature and its creatures. Traditionally, wild animals were hunted and killed during all seasons to put meat on the table for the family.

Cows that were going to provide milk for a family for a long time were given names. Most of the time female calves were kept for future milk cows. The male calves were sold or were placed in a remote pasture, unnamed and untouched by loving human hands. When the time came, they were killed for beef.

Hogs were cycled through one year—fed, fattened, and killed for meat. Dad told us that we couldn't give the hogs names or pet them because they were going to be killed. The pigpens were built far from the regular paths of playing children.

Reverence, deep loyalty, and responsibility toward animals reflected the deep loyalty and responsibility to family, kin, and the community as a whole. There were no individuals in Hopkins Gap. Each person was a Shifflett, a Morris, a Conley, a Crawford, or one of the other family names. If there was any kind of assault, verbal or physical, on any person, the unwritten rule was one for all and all for one. Sometimes there were rivalries between communities. Often during the days of moonshining, Hopkins Gap moonshiners would have a price war with moonshiners in the Peak. When this happened, the families in Hopkins Gap became the "Gappers" standing together against the "Peakers."

As I have stated, power and status shifted from task to task and evolved as special talents passed to the younger generations. The focus was not on individual competition to grab and hold on to power and status. No special talent was considered more important than any other. Rather the focus was on the purpose at hand and the person who needed to be in charge at any given time.

Plants had good and bad qualities as well. Nightshade, a plant that grew among the weeds in the garden, was poisonous to hogs; but it was also the source of salve useful for various ailments. Polk weed, once in full maturity, produced berries that stained and had a horrible odor; but, in the early spring, young polk-weed shoots were a main ingredient in "weed greens" gathered, boiled, and eaten to cleanse the body on Green Thursday, the day before Good Friday.

Skunks were pests that raided the hen house for eggs and sprayed the dogs; however, in the winter their skins were a source of extra money for the family. The fat scraped from their skin was rendered into "skunk grease" that was rubbed on a warm red flannel rag and placed on the chest at bedtime to break up a winter cold or to treat pneumonia.

Hardly anything existed that didn't have a purpose. Plants, signs of the moon, snakes, and every animal in the woods had good as well as bad in them. Even dead black snakes, handled in just the right way, could bring rain in a dry spell. You had to hang the snake on a fence with its belly facing the west.

Most amazing, I think, was the way that people were viewed. It was basically understood that everybody in the Gap had some good and some bad in them. The best way to deal with people was to know them well enough so you could avoid the bad stuff while you let them make their unique contributions to the community.

The Morris and Shifflett Families

Morris

Andy Lam & Ellie Lam	Adam Morris & Jane Crawford
Victoria	William
Charles	Jane
Ed	Joseph
Grandma Mary Ellen Lam	**m. Grandpa John Wesley Morris**
Nang	
Nettie	

Grandma Mary Ellen Lam & Grandpa John Wesley Morris
Children: (There were eighteen children born, six died in infancy.)

Zilla Morris m. Russell Carr
> Jean, Irene, Anna, Russell, Richard, Ruth, Leonard, Pearl, Grace and Helen Carr

Carl Morris m. Gladys Shifflett
> Vernon, Carl E, Arbutis, Lillie G., Pete Morris

Charlie Morris m. Madeline Dove
> Sylvia, Janet, Eunice, Helen, Mildred Morris

Gilbert Morris m. Lula Crawford
> Renetta, Tucker, Margaret, Shirely, Fern, Spencer, Emory, and Arbutis Morris

Jim Morris m. Hazel Crawford
> Loretta, James and Christine Morris

Dorothy Morris m. Olin Kephart
> Genevieve, Douglas, Mildred, Grace, Lawrence and Elwood Kephart

Goldie Morris m. Rob Crawford
> Ruby, Joyce, Randy and George Crawford

Shirley Morris m. Ethel Crawford
> William, Billie Jean, Shirley, Charles, Sam, Gary C., Bonnie, Paul, Arvona, and Betty Morris

Gladys Morris m. Vernard Shifflett
> Troy, Roy Charles, Janice Faye, Donald, Nancy J., and Roger Dale Shifflett

Stella Morris m. Clarence Payne
> Mary, Gifford, Nelson, Charles, Bus, Myrtle, Faye, and Conard Payne

Robert Morris m. Hulda Pietsch
> Richard G., Randy E., Dennis P., and Ellen Morris

Myrtle Morris m. Norman Shifflett
> Peggy Ann, Larry, Brenda, John, and Warnie Shifflett

Peggy Ann Shifflett

Shifflett

Hiram Banks Shifflett and Frances Crawford (never married)

Children:
>Warnie
>**John Austin Shifflett**

John Austin Shifflett m Molly Frances Crawford
Children:
>Vernie m. Charles Conley
>>Leonard, Ethel, and Hazel Conley
>Lena Shifflett
>>Bootsie, Vivian, Jennings Shifflett
>Mabel Shifflett m. Dave Ritchie
>>Catherine Ritchie
>Larry Shifflett m. Anna Garber
>>Rebecca, Betty, Patsy, Donald, and Carroll Shifflett
>Floyd Shifflett
>James Shifflett m. Beulah Crawford
>>Melvin, Mildred, and Robert Shifflett
>Viola Shifflett m. Robert Fagg
>>Jackie, Bobby, and 2 other Fagg children
>Hattie Shifflett m. Earl Stoutameyer
>>Shirley, Carolyn, and 2 other Stoutameyer children
>Pauline Shifflett
>**Norman Shifflett m. Myrtle Morris**
>>Peggy Ann, Larry, Brenda, John, and Warnie Shifflett

Part Two

MEMORABLE CHARACTERS

"The night is beautiful,
So the faces of my people.
The stars are beautiful,
So the eyes of my people.
Beautiful, also, is the sun.
Beautiful, also, are the souls of my people."

Langston Hughes (3)

O ver the years I have come to recognize how much the traditions Hopkins Gap people used to survive on a day-to-day basis
influenced their lives.   The communal spirit necessary for survival
in the early days shaped their characters to care for other people
and to share their resources. Later, when moonshining became the
major way of surviving, some of those same characters took on a
darker element that came out as distrust and suspicion of strangers.
Growing up in this setting had a major impact on how I viewed the
world.   I have always been able to share all kinds of resources
including material things such as money and nonmaterial things
such as ideas; but at the same time, I am suspicious of strangers who
want to get too close to me. I feel as if they want some part of me
such as information that can be used against me. I firmly believe
that growing up in Hopkins Gap in a culture that was rapidly
changing during my early life from an honest, caring, community
surviving by cooperation to a community that survived by the
illegal activity of moonshining, that required secrecy and distrust of
strangers, is the source of much of the conflict I have experienced in
my life. You will see as you read about the memorable characters in

my life, including Mom and Dad, were very complex people with both positive and negative elements in their personalities.

Norman Shifflett and Myrtle Morris Shifflett:
Their Courtship and Early Marriage

The two most memorable and influential characters in my life were Mom and Dad. They married young and committed to the role of housewife and mother and husband and father. Since they wanted to be a mother and a father, they didn't wait to start their family. Mom was pregnant by the tenth day of their marriage.

Although Mom and Dad were very much in love when they got married, they saw their union in a different light than most young folks do today. She told me she got married to be a wife and a mother. Dad never said why he got married, but his behavior said it for him. He always kept a job and never missed a day of work even when he was sick.

Their marriage was not without major and minor disagreements because they came from two families that had competed in the moonshine business in Hopkins Gap. Many of the fights Mom and Dad had during their fifty-four year marriage would end up delving into old arguments about moonshine quality and price wars from the 1930s and 1940's. She defended Uncle Rob who raised her, and he defended Grandpa Austin and his brother, Uncle Jake.

Mom said, "Rob made the best moonshine and even though he raised his price from $2.00 a pint to $2.50 a pint, his customers were faithful." Dad responded, "Rob tried to run my family out of business by raising his prices." They wouldn't speak for a day or two then things would return to normal until the next disagreement.

When I heard them arguing after I got old enough to talk back some, I asked them, half jokingly, "Why do you all stay together? Why not get a divorce? They stared at me with a curious look on their faces, as the reason they were arguing was suddenly forgotten. Finally, Mom said, "I got married for better or for worse, and I'd never think about a divorce."

Norman and Myrtle Shifflett in 1944

Mom and Dad shared a strong commitment to their children, their home, and their extended family in Hopkins Gap. In spite of their arguments, I could expect to smell supper being prepared as I walked home from the school bus stop. The aroma of a fresh pot of pinto beans and homemade bread greeted me nearly every day. I knew Dad was going to work every morning; and, at 5:00 in the evening, Dad was coming home from work. On Fridays he handed all of his pay to Mom except for five dollars to buy his lunch the next week. She used the money wisely to provide for the family.

Although they lived very close to each other as children growing up along the Shoemaker River in the Gap and went to White Hall School together, they didn't really know each other. Mom explained, "I never considered him as a boyfriend because he was a Shifflett. Morrises and Shiffletts didn't have much to do with each other." They didn't pay any attention to each other until Dad was nineteen and Mom was eighteen. And their meeting and courtship occurred outside Hopkins Gap.

When Dad was about eighteen years old, he was arrested for making moonshine. He was working for one of the more prominent large-scale female moonshiners in the community. He went to prison for four months. When he was released, he went to work for her again. Two weeks later, he was arrested once more. After serving another eight months in prison, his brother, Lurty, noticed that Dad was becoming a heavy drinker. Uncle Lurty told Dad he had to get out of the moonshine business or he would spend a lot more time in jail. He convinced Dad to move away from Hopkins Gap to live with him. Lurty helped him get a job in a shoe factory.

Mom had recently moved from Hopkins Gap with Aunt Goldie and Uncle Rob. She was eighteen and by Hopkins Gap standards, long overdue for marriage and motherhood. When I asked Mom how she became interested in Dad, she told me, "I wanted to see a Laurel and Hardy movie and so I caught a ride to Harrisonburg with Jim and Hazel. The movie cost ten cents, and I didn't have it, so I asked Marshall Kirkpatrick if he would take me to the movie. He grinned and said, 'Sure, I'll take you.'" Mom said, "Then I got scared and didn't want to go with him by myself, so I asked him if he would also take Hazel. He said, 'No, I ain't takin' nobody else.'"

"I figured right then, Marshall would want to get paid for spending ten cents on me, so I told him to forget it," Mom said. "But I wanted to see the movie so I looked around the restaurant for somebody else to ask and there set Norman Shifflett. He had stopped in for lunch when his shift ended at the shoe factory. I walked over and asked him if he would take me and Hazel to see Laurel and Hardy." He answered right away, "Yes, I'd be glad to take you all to see it." Mom smiled and told me, "That was the beginning of us gettin' together."

Their dates consisted of meeting in Harrisonburg on Saturdays, going to the movies and stage shows. They saw many movies but the one that Mom remembers most was "Gone with the Wind." They saw Tex Ritter, Roy Rogers, and Gene Autry on stage. After the movie they would eat a hamburger or a hotdog at Layman's Restaurant on Liberty Street. After each date, Mom went home with Rob and Goldie, and Dad went home with Uncle Lurty.

Once they had been seen together more than one time at Layman's Restaurant by the folks from Hopkins Gap, they were

70

considered a couple, and speculation began about the timing of an upcoming wedding. On Sunday afternoons Dad visited Mom when he could get a ride to Aunt Goldie's house where they were under the supervision of Uncle Rob and Aunt Goldie. During the week, they wrote wonderful love letters to each other, although they lived only three miles apart. There were no telephones.

Mom gave me some of the letters she got from Dad during their courtship. In one letter, dated June 11, 1940, they had apparently talked about getting married. He wrote: "Myrtle darling I would love to do what you said Sunday evening right away for if I don't soon get you where I can be with you all the time I will blow my top and you know that would be bad. There is only one thing holding me back and that is the money problem. Of course, if you want to we will make it right away. It is all up to you." He always signed his love letters, "This letter is from a boy who loves you X X X X X X X X X X X , Norman Shifflett."

It is obvious from the letter that Mom asked Dad to marry her. Norman Shifflett married Myrtle Morris, in a group wedding, on July 27, 1940. Nine months and ten days after their wedding, I was born. Within three years, I had a brother and a sister.

Peggy Ann Shifflett at the age of three months.

Three of us kids

Dad was known as a singer, guitar player, and a dancer. According to Uncle Shirley, he could sing, dance, and make people laugh with his antics, but his guitar playing left something to be desired. He teased Mom a lot when they first got married with this song:

> *When I was single, oh then, oh then,*
> *I got me a wife, oh then, oh then*
> *I got me a wife, oh then*
> *I got me a wife, the pride of my life.*
> *I wish I was single again.*
>
> *She beat me, she banged me, oh then, oh then*
> *She beat me, she banged me, oh then*
> *She beat me, she banged me,*
> *She swore that she'd hang me.*
> *I wish I was single again.*

My wife she died, oh then, oh then
My wife she died, oh then
My wife she died,
I laughed 'til I cried.
To think I was single again.

I got me another, oh then, oh then
I got me another, oh then
I got me another,
She was worse than the other.
I wish I was single again. (4)

Shortly after I was born, Mom and Dad rented a small, four-room, yellow stucco house from "Pop" May and his wife, Minnie, neighbors of Aunt Goldie and Uncle Rob. It was a long house with a cement slab for a front porch. In front of the slab was a parking space for a car.

The house had a fairly large living room and one small bedroom on the right as you entered the front door. As you walked toward the back of the house, there was a narrow dining room then a kitchen. A steep staircase dropped from the kitchen door into the back yard. A huge black-heart cherry tree stood beside the steps and provided shade for us as we played in the back yard. There was no basement just a dirt crawl space under the house.

I would get on my tricycle at the front door of the house and speed through the living room, the dining room, and kitchen. When I reached the kitchen door, I would "put on my brakes" so I didn't roll down the seventeen steps that dropped rapidly from the kitchen door to the back yard below. Mom warned me many times that my "brakes would fail," and for sure they did fail one day. My tricycle and I rolled down the steps resulting in a huge goose egg knot on my forehead. Until the day she died, when I told Mom I am going to do something like ride a raft down the Grand Canyon, I could see the fear in her eyes. She caught herself, curbed her protective impulses, and gently said, "Remember the time when your brakes failed."

Mom and Dad's marriage was a bit rocky at first because he still had a taste for whiskey. Occasionally, he came home late from work and reeked of alcohol. They argued, and Mom told him he had to stop drinking or he would be sorry. Well, lots of Hopkins Gap women threatened their husbands with various consequences, so Dad, I guess, assumed she wasn't serious. He came home drunk one more time.

When he parked his car on the cement slab that was the front porch, she knew he was drunk again. Instead of running out to the car and helping him in the house, Mom just waited. After he sobered up some, he staggered to the door and opened it. She was just inside the door. She balled her fist up and the first blow landed on the side of his head. I didn't see the rest of the fight because I ran into the bedroom and got under the bed. The fight went on for a while. Mom told me later, "I beat the shit out of him. I was hittin' him so fast; he couldn't get a lick in on me." It was many, many years before Dad came home drunk again.

Our first house was heated by a coal stove in the living room and by Mom's wood cooking stove in the kitchen. There was no bathroom and no running water. Mom carried water from a cistern at the end of the back yard. We all went to the bathroom in a chamber pot that Mom faithfully emptied every morning. As my brother, Larry, and sister, Brenda, got a bit older we invented our own competitive game around our bowel emptying needs. There was a chicken house right next to our house. Pop May had built slanting roosts for his chickens to roost on at night. We went to the bathroom in the chicken house, three of us at the same time usually. We climbed up on the roosts and pooped. We each had our own spot. The competition was about seeing how high the pile could get before it fell over. Whoever lost that game had to find a new spot on the roosts and start building his or her pile from the floor up again.

There were holes in the floor of our house; and, in the wintertime, big rats would stay under the house and occasionally come up through the floor. I was only three years old when I awoke to the sounds of Mom and Dad struggling and my tiny baby sister, Brenda, crying hysterically. She was less than six weeks old and had been sleeping in a crib next to their bed. Mom lit the lamp when she heard Brenda screaming and saw a large rat jump out of the crib. Brenda was bleeding profusely from the back of her tiny hand.

Mom and Dad frantically jumped out of bed and once they realized what had happened, Mom grabbed the baby and stopped the bleeding while Dad put a heavy board over a hole in the kitchen floor where the rat had come into the house. They recovered from the horror and went back to bed. In a few minutes, the baby was whimpering again because the rat had moved the heavy board and was back in her bed. This time Dad placed a ten-gallon sour kraut jar upside down on top of the hole in the floor and slid a board part of the way under the jar. The rat came in the third time and awakened them as it struggled to get out of the ingenious trap. With the rat trapped, Dad slid the board all the way under the jar and skillfully used it to choke the rat to death.

Shortly after that horrible night, my dad was drafted into the army. He received his call in June, 1944, immediately after the Normandy invasion, where thousands of American soldiers lost their lives. He had to leave quickly as part of the replacement army.

Suddenly my life was filled with fear. I was too young to understand what was happening, but I knew it was bad. Mom tried to hide her tears from me, but I knew she was crying all the time. She kept her back to me a lot. Dad was sad and paid extra attention to us, buying us little gifts and candy nearly every day when he came home from work. I would wake up in the night and hear both Mom and Dad crying and talking.

Dad let me "help" him change a tire on his car. We worked on the cement slab front porch. He was very patient with me as he explained each step of the process. When he finished with the tire, he quietly drove the car, with me in the front seat beside him, into "Pop" May's garage. I knew by the way he looked at the car as he closed the garage door that it would be a while before we rode in the car again.

I also watched him chop some firewood for Mom just before he left for the army. I was leading my little brother, Larry, by the hand, and he was just beginning to say "daddy." Dad looked so handsome standing on the woodpile with his axe in his hand. His curly brown hair was moist from perspiration and hung in ringlets across his forehead. He stopped chopping wood and picked up my brother, and held him close for a while. Tears were running down his face as he said, "I love you, son."

While he was away, Mom cried a lot and waited every day by the mailbox for a letter. Dad sent us Christmas cards and birth-day cards addressed to "My darling daughter" or "My wonderful son." He sent us a toy rifle like the one he was carrying in Germany. We were thrilled with it, but immediately lost it in a crack in the foundation of Pop May's barn. We searched and searched but never found it.

Dad came home for short visits before he went to Germany. He didn't have any of his curly hair left; it was cropped short, thinner on top, and had a strand or two of gray in it. He was quiet and his face wasn't the same. His ever-present smile was gone. He didn't want us to hang on him as much as he did before he left. But Mom told me how much he loved all of us and that he was just worried. "Everything will be okay when he gets home," she assured me.

Dad was gone to the war for nearly two years. It seemed like forever to me. Once in a while, I would sneak into Pop May's garage and look at Dad's car. At first it was still clean when I went to look at it. Then, I started noticing a layer of dust on the windshield and hood. Each time I visited the car the dust was thicker. I wondered if the car would start when Dad got home. The thicker the dust on the car, the longer I knew he had been gone. I worried I would never see Dad again.

Finally, the war in Germany was over. Mom was beside herself with joy and promised us he would be home soon. Dad did get home, but it was for only a brief time. He had to go back to the army and was going to be shipped to Japan. He was in Oklahoma on a train heading for California when the Japanese surrendered and the war ended.

He got home to stay in the late fall of 1945. I remember the morning when he finally came home to stay. I was five years old. I got out of bed and saw him lying across Mom's bed. He was still in his uniform. I jumped up and kissed him. He took his arm and knocked me away and said, "Get the hell away from me."

Brenda, who was now two years old, had gotten out of bed. She was standing in the bedroom door. Only a curtain separated the bedroom from the living room where Mom's bed sat in the corner. Brenda had her little arms wrapped around the curtain and was sucking her thumb as her big brown eyes stared at the strange man on the bed with Mom. The image was planted in my brain forever.

Dad sat up on his elbow and looked at Brenda. He said, "That's the ugliest kid I have ever seen." Mom said to him, "She looks exactly like you." That was the start of our family life after Dad returned from the war.

Mom tried to explain to me why Dad had changed. She said, "The daddy you knew before the war never came back home. The army took a good husband and daddy and sent a mean one back to us." I longed for the hugs that I got from him before he went away, so I figured out a way to get physically close to him without him knowing what I was doing.

Just about every evening after supper, he would get us all in the car and go over the hill to visit Aunt Goldie and Uncle Rob. One night I fell asleep before we left for home, and he had to carry me to the car. I woke up as he was carrying me securely against his chest. He smelled like soap and tobacco smoke, and he felt physically powerful. I loved how safe I felt, but I knew I had to keep quiet or he would put me down and tell me to walk. Guess what? I fell asleep every time we visited Uncle Rob and Aunt Goldie in the evenings so Dad would have to carry me to the car.

77

He never deliberately hugged me or touched me again in my life until he was on his deathbed, and then I hugged him and kissed his cheek. He kissed me back. After he died, I found a picture of me in his wallet. It had been taken on the day I defended my doctoral dissertation. It wasn't until that moment that I knew he was proud of me.

In April of 1946, my brother, John, was born. Mom had gotten pregnant when Dad was sent home for a brief leave before going to Japan. John was born at home on the bed in the living room. Grandma Molly and Nettie Conley, the midwife, helped with his birth. When the pains started, Dad put us in his car and took us to Aunt Goldie's house. He came to get us as soon as John was born. He was a big baby, weighing ten and a half pounds, I learned later, and he was still wet when we walked into the house to look at him for the first time.

I started asking questions about where babies come from after John was born. Mom wasn't ready to answer my questions, so she told me, "Your daddy brought him home from Germany in a buzzard egg." I began to wonder if that was why Mom seemed to love him so much more than the rest of us.

In September of 1946, Uncle Rob suddenly died. He left his fields full of crops to harvest. Aunt Goldie's sons were too young to do all the work, so we temporarily moved in with them. Dad helped Goldie get the crops into the barn before winter. Then we moved back to our own house.

Not too long after John was born, mom got pregnant again. She told us we were going to have a little brother or sister, and, of course, we were excited. One Saturday morning, Dad woke us up really early and put us in the car. I could tell he was really scared and upset. As he drove us over the hill to Aunt Goldie's house, we met an ambulance coming down the hill toward our house. I looked at Dad, but he just drove on and didn't say anything.

Later that day, Dad took us back home with him to get us clothes to stay a couple of days with Aunt Goldie. I was a very curious child, so while we were at our house, I took my brother,

Larry, into the room where Mom and Dad had been sleeping. The bed was covered with blood and there was a washtub setting by the bed with bloody sheets in it. I pulled the bloody sheets apart, and there was a tiny dead baby. Both my brother and I started screaming because we thought Mom was dead too.

Dad came running and gave us each a whack or two across the butt. I managed to ask him between sobs, "Where's Mama?" He told us, "She is in the hospital and will be home in a few days." He had no choice but to tell us the baby had died. "Your mama woke up sick in the night and I ran over to Mr. May's house and Minnie called the ambulance. The baby was born while I was at their house. It was a little boy, and he died."

Aunt Goldie was struggling with finances after Uncle Rob died, so she had to get a job. Although I was only six years old, I worried about Aunt Goldie not having any money. One night I dreamed that I broke into my piggy bank and found nine pennies, all the money I had. I took the money to Aunt Goldie's house. She was standing at the foot of her stairs crying when I put the nine pennies into her hand. I never forgot that dream.

Aunt Goldie went to work at a silk mill in Harrisonburg but soon discovered that she couldn't work and manage the farm. Shortly after Mom's miscarriage, in 1951, Aunt Goldie told Dad she couldn't continue to handle the responsibility of her farm and keep her job. She asked Mom and Dad if they would rent the farm and take it over. They said yes, and we moved from our first house to Aunt Goldie's house just across the hill.

We hadn't lived there long until the Korean War started. I watched Dad listen to the radio to get the news about the war. The reception wasn't very good, so he sat in a stooped position with his ear glued to the speaker. He was so scared he would be called back into the army. I was scared too. Two young men who were drafted from Hopkins Gap were killed in Korea.

When we moved to her farm, Aunt Goldie moved into the washhouse that she had fixed up for her oldest daughter, Ruby, to live in when she got married shortly after Uncle Rob died. I was ten years old by now and Aunt Goldie offered me a job. She asked me to feed a pig for her and wash her dishes every day. She paid me a quarter each week for washing her dishes and, after I fed her pig for two years, she gave me a five-dollar bill. I had never had a bill that big in my hand so I thought it was wonderful.

While we were living at Aunt Goldie's farm, Mom got pregnant again. In February of 1952 my brother, Warnie, was born. Times had changed by then and Mom had Warnie in the hospital. She had a very difficult delivery, so the doctor recommended she not have any more children. She had an operation. While she was in the hospital, Dad took the rest of us to two movies showing at a theater in Harrisonburg.

One movie was "Old Yeller," and the other one was "The Lawless Breed" starring Rock Hudson and James Garner. The reason I remember this is that Dad made us so mad we could have killed him. He made us leave the theater about five minutes before the movies ended. We didn't get to see Old Yeller get shot at the end of the movie. Just as he made us leave, the little boy in the movie was crying as he pointed the gun at Old Yeller.

Dad told us he had to have a cigarette; but at a later time, I heard him say he couldn't stand to be in a crowd of people. Learning that he didn't like crowds helped me rethink my anger toward him for taking us out of the theater before the end of Old Yeller, and I promised myself at that moment that I would see Old Yeller again. Later in my life, I rented the movie and watched it all the way through to relieve my feelings of having missed something important because of my dad.

Two years later in 1953, a farm near Goldie's house came up for sale. Mom talked Dad into buying it. She tried to get Dad to apply for a Veteran's Loan because the interest was lower, but in a mountain man's way, he told her he didn't trust the government, "Sometime or another, they'll come and take the farm away from us." So he borrowed twenty-eight hundred dollars from a bank and bought the farm.

We moved into our new home in August of 1953. The home that they bought was known as the old "Shifflett" place. At least fifty years before, it had been built by a Shifflett family. The early Shiffletts lived there and raised their family. When they died, the farm was sold and used as rental property. It had received minimal upkeep over the years and was very run down. There was no running water and an outside toilet. There were cracks in the outside walls of the house that we could see light coming through.

After we moved in, Dad had me to help him move our hay from Goldie's barn to our barn. I was helping him unload a wagon full of hay bales into the loft. We got all the hay in; but when he stepped off the wagon into the barn to help me stack the hay, the whole barn collapsed. I was thrown clear, but he was buried deep among the hay bales. I called his name and when he answered, I started crying. The only thing that happened to us was that he lost his glasses and had to buy a new pair.

After the barn collapsed, we had no place to keep the hay for the cows. We could not afford to build another barn so, luckily, Grandma Molly had a chicken house she wanted moved or torn down. Dad tore the chicken house down in sections and rebuilt it in a spot of level land near the collapsed barn. The building was free except for the hard work of tearing it down and rebuilding it. The chicken house replacement for the collapsed barn still stands on the home place.

After the scare we had with the barn falling in, Mom and I went to work trying to patch some of the cracks in the house so we wouldn't freeze in the cold months ahead. We used newspapers and old blankets to stuff the cracks shut. She put a blanket over the back door to the cellar and nailed the door shut for the winter.

Mom worried about us being cold, so every night she stoked the coal stove in the living room until the stovepipe was red hot nearly all the way to the ceiling. I heard her say she was scared the house would burn down with all of us in it. My brothers, Larry and John, slept together in one upstairs bedroom and my sister, Brenda, and I shared another upstairs bedroom. Mom warmed old bricks and rocks, filled bottles with hot water, and put them in our beds to keep us from freezing. There was absolutely no heat in the upstairs.

I felt a strong sense of responsibility for the family. I lay awake at night for as long as I could so I would smell smoke and wake everybody if the house caught on fire. Mom and Dad were always tired, so I knew they needed their sleep. I awakened many mornings with frost in my nostrils.

The following summer, while I was out of school, Mom and I worked on the house. We wallpapered the upstairs bedrooms and her bedroom downstairs. We patched holes and painted. By the time school started, we had the house looking pretty fine. My mom lived in the "old Shifflett place" until her death two years ago.

Over the years, as we could afford it, we fixed the house so it was more comfortable. In 1969 Mom told Dad she was tired of walking through the ice and snow to go to the toilet. She asked him if she could borrow the money to fix the cellar for her canned food, add a pantry off the kitchen, and put in a bathroom with a tub and shower. She already had the estimates; it was going to cost three thousand dollars.

Dad told her absolutely not. He didn't want to go in debt for a bathroom. They argued for days. He said, "I don't want a toilet in the house. It ain't healthy to shit where you eat and sleep." She called him names such as Peter Tumbledown. That name was always her favorite for him. She yelled, "You'd set here and let the damn house fall in on all of us. I'm borrowin' the money anyway. I'll pay it back myself with my milk money." She went to the bank and borrowed three thousand dollars and brought the papers home for him to sign. He signed them.

In the 1980's Mom was getting tired of carrying wood and coal for the stove, so we put central heating in the downstairs. Later on, we put vinyl siding on the house. The upstairs still had no heat in the winter.

Mom: She Was the Queen of Her Hearth

Mom was the fifteenth child of eighteen children. She was orphaned at age five by her mother, Grandma Mary, and by her father, Grandpa John, at age nine.

"I worshipped both Mom and Dad," she always told me, and I really missed Mom after she died. I almost starved. Dad made my older sisters, Goldie and Dorothy, do the cookin', but they either burnt everything or left it half raw. I wished I was old enough to cook for my daddy."

For most of her life Mom never cut her hair. At the longest point, her hair reached the back of her knees when she let it down. In her younger years, it was dark brown, very thick, and wavy. She wore it up around a long cloth bun that reached from ear to ear and wrapped around the front of her head.

When she washed her hair, it took all day to dry. It was beautiful as it billowed down her back. I loved to watch her when her hair was down. She had to be careful to keep it out of whatever she was doing. One time she got it caught in her wringer washer. She said, "It's a good thing my hair is so long. I got the wringer stopped before it tore my head off."

After that dangerous incident, I asked Mom, "Why don't you get your hair cut?" She answered, "I can't cut it. Just before he died, my daddy asked me not to ever cut my hair."

"But Mom," I pointed out, "Grandpa's been dead for twenty-five years." "Don't matter how long he's been dead, I made him a promise and I'm gonna stick to it," she stated, with a resigned expression on her face.

Years later, long after her long brown hair had turned gray, Mom started having constant headaches. Her doctor told her the weight of her hair was causing her problem. She came home from the doctor and said to me, "What am I gonna do? I promised my daddy, I wouldn't cut my hair."

She struggled for several months with the choice of constant headaches and her promise to Grandpa John.   Finally, she asked me to take her to get her hair cut. While we were at the beauty shop, I talked her into cutting it short and having a curly permanent put in it.

When we left the beauty shop, she was ecstatic. Her headache was gone. She said, "I feel so free. I feel like I could just fly. My head is so light." She never stopped mentioning her promise to her daddy but justified her short hair by saying, "I don't think he would have wanted me to suffer with headaches." I always reassured her, "I know he wouldn't, Mom."

Mom strumming "Wildwood Flower" the guitar

Mom never attended funerals of people who died in the community, and I always wondered why. After we bought the tiny farm where she still lives, we had a well drilled in the back yard. She could not stand to walk out the back door and see the red clay where the drill was working. One day she realized that it reminded her of her parent's graves. Mom associated the red clay with loss and grief she suffered as an orphan.

Realizing what red clay meant to her did not help her cope with death. She never attended the funerals of her sisters and brothers and even my daddy. When the time came that she knew she was too sick to get well, she sat in her chair for five years somewhere between life and death and could not make the transition. I am sure her clinging to life had something to do with the finality of the red clay around the grave. She did not want her children to suffer the pain of her loss as she suffered throughout her life.

After she was orphaned at age nine, she was passed from one older sister to another for a year. She spent part of that time with her oldest sister, Zilla, who was extremely abusive. Zilla was a promiscuous woman, and she told Mom, "As soon as you start 'bleeding like a little pig' you'll be screwing around with men." Mom told her sister, Goldie, what Zilla had said to her. Aunt Goldie, who was twelve years of age, was in love with a young man named Robert Crawford. He was twenty years old. Partly in keeping with mountain tradition and partly to give Mom a home, Goldie married Rob at age twelve. They immediately established a household and took my mother to live with them. They raised her from age ten to age eighteen, when she reconnected with my father and got married.

*Rob and Goldie Crawford's family. L-R: Joyce, Ruby,
Goldie, Mom (standing), Rob, Randy, and George*

My mother told many stories about her place in her sister's home. She slept in an attic room; and, after Goldie had her own children, they slept in the bed with Mom. "There were cracks in the walls of my room, and at night I could see moonlight shining through them. In the winter when it snowed, I woke up many mornings with a skiff of snow on top of my comforters," she told me.

"I had to do most of the cookin'. Rob wanted his food cooked just right so when he told me how to fix something, I made sure I did it his way," Mom said. "A couple of times, he threatened to whip my ass because I didn't get enough salt in the beans. Rob was a pretty good teacher when it comes to cookin'."

Mom told us she was given all the dirty chores and was responsible for taking care of Aunt Goldie's four children. She tells stories of how those children did mean tricks to her by running ahead of her as she was going to the outside toilet, sitting on the seat, and not letting her use the toilet. She often told me she got married to escape the horrible situation and to have children of her own, "I couldn't wait to get married and have my own house. I wanted six kids to love and care for and a warm house to keep clean."

There was not a lot of money to go around so Aunt Goldie's kids, including my mother, never enjoyed any of the luxuries of life. Mom told me, "Rob and Goldie somehow found extra money for themselves though. Many evenings they got in the truck and went to Bridges Service Station where several couples gathered to drink cokes, eat moon pies, and dance. They never brought me and the kids anything."

Uncle Rob was a moonshiner and also owned a sawmill; so many young single men hung around his house. As Mom developed into a young woman, she was often sought after for courtship and sexual favors. "I learned to defend myself anyway I could. One time, while I was peeling potatoes for supper, Rob Craig reached out and touched my breast. I took the knife and hacked into his knuckles. He called me a son-of-a-bitch. His hand bled like a stuck hog. I'll bet you he never touched me again." After that incident, Mom developed a reputation for defending herself, and all the men left her alone.

Mom sweeping the front porch of the house where she and Dad raised our family.

Mom was always overweight. She told me, "When I was nine years old, I weighed ninety-nine pounds. Rob always made fun of me because I was fat. One time he really hurt me. He told me, "Myrt, you look like a bail of hay with the middle string busted." She remained conscious of her weight all of her life. I always thought she looked pretty compared to some overweight women in Hopkins Gap, because she wasn't sloppy fat. There was a lot of muscle under there, too.

Mom sat in her chair a short time before her death and speculated on whether she would go to heaven or hell when she died. She thought back over her life stating that she had never slept with any man other than my daddy. She had cursed some, but only when she was mad. She said she had asked forgiveness for those times. She never mentioned hacking Rob Craig's knuckles. I guess she felt totally justified in that act.

Finally after a long time of reflecting on her life, she concluded that she had committed only one sin and that she wasn't sure she had been forgiven for that one. I asked her to tell me what she had done. I was expecting to hear that she had murdered someone since she was so serious. She sat there staring off into space. I said, "Tell me, Mom. Maybe it wasn't so bad."

Finally, she started to speak.

I went to Mary Kirkpatrick's store and post office with Bonnie Crawford many times. Bonnie was a thief and was always asking me to cover for her while she stole things from the store. I wouldn't help her for a long time. Then one day she hit on one of my favorite things — Vienna sausages. Bonnie asked me to help her steal a can and we would share it on the way home. I hesitated because I knew if Mary caught me she would tell Rob, and I would get a helluva beating. Bonnie assured me we wouldn't get caught, as my mouth began to water for Vienna sausages. I had a paper bag to carry my groceries home. She told me to watch and when Mary turned her back to put up the mail, I was to hold my bag open. When Mary turned her back, I opened the bag, and Bonnie threw in a can of sausages. We casually left the store and hurried up the road to a grove of pine trees where we sat down to share the stolen goods.

The can had to be opened with a metal key that hooked onto a little metal tab. As soon as we started to turn the key to open the can, the metal tab broke. There was no way we could open the can. We both cried and finally threw the can down and walked home.

Everyday we went back to the pine grove and watched the ants crawl in and out of the can as they ate the sausages. I swore never to steal another thing as long as I lived, and I never have.

This is Mary Kiripatrick standing in front of the building that was once the Post Office and general store where Mom helped to steal the Vienna sausages. (1958)

I tried to assure her that when God measures her sins, that can of Vienna sausages would not keep her out of heaven. I said to her, "Besides, half of that sin belongs to Bonnie Crawford."

Mom married Dad in a ceremony with two other couples. As I said before, it was a kind of group marriage. When my mother got mad at my dad over their fifty-four years of marriage, she would tell me she really wasn't married to him because her mind had drifted when it was time to say "I do." The preacher never knew she didn't say it, because the other two couples said it very loudly at the right time. That bit of information was somewhat upsetting to me as a child. I expected my mother might leave my dad at any moment.

While Dad was a wonderful worker and didn't waste his money, he was also an intellectual type. He simply was not good with a handsaw and a hammer. Mom discovered this problem early in their marriage when she asked him to nail a board over a hole in the cow barn. He didn't do a very good job. She took the hammer and handsaw to the barn and fixed the hole the way she wanted it fixed.

From that point on, when she wanted something done that involved measuring and carpentry, she didn't ask Dad anymore. She simply said, under her breath, "I'll do it myself said the little red hen." One day I asked her, "What does that mean, Mom?" She answered, "When I was in school, I read a story about a little red hen who couldn't get any other chickens to help her around the chicken house. After a while, she got tired of asking and said to herself, 'I'll do it myself'. So I'm like the little red hen. If I go on and do it myself, it'll be done right in the first place and save me time in the long run." Mom was extremely talented with her hands and could repair most anything. My brother, John, always asked her to fix his broken toys. His pet name for her was "Mama fix it."

At that time, some animal feed and flour was sold in printed cotton sacks. Sometimes they had flowers on them or little designs and sometimes they were solid colors in red or yellow. Mom told Dad to always get her cow feed and flour in printed sacks. She washed them and made our school clothes out of them. By the time school started in September, she had all our clothes made including our underwear. She saved the scraps and made comforters to keep us warm in the cold weather.

Mom was known far and wide as a good cook. Folks in and out of Hopkins Gap sought her food, especially her fried chicken and banana cake. Often when people pushed back from her table, they said, "That meal was so good it would make your tongue slap your brains out." She was rewarded adequately by those comments.

She knew more about oven temperatures and the effect of altitude on baking than anyone. One of my favorite memories is of the time when she was trying out her oven at the new altitude, shortly after we moved to where she lived the remainder of her life. The first cake she took out of the oven immediately fell flat. She adjusted her oven temperature, mixed another cake and put it in to bake. When she removed the second cake, it immediately fell.

Since she was persistent, she adjusted the temperature again and went through the whole process the third time. I was in the kitchen watching her because it was like watching a scientist solving a major problem. I knew how much her cooking meant to her. If she couldn't bake a banana cake, she no longer needed to live.

Well, the third cake came out of the oven as flat as a pancake. I could tell she was mad, because she started to cry. Crying made her even madder. I kind of hung around the door, because I knew something was going to happen. My little sister, Brenda, was innocently playing in the kitchen for the warmth of the stove. She had no idea that something loud and destructive was about to happen.

Suddenly, Mom threw the cake pans, with the cake in them, in the floor and jumped up and down on them until they were flat. That didn't take too long because, at that time, she weighed a hefty two hundred and thirty-six pounds and was often described as "two axe handles across the ass" which made me fighting mad when I heard it. I was old enough to enjoy the stomping show, but my sister, Brenda, was terrified because she was taken by surprise.

I responded to Mom's frustration with a variety of feelings. In some cases I wanted to laugh — like with the cake pans. It was a funny sight with her jumping up and down on the pans with chunks of yellow cake sticking to her shoes and flying through the air. At the same time, I felt really bad for her because she worked so hard. She had varicose veins in her legs and by the end of every day, they would be swollen and throbbing from her working hard all day. I always wanted to grow up fast, get a job, and buy her a new stove or a new whatever was frustrating her at the time.

Another time, Mom was making strawberry jelly. We had all crawled on our hands and knees up a steep hill to pick tiny wild strawberries. We had all sat around in the evening capping and cleaning the fruit. In other words, Mom and all of us kids had a large investment in the jelly project. She boiled the jelly in a large dishpan with handles on the side. When it was ready to remove from the stove, she stuck two large spoons in the hot handles on the pan and proceeded to lift the jelly off the heat. I had watched her lift a hot pan this way a thousand times before so I had no reason to doubt her skill now. Just as she turned around, the spoons slipped and the jelly spilled down the front of her apron. She dropped the pan to the floor. She clamped her lips tight together, reached behind and untied her apron, leaned forward and removed the apron so she wouldn't get burned. I knew something was about to happen. Without saying a word, she stepped on top of the dishpan and stomped it beyond recognition. Then she quietly cleaned up the sticky mess. My brother, Larry, also witnessed this trauma and remembers it to this day.

Dad had a short temper after he returned from the war, so Mom didn't trust him with our discipline. She took care of that herself in a variety of ways depending on which of us needed her attention. Quietly and calmly she shaped each of our lives as needed. I can still hear her say to me when she caught me in some bad behavior, "Go get me a switch off the lilac bush and bring it here." She learned early in our lives that Larry and I responded to a lilac switch. My sister, Brenda, always changed her behavior after a good lecture. My younger brothers, John and Warnie, were brought in line by a few whacks across the buttocks with the fire shovel. If any of these methods failed, she simply said, "I'll tell your daddy when he gets home." We all responded to that warning because we remembered the width of his belt—at least ten inches in my memory—when he took it off and used it.

As I think about my mother now, I realize she didn't have many close friends other than my Aunt Ethel, Uncle Shirley's wife, and I doubt that she ever really confided in anyone. Most of her conversations with other women were about cooking and sewing. I know that she listened to Aunt Ethel's problems while they cooked on Sundays, but I never heard her talk about her life to anyone.

Mom seemed more inclined to spend time with her children than with women her own age, but she also never told us much about who she really was, about her feelings as a person other than a mother. I know there were dark secrets in her younger life, because evidence revealed itself in the things that made her angry and the things that made her cry.

I have always believed that she was physically and sexually abused when she was too young to defend herself. I asked her several times, "Mom, did anybody ever hurt you when you were little?" Her response was always the same, "What's in the past is over."

While she was proud of her clean white clothes on the line early every Monday morning, her comforters, and the clothes she made for us, Mom's main identity was wrapped up in her cooking. When people showed up at the house unannounced, she often said, "If I knowed you was comin' I'd have killed a chicken and churned," or "I'd have baked a cake." She appeared to most as very gracious when she made these comments, but I knew she was subtly telling people they should have let her know they were coming so she could have planned a great meal for them.

Nevertheless, she was always able to feed any number of people who arrived unannounced. If she knew ahead of time that a large number of people were coming to eat, like on hog killing day, she would say to me, "I'll have to put the big pot in the little one." For many years, I didn't ask her what that meant because I figured it was some kind of magic she practiced to cook a lot of food. Finally, I asked again, "What does that mean?" She responded, "I am gonna have to use every pot I have to cook enough food for these people."

The simplicity of her answer was a shock to me, because I did, and still do, assume a deeper meaning in just about everything I hear. I have always assumed everybody else is smarter than I am and can express themselves in more meaningful ways.

After a long day of cooking, cleaning, and taking care of kids, Mom would say, "I'm as jumpy as a long-tailed cat in a room full of rockers," "I'm as nervous as a whore in church," or "You don't have to be crazy to live here, but it helps."

Mom worried about skinny folks not eating enough. Perhaps this reflected her discomfort with her own weight. She was

93

never allowed to forget her weight because of the men in the extended family were always saying things to her such as, "Myrtle, when I walk behind you, your ass looks like two kids fightin' under a blanket." Because she heard these kinds of comments, she always thought she was ugly. I thought she was really pretty and many other people did too. I often said to her, "Mom, you are so pretty." She always got upset and sometimes responded, "Yea, I look like I was shot at and missed and shit at and hit."

She described skinny people as "having to drink muddy water to keep the sun from souring their guts." When I was about twelve years old, I wouldn't eat anything in the summer time except tomatoes. I always got really thin. Mom yelled at me for not eating. She said, "I can read the Bible through your ribs."

As I said earlier, I was born almost nine months and ten days after Mom and Dad's wedding. As was the case with all the women in Hopkins Gap, she wanted a boy as a first child and had already picked his name. He was going to be named William. But, my being a female threw her for a loop. She had no name picked out. So the local funeral director's wife suggested she call me Peggy Lois. I ended up being called Peggy Ann. My mother never explained the change.

Mom always let me know that she was disappointed in my gender as her first child. She told me she had wanted a black-haired, brown-eyed boy to start her family. I had platinum blonde hair and Grandpa Austin's blue eyes. I began my life feeling inadequate and misplaced in the scheme of the family. A year and one-half later, she gave birth to my brother, Larry, who had black hair and brown eyes. This did not help my situation. She had the perfect child.

Many times I sat on the kitchen chair crying and saying to her, "I wish I was a boy with black hair and brown eyes." She would say to me, "I asked for a boy when you were born, and I got you instead."

The third child was a girl. Destined to be the middle child and having been a girl, my sister, Brenda, suffered even more than I did. She was lost between two boys. She spent her entire childhood, and her adulthood, seeking approval from Mom and Dad.

While Dad was in the army, Mom had a rough time taking care of the household and three small children. Many times she told me how, in cold weather, she went to the barn to milk her cow and left me in charge. I asked her, "How could you trust me to stay with the little ones. I was only three or four years old?" She replied, "I put all three of you in the baby bed. I pulled up the side of the bed so the little ones couldn't fall out. I told you to sit there and watch them. When I got back from the barn, you were always exactly where I put you and the little ones were just fine."

Leaving me in charge did not work one time when she went to the woodpile to chop some wood. She told me to watch Brenda who was just beginning to walk by this time and very curious about everything. Mom had left a ham hock boiling on the kitchen stove. Brenda went into the kitchen, pulled a chair up to the stove, and grabbed the handle of the ham pot. She burned her hand and, in her panic, upset the pot of boiling broth down over her body. She slipped and fell off the chair.

When I heard the noise and screaming, I ran to the kitchen to find her floating on her stomach in the greasy hot ham broth. I ran to the front door to get Mom, but found I couldn't reach the latch to open the door. I just started to scream and pound on the door. Mom heard me and came running.

Brenda had third degree burns on her belly and still carries the scar today. I have always felt guilty about that scar on Brenda's belly but certainly came to realize that it was not my fault. I have also forgiven my mother for giving me too much responsibility at such a young age. She was doing the best she could since she was both man and the woman of the house while Dad was away.

Mom got lonely sometimes in the evenings, so she would walk across the hill about a half of a mile to Aunt Goldie's house. She carried the two little ones, and I walked alongside. She often stayed until after dark before she started home with us. As we walked home in the dark, she talked to me about the stars and about how far Dad was away from us. I got sleepy on these late evening trips home, and I would say, "Carry me, too, Mama." She would put her hands together and stoop down so I could sit on her hands. With a baby in each arm and me sitting on her hands, we all made it home safely.

Two years after my sister was born, my brother John came into the world. He had blue eyes and blonde hair. He didn't fit her image of the perfect child but somehow turned out to be my mother's favorite. By then, I was five years old. Many times as she changed John's diaper, she let me watch and pointed out the difference between boys and girls. She said that when God made a boy he had extra material, and he carefully shaped the extra material into the penis. But, when He made a girl, he ran out of material and had to leave a gap.

Once again after being born first when Mom wanted a boy, I felt very inadequate as a female and could sense God's disappointment when He realized he had not bought enough "materials" for his baby-making project.

While my mother never worked on a job outside the home, she consistently contributed to the family income. When Dad left for the army, Pop May encouraged Mom to buy a cow to provide milk for us. He sold her a jersey heifer for fifty dollars and provided free barn space.

Mom's army income was one hundred and twenty dollars each month. That money didn't cover all her expenses and meet her dream of saving enough money for a down payment on a small farm. Again Pop May suggested she sell the extra milk from her cow to the local dairy.

She made arrangements with Charlie Henkel, the milkman. He brought her a five-gallon milk can. She filled it with her extra milk, and Charlie picked it up every other day. Her first milk check was thirty dollars. The extra money went a long way toward paying her rent and buying groceries, so she was able to save a portion of her army allotment each month.

Mom saved two thousand dollars toward her dream of owning a small farm. Just before Dad came home from the war, a nice farm came for sale, and the price was two thousand and seven hundred dollars. Mom asked Uncle Rob if he would loan her seven hundred dollars so she could buy the farm. He said he couldn't loan her the money. The farm was sold to someone else by the time Dad got home.

Mom was having good luck with selling milk, and she wanted to buy some more cows, so she jumped at the chance to take over Aunt Goldie's little farm when it was offered. Goldie's farm had thirteen acres. With the extra land, Mom was able to expand her herd to six cows; and her milk sales were booming.

Uncle Rob had built chicken houses on the farm before he died, so Mom started raising chickens for sale. Her first flock was five hundred chicks. She raised them to six weeks old. A poultry buyer came to look at them and paid her the top price. She cleared five hundred dollars on her first sale.

Two years later, the same farm that Mom had wanted to buy came for sale again. Meantime, the land had been split and the best pasture sold to John I. Myers. At this time, the farm had only seven acres. Mom and Dad bought the farm. She decreased her herd to four cows and continued to produce milk. Charlie Henkel still drove past the house to haul her milk to market.

During the summer of 1954, the polio epidemic reached Hopkins Gap and the surrounding area where we lived. Several children in school with me were stricken with the disease. Mom panicked. She heard all the stories on the news about children being in iron lungs and dying from the disease. As usual when she got scared, she went into action. She quarantined us for the whole summer. She didn't let us go anywhere. She met visitors at the road and wouldn't let them come in the house.

By the following summer, the Salk vaccine was available. She would not let us take the shot because she believed that the vaccine could cause us to get polio like it did some children when it

97

first became available. She always bragged that she kept us from getting polio.

Dad was working hard at a local feed mill; but his bring-home pay was only forty dollars a week. There were five children to support and a house payment of twenty-five dollars a month. I was in high school taking courses to be a secretary. I had to pay a fee to use the typewriters. It was two dollars and fifty cents a month. Dad's pay and Mom's milk money were not enough to cover that extra expense, so Mom walked to Aunt Goldie's house to wash and iron her clothes for $2.00 a week; thus, my typing fee was paid and extra things were purchased.

After several years of selling milk, the local dairy changed hands and stopped hauling small amounts of milk. Mom got very upset, but she didn't give up her cows. She passed the word to the neighbors that she was selling milk by the gallon. The news spread, and folks started coming to the house to buy milk.

She bought a butter churn, started making butter and cottage cheese and offered these items to her customers. She still had extra milk, so she bought newborn calves from local dairy farmers and raised them to sell for veal. With this money, she was able to buy a freezer and maintain the farm.

By this time, Dad was making a little more money at the feed mill and three of us kids had incomes of our own. I had my job as a secretary; my brother had a job at the Bridgewater Furniture Plant, and my sister worked as an office manager. The financial need for the cows was less important; and, in fact, Dad showed Mom on paper many times that the cows were not giving enough milk to pay for their own feed. She argued with him, "Okay, Norman, you stop at the store on your way home for work every day and bring me two gallons of milk. I'll soon show you how much money the cows save you."

After a time, it was obvious that she was sentimentally attached to her cows, and it really didn't matter to her if she was making any money or not. She expressed this sentiment by telling the stories of how she took care of three small children and went to the barn to milk while Dad was in Germany.

She told me, "After Brenda got a little older and Larry started walking, I got me two little baby bottles. I took you, Larry, and Brenda to the barn with me. You and Larry stood by my knee, and I laid Brenda across my lap. She lay there while I milked the cow. Before I started milking in my bucket, I filled the little baby bottles with warm milk straight from the cow. I handed you one and Larry one. I kept y'all suckin' warm milk from the bottles while I finished milkin'." I have faint memories of those times and got quite a loving picture as I heard Mom repeat that story many times.

Her sentiment was also expressed in other stories about her cows. Each cow had a name—Ole Jerse was her first cow. Ole Jerse had a female calf; Mom named her Hommy. Hommy had Nanny, and Nanny had Betsy. She often bragged that she had four generations of cows represented in her herd beginning with her first cow. She could relate stories of each cow's birth—how she had to "pull them out" of their mother. She knew each cow's milk output.

She related stories of "drenching" them—giving them medicine when they were sick—and how she figured out how to handle a cow without any help. "I stuck two fingers in the old cow's nose, put my hip against her front shoulder, and pulled back on her nose," she bragged. "When her mouth came open, I stuck the medicine bottle in where her teeth couldn't bite it. I poured the medicine down her throat, so she had no choice but to drink it."

She knew how each cow eventually died; and for many years, she cried about Betsy when she died after she got into the hog feed and bloated. She used the cows to teach my sister and me about sex and having babies.

When I was about nine years old, she told me about menstruation. Shortly after that, she sent me along with my dad and Ole Jerse when he took her to the bull to be bred. I saw enough of the breeding process to fill my head with curiosity. I think that was part of her plan. When I got home, I started asking her questions.

She used her wringer washer for the next step in my education about the birds and the bees. The drain hose lifted up and was hooked into a hole in the side of the washer. She took the drain hose out of its hole, compared it to a penis, and showed me how a man sticks his penis into the woman's vagina as she put the hose back in the storage hole. I was anxious to have more information, so I asked her, "Tell me how babies are born." She answered, "Not now, you're not old enough yet."

When I was twelve years old, she taught me about birthing babies. Hommy was about to have a calf, so Mom took me in the chicken house; and, through the cracks in the wallboards, we watched the calf be born. She explained every part of the process — the birth pains, the water breaking, the calf emerging head first, and finally the releasing and consumption of the placenta by the cow. She quickly told me humans did not eat the placenta, and they did not lick their babies clean. That was a relief to hear.

Mom protected her cows nearly as much as she protected her children. She never allowed Dad to get close to the barn while she was milking. She explained to me, "He talks too loud and the cows don't like it when he cusses. They won't 'let their milk down' because he makes them nervous." In fact, she didn't want any males to be near her cows. She taught me how to milk so I could fill in for her in case she got sick.

One time, an agricultural extension agent dropped by the farm and told her she had to have her cows vaccinated for bangs disease, a common name for brucellosis — an infectious disease of cattle that can be transmitted to humans through the cow's milk. He warned her that we could all get a serious disease called Undulant Fever from drinking her cows' milk. Dropping by the farm was the agent's first mistake.

Mom lit into him like a wet hen. "My cows are not sick and you're not doing anything to them. When they get sick, I treat them myself and if it's something I can't take care of, I'll call the cow doctor."

The agent tried to argue with her. That was his second mistake. She picked up a stick of wood from the woodpile and started walking toward him. Her face was beet red. She said, through clenched teeth, "You get off my property right now, and don't you ever show your face around here again." I remember him shaking his finger at her as he backed away toward his car, "I won't be back, but somebody will." Mom answered, "Tell 'em to come on, I'll run them off too." Nobody else ever showed up to vaccinate her cows.

The time came when Mom's first cow, "Ole Jerse," was too old to breed anymore. The cow was about twenty-two years old. Not being able to breed meant she would soon stop giving milk. With the pressure from Dad about feeding a nonproductive cow, Mom finally agreed to sell "Ole Jerse." She called Russell Crawford and asked him to haul the cow to the Saturday stock sale in Harrisonburg.

When the truck arrived to pick her up, Mom made sure Russell got her on the truck without hurting her, and then she asked him to wait until she went inside the house. He drove off with "Ole Jerse" looking very frantic on the back of his truck. Mom stayed in her bedroom for a long time. We could hear her crying. When she came out she never talked about "Ole Jerse" again for a long, long time.

By the late 1980's Mom was over sixty years old, and her energy was declining. She still fed her veal calves, made butter, and cottage cheese and sold raw milk. The work was time consuming since she had developed friendships with her customers. When they picked up their products, they frequently visited for twenty to thirty minutes.

To make up for the extra time and energy, Mom turned the milking over to her daughter-in-law, Hilda. She paid Hilda with free milk products for her growing family. It was quite a moving picture to watch Mom, Hilda, and Hilda's little girls gather the milk buckets and head to the barn to milk.

Peggy Ann Shifflett

The milk business was now a three-generation operation that had both good and bad aspects. The fact that Mom needed help with her cows reduced her personal satisfaction. She often said: "It used to be a peaceful time — quiet — I used that time [while milking] to pray for my son not to go to the army. When he went, I cried about him being in Vietnam and prayed for him to return safe. I prayed for Randy when he was sick and worked out a lot of my problems beside my old cows." Randy was Aunt Goldie's son and it turns out that Randy died May 17, 1972, and Dad gave Mom the news early that morning while she was milking. When he came back to the house, I asked him how she was doing. He said, "She never looked up from the milk bucket."

Three generations of milking women -- Hilda, Vanessa, Paula and Mom in the back hiding from the camera. They are returning from the evening milking.

Mom kept her cows until she had a debilitating stroke five years ago. She had reduced the number to two cows, and Hilda did

the milking every morning and evening with the same compensation — all the milk she needed for her family.

During late 1970's and early 1980's, I was in school in Texas finishing my education and starting my teaching career. By this time, I was thirty-eight years old. On one of my trips home from Texas, Mom asked me to go for a walk with her. As we walked down the gravel road in front of her house, she took my hand. She remained quiet for a little while then she started to talk to me. She said quietly, "Peg, people in the family have always asked me why you never got married and had kids like everybody else. For a long time I let their questions bother me. I made excuses like you hadn't met the right man yet or I would say, 'She'll come home when she's finished her school, and she'll get married'." I listened quietly while wondering where this little speech was going. She continued, "I know I've bugged you over the years about getting married, but my main reason for wantin' you to get married was so you'd have kids to take care of you when you get old."

She squeezed my hand a little tighter and went on, "I've done a lot of thinkin' while you've been in Texas, and I've decided to tell you its okay with me if you never get married. I just want you to be happy in whatever you choose to do." I was astounded at how much she had thought about me not getting married. I sensed the extent of her conflict. She had helped me get the money to go to college while at the same time she was being pressured by the family to have me fulfill the mountain girl's role of getting married and having a family. I felt a weight lifting off my shoulders because she had questioned me over the years about getting married. I said, "Mom, I am so happy that you're okay with the way I am living my life. It will relieve me of a lot of guilt." We turned around and walked slowly back to the house.

Dad: He was the King of His Garden

My dad, Norman Shifflett, was the ninth child of ten. He never talked about his early childhood, but Uncle Shirley grew up

103

with him and has shared a lot about his early life with me. When Dad got home from school in the evenings, Grandpa Austin told him to hitch up the mule and plow the corn.

Uncle Shirley said, "Your daddy was so little when Austin made him plow corn that he couldn't reach the plow handles good enough to hold the blade in the ground. I saw him put his feet on top of the plow blade to get up high enough to keep the plow in the ground. Across the field he went with his feet never hitting the dirt."

Dad had a nasty scar beside his nose. Uncle Shirley told me it was from the mule kicking him in the face while he was buckling the harness. "The mule kicked him square in the face. His nose was broke and cut real bad. He didn't even go to a doctor."

Dad had a seventh grade education because that was all that was available at the one-room school in Hopkins Gap. He finished seventh grade and took it over one more time because he loved learning so much.

He was a self-educated man. Throughout his life, he read every book or newspaper he could get his hands on. He studied the history of the Jews and studied the Bible especially the Book of Revelations. He predicted that Israel would someday defeat the United States in a final world war. I always think about his predictions when I hear the news about the crisis in the Middle East. He would have made a fine preacher or professor.

He was the Hopkins Gap community historian. He could trace every member of the community several generations back in their family tree. People came from miles around to ask him about this or that person's history. He borrowed a camera many times and photographed the oldest people in Hopkins Gap. He took the only picture of Mary Kirkpatrick, just before she died in 1961. She was standing in front of the building that had been the Palos post office and general store in the Gap. That picture hung on the dining room wall until the morning before Mom died.

At the end of his life, he was working with a woman from Austin, Texas. She had traced her roots back to Banks Shifflett, my

great grandfather. Dad took her to the cemeteries in Greene County and the Gospel Hill Mennonite Church cemetery looking for clues to connect her more directly to our family line. He had an incredible memory that he passed on to me so that I could name all my twenty-two aunts and uncles, my ninety-nine first cousins, and eventually tell the story of growing up in Hopkins Gap.

He voted in every election and was a rabid democrat. Only once in his life did he admit to voting for a Republican, although he didn't say who got his vote. He was very private about his voting record, but I assumed he voted for President Eisenhower because he had seen him several times when he was a soldier in Germany, and he admired him as a general. He never admitted that he voted for Eisenhower, but he also never denied it.

Dad was a small man of about five feet and seven inches. He was thin and wiry like Grandma Molly and never weighed over one hundred and fifty pounds soakin' wet, but he was very strong. When he was young, his hair was dark brown and curly. He didn't lose any more of his hair after he returned from the war but by the time he died it had turned gray like Grandpa Austin's hair.

Before he went to the war, he had Grandma Molly's sharp brown eyes with a twinkle that revealed his quick sense of humor. Uncle Shirley described my pre-war Dad many times. "We were the best of buddies. We made moonshine together, fought off the Peakers, and drank a lot of whiskey before we got married."

Not long ago, Uncle Shirley was telling me about Dad's sense of humor when he was a young man. He told me about a time when he and Dad got drunk and ended up at Grandpa Austin's house. They partied and drank some more whiskey until they passed out on the floor. Dad woke up the next morning and apparently had a very bad taste in his mouth.

Uncle Shirley said, "Your daddy woke up and punched me. He said, 'Shirley, did you see a man in this room just about five minutes ago?' I said, 'No, I was asleep until you punched me.' Your daddy said, 'I wish I had been awake just five minutes ago. I would have caught the man who took a shit in my mouth'."

105

Dad was not the same man when he returned from the war. His hair was short and had lost its curl. He looked tired and old. The sparkle in his eyes had dulled and had been replaced with a studious and reflective gaze, but most often his eyes were filled with fear and stress. His sense of humor, while still with him, was sporadic and very unpredictable. He was very moody. He would occasionally talk about his experiences in Germany with his men friends. He told a hair-raising story about crossing the Rhine River with General Patton's army. The soldiers were in pontoons as they crossed the river. They were vulnerable targets for the German sharpshooters. As the pontoons left the shores of the Rhine, the German snipers started shooting. They killed or wounded every soldier in the first pontoon and started shooting the soldiers in the second pontoon. Dad was in the second pontoon. They shot every man right up to where Dad was sitting in the middle. The man next to him was hit in the shoulder. The next shot rang out and slightly clipped the end of Dad's finger. The shooting stopped. His pontoon landed safely on the opposite shore of the Rhine River.

I often heard him describe the necessary mental work he had to do to survive the war. He told Mom he had to make us "little in his mind" so that his love for us, and the fact that he was missing us, did not distract him and make him vulnerable to deadly mistakes. He told us what happened to men who took the time to cry about their loved ones at home. He said, "Many of them didn't make it through the next battle."

After Dad returned from the war, he had nightmares. Mom told me that when he awoke after a nightmare he would cry and tell her how scared he was that he would never be able to make his family "big in his mind" again.

The shoe factory was closed when he returned from the war so Uncle Lurty got him a job at Rockingham Milling Company. He stood over an open hole in the floor and poured the ingredients for animal feed into a mixer below. It was a very dusty and dirty job. I hate to admit that many times in my life I was ashamed of him because he always smelled like chicken feed and had feed dust on his clothes and shoes.

He worked there for thirty-six years. For a short period of time, he was trained by his company to diagnose and treat illnesses in chickens and turkeys. For those few years, he wore clean clothes, gained a little weight, and looked really nice in his white "doctor" jackets as he left for work to vaccinate sick poultry.

One summer he took a week's vacation to spend time with his family. He bought a nice hat and a khaki trench coat and took us all out to eat at Layman's Restaurant on Liberty Street. He took off his hat and hung his trench coat on the coat rack. We all sat around a table as a family. We always had family meals at home, but this was the first time, and only time, we ate in a restaurant as a family. Of course, I immediately went into fantasy mode. Ever since I started school and read about Dick and Jane, I wanted a daddy with a briefcase, necktie, hat, and trench coat. I wanted Mom, who was always overweight, to be slender and wear nice dresses with a modern hairdo. I wanted to live on a street in a town. In my fantasy, I was "Jane" in my first-grade reading book. My brother was "Dick" and the other kids didn't exist in my fantasy. Dad was "Dick and Jane's" father, he had a briefcase, and we lived on a street, with a street address, rather than on Route 4, Box 10.

For the remainder of his life after he returned from Germany, talking about the war seemed to put him in a good mood for a few days, yet it haunted him for the rest of his life. After he returned from the war, I saw him cry only once. In 1963, when we drove my brother, John, to the airport to leave for Viet Nam, Dad asked me to drive the car back home. That was an unusual request because he didn't really trust my driving. He got in the back seat. I glanced in the rear view mirror and saw him wiping the tears with his big white handkerchief. He never made a sound.

Dad loved fried potatoes; and, in the same way his daddy, Grandpa Austin, had to have bird egg beans every meal, Dad had to have fried potatoes every day and twice on Saturdays. He raised wonderful potatoes in his garden every year.

*Dad in his garden hoeing potatoes after a
long, hard day of work at the feed mill*

My favorite memories are of him in his potato patch. I think now that the only real peace Dad had after he returned from the war was when he was in his potato patch. I have a picture of him hoeing the weeds between the rows. I always wanted my Dad to have peace in his life. Perhaps that is why I treasure the picture so much. Every time I look at it, it is as if I am standing there with him.

As soon as the potato plants peeped through the ground, he was out there gently digging around them. He despised potato bugs. When he saw the first one on his potato plants, he grabbed his spray and soaked the whole patch. As soon as he sprayed them, he walked slowly up and down each row and handpicked the bugs off the plants, put them in a tin can with kerosene, and then set the can on fire.

Every harvest time he would try new ways to get his potatoes out of the ground. The garden had a six-foot wire fence around it that he had built to keep out the cows and chickens. It was hard to use a tractor in the small space. One year he took the car out into the pasture behind the garden and hooked long chains to the plow. He put my brother and me behind the plow to guide it through the potato row while he pulled the plow with the car. That method didn't work because we were too small to hold the plow in the ground.

Another year, he made a harness for my brother and me and hooked us to the plow while he held it in the potato row. We were too weak to pull the plow with its blade stuck in the ground. Much to his dismay, he ended up digging his potatoes by hand every year. But it was a labor of love, because he enjoyed comparing the yield each year to the one from the year before.

Some of the biggest arguments between Dad and Mom happened when she went into his potato patch and "grubbed" some new potatoes before the vines died. He would say, "Myrt, how in the hell am I gonna know how many potatoes I got this year with you out there "grubbin'?" His fussing never stopped her. Year after year, she "grubbed" and he fussed.

Dad always wanted a tractor, but Mom wouldn't let him buy one. She thought he would use it to trim the pasture where her cows grazed. She told me many times, "If I let him buy a tractor, he'll cut every blade of grass. I want the grass to be tall so the cows can eat in the dry months. I won't have to buy as much hay in the winter." She continued, "He takes the lawn mower out in the field and cuts some of the cows' grass every chance he gets anyway." There was always a conflict between what Dad wanted to do and what Mom wanted for her cows.

Dad worked around the problem by using the car as a tractor. One time I was helping him make hay. He was pulling an old hay rake that had a foot pedal to release the hay to make a windrow for the hay bailer. He drove the car while I worked the pedal on the hay rake. We were moving along fine until he made a sharp turn in the corner of the field. The large wheel on the rake got caught behind a fence post and snapped the axle in two pieces. Dad heard the crack, stopped the car, got out and walked toward the rake and me. I expected a major whipping, but he just stood there looking at the rake and said very calmly, "I'll be a lop-eared cock sucker."

Dad was a faithful worker. The thirty-six years he spent working in a feed mill ultimately killed him. He breathed feed dust all those years, and smoked cigarettes as well. He died some years ago from brown lung. He was only seventy-five when he died. We didn't realize how sick he was because he never complained. After he died, our neighbors and extended family members told us that he had been sick for a very long time.

A few months prior to his death, I got a clue that he was very sick when he started driving his truck to get the mail. The mailbox was only fifty yards from the house, but it was down the hill some. I thought he would be around a while longer, so I had not formally recorded his community history. Not only had I failed to record his voice, but I also felt bad for the community.

I never realized what a treasure my daddy was to our family and to the Hopkins Gap community. Unlike other men who depend on their wives to maintain family connections, Dad was the one who visited people in the hospital, nursing homes, and attended every funeral of people in the Gap. When he died, his sister, Vernie, was in her nineties and living in a nursing home. Dad was her most faithful visitor. I wondered who would take his place in her lonely room.

Dad lost a few of his brothers and sisters before he died. He made sure their graves were marked with headstones. When I visit his grave now, I notice that his brothers who have died since him do not have headstones, and they probably never will. It seems that nobody else in the family cares as much as he did.

Now as I write, I depend on notes in the margins of books, on envelopes, and bits of paper. I wrote these notes as I listened to him talk over the years, always intending to record him. I am thankful for my scattered notes.

Influence from the Grave

Other influential characters in my life died long before I was born. Their contributions to my childhood were given in stories about their lives passed on to me by my mother. They were also the characters in much of the oral tradition so freely given to my generation by my uncles and aunts. Whenever I found myself in a quiet setting with Uncle Shirley, Uncle Jim, my mom, or dad, I could expect to hear a story. Amazingly, the stories were told the same with each telling giving me the sense that I was being read to from the Hopkins Gap history book. Not a detail was left out and the colorful and vivid descriptions placed me in the midst of the story as if I had been there when it happened.

Some of my favorite times were cold winter evenings in the kitchen by the wood stove when Uncle Shirley would drop by or long Sunday afternoons in the summer on the front porch at Uncle Jim's house. I could tell when a story was about to be told. Uncle Jim would stop rocking his chair, take a toothpick out of his mouth, lean forward, and look up into the leaves of a huge red oak tree that shaded his front porch. Finally, he would start his story with "Have I ever told you about the time...." I may have heard the story ten times before, but I always acted as if it was the first time. As Uncle Jim got older he suffered from untreated maturity onset diabetes. His blood sugar was always so high that his saliva was sticky. As he told his stories, his lips made a little popping noise as he talked but the sound never distracted me from his fascinating stories about hunting and moonshining.

111

Peggy Ann Shifflett

Grandpa John Morris and Grandma Mary Morris

Mary Ellen Lam married John Wesley Morris when she was fifteen years old, and he was twenty-one. Grandma Mary died in 1926 at the age of thirty-nine. She had just given birth to her eighteenth child, and he was four months old. Grandpa John took Gandma Mary across Little North Mountain to stay with her sister because he was afraid he would get her pregnant again. She never returned to her family and died at her sister's house. According to Aunt Goldie, she died of "heart dropsy." It was believed that childbearing weakened her heart so that it "leaked fluid" into her chest until she could no longer get her breath. Today we would say she died of congestive heart failure.

Twelve of her eighteen children lived to adulthood while three died as young children and three were stillborn. The twelve who lived gave birth to a good portion of my ninety-nine first cousins that I brag about to my students and anyone else who will listen.

Although we never met, Grandma Mary influenced my life through my mother's tales of her wonderful cooking and the loving descriptions of her beautiful, bright calico dresses that she made for herself. "My mother's waist was as 'thin as a wasp'. Her clothes fit really nice when she wasn't pregnant," she told me. "Her long skirts were gathered full around her hips, and there was always an apron pinned to the front of her dress above her breasts and tied behind her back. Her light brown hair was naturally wavy, and she wore it up in a bun on the back of her head." One of Mom's favorite memories of her mother was watching her brush her hair at night before she went to bed.

As a young child I listened to these vivid descriptions; however, as I grew older and became more curious, I wondered about Mom's descriptions. After all, she was only five when Grandma Mary died. However, someone in the family located an old family picture of Grandpa John and Grandma Mary with their three oldest children, and, sure enough, Mom's description of her mother was perfect.

112

John and Mary Morris with the oldest of their eighteen children
— Aunt Zilla, Uncle Carl, and Uncle Charlie (circa 1930)

After my father died, I was sorting through his papers and came across his birth certificate. I was surprised to learn that the midwife who brought him into this world was Grandma Mary Morris. I had never been told that she was a midwife. She delivered my daddy just a few months before she got pregnant with my mother.

Grandma Mary's life still enriches my life because it was so extreme — eighteen single births by age thirty-nine! Her story gives me lecture material on birth control and failed birth control, changing death patterns and birth patterns. She and my Grandpa John worried a lot about having so many children and having to work so hard to support them. According to my Aunt Goldie, they tried to not get pregnant, but their method didn't work. She said, "He tried to keep from getting Mom pregnant by pulling 'it' out before he finished; but, then he just put 'it' right back in again." Obviously, "coitus interruptis" doesn't work if it is practiced as "coitus interruptis coitus!"

Grandpa John was a strong man and was respected as a good worker. Uncle Shirley often told me his daddy was "the workinest man he had ever seen." His labors included carpentry, butchering, and apple orchard tending. One of the houses he built for his family still stands in Hopkins Gap. When I drive past it now, I am always reminded of my mother pointing out the crooked windows in the second-story level. Her face beamed with pride as she told me, "I think he did a good job. His only tools were a hammer, a handsaw, and a carpenter's square."

Uncle Shirley told me that Grandpa John butchered for everybody in Hopkins Gap. He sometimes butchered for folks across Little North Mountain in the Valley. "He never got any pay except for a 'mess' of meat for his family; but, I guess with the size of his family that would have been a lot of meat."

Grandpa John moved his family out of Hopkins Gap for a short time to take an orchard job in Twin Mountain, West Virginia. While he and Grandma Mary lived there my mother was born. She was child number fifteen. Uncle Charlie was old enough by that time to help in the orchards. Uncle Shirley said, "My daddy could take care of two rows of trees and help Charlie with his row. He was a 'work horse'."

When Grandma Mary died, Grandpa John tried to take care of his smaller children with the help of his oldest daughters. Aunt Goldie and Aunt Dorothy were still at home, and they tried to cook for the family. Mom, who was five years old at the time, told me that everything they prepared to eat was not fit to eat. "I used to get up from the table and go stand on the porch so I could smell Aunt Millie's supper from down the hill," she told me. "Sometimes Aunt Millie asked my daddy to come down to her house to eat, but she couldn't afford to feed all us kids."

After two years of trying to keep his household together with the help of his young daughters, Grandpa John went down the road to Mike and Cass Lam's house. He knew they had a daughter in her late twenties who was still single. Her name was Ivy Lam. Mom said, "My daddy asked if he could marry Ivy so she could cook for him and help with the younger children. Mike and Cass said yes."

Mom always emphasized that it was not a marriage for love. "My daddy just needed a cook and a housekeeper," she told me. "Ivy spoke Pennsylvania Dutch, and she was mean to me. She made me sit on the hill above the chicken lot for hours every summer day to make sure the chicken hawks didn't get her chickens. Ivy told me the chickens were important for the survival of our family. I didn't believe her then with the hot summer sun beating down on my head, but now I remember Ivy dragging me by the hand as she walked about five miles to Doug Brenneman's store with eggs and homemade butter. Sometimes she grabbed a live chicken and carried it by the legs to the store. She traded the chicken, eggs, and butter for staples such as sugar, salt, and flour."

Four short years after Grandma Mary's death, Grandpa John died of a heart attack at age forty-nine. Uncle Shirley told me, "He was butchering for somebody over in Linville and cut his hand really bad. He took thirty aspirin during that day for the pain and lost so much blood his heart stopped."

According to Aunt Goldie and Mom, Grandma Mary was often the victim of her own mother, Ellie Lam, who was thought to be an evil witch. Ellie never liked Grandpa John, and she constantly cast spells on her always-pregnant daughter. Aunt Goldie told the story that happened when Grandpa John and Grandma Mary lived at Twin Mountain, West Virginia. My mother was a tiny baby when Grandma Ellie left Hopkins Gap on a trip to visit her daughter and the new baby. While Ellie was there she got into a fight with Grandma Mary and was asked to leave. Ellie walked out of the yard and looked back to say to Grandma Mary, "You will be sorry for what you did old girl." As soon as she was out of sight, my tiny baby mother-to-be started crying. She cried for several days until Grandma Mary called on a West Virginia Granny Woman to remove the spell Ellie had placed on the baby to make her cry.

115

It was said that Ellie could turn herself into a cat and come through the eaves of the house or reduce her size and come through the keyhole in the door. According to Aunt Goldie, "She made mom [Grandma Mary] sick and gave the babies colic so they cried all the time. Mom hated her own mother."

Grandpa Austin and Grandma Molly Shifflett

My daddy's parents, Grandma Molly and Grandpa Austin lived for some time after I was born. Grandpa died in 1958 when I was seventeen and Grandma died in 1971 when I was thirty years old. They were no slouches when it came to having children. They had ten children and raised all ten to adulthood. Even my Aunt Lena, who had five children and had never married, lived with them. They helped raise her children.

Three of their children were born deaf and mute. Mom told me many times, "Austin and Molly were half brother and sister because of Banks Shifflett's runnin' around. No wonder they have three kids who can't hear and talk." She added, "I worried a lot about you kids being deaf so the first thing I did when you all were born was to check to see if you could hear. I clapped my hands close to your ears and if you didn't jump, I screamed into your ears. That made you jump awake."

Grandpa Austin and Grandma Molly were very serious people with little to say. It always seemed that they were angry because they were born and had to survive and raise children. There was little fun and no laughter in their house. It seemed that all they did was cook and wash dishes, but that was because I mostly saw them on Sundays. I also noticed a huge vegetable garden, a barn, several cows, a chicken house, and a hog pen. There was a root cellar filled with potatoes and canned vegetables, fruit, and pork. They obviously worked hard during the weekdays.

They cooked the same thing all the time. Breakfast was bird-egg beans known today as cranberry beans, home-canned

116

peaches, homemade bread, sausage, and gravy. Grandpa Austin loved bird-egg beans, and bought them by the one hundred pound sack. He often placed his order with my daddy before we left for home on Sundays. He would say, "Norman, how about bringin' me a hundred 'lubs' of beans next Sunday?" (Grandpa thought the abbreviation for pounds, lbs., was pronounced as "lubs.)

Grandpa Austin Shifflett (left) with his brother, Warnie Shifflett

The noon meal was bird-egg beans, homemade bread, ham or sausage, canned peaches, and fried potatoes. The evening meal was bird-egg beans, boiled potatoes, canned peaches, and ham or sausage. In season, they substituted homemade applesauce, dry-land cress gathered from the cornfield, and green beans. Sunday dinner was the same, but in larger quantities to feed us when we arrived after church.

Over the years my mother introduced banana cake and fruit pies into their diet. It was as if they had discovered a pot of gold; they loved her desserts. She got tired of baking for them so she tried to teach Aunt Lena. It was the most frustrating thing Mom ever tried—she could not teach Lena how to bake a pie. Mom always liked to talk about how backward my dad's folks were when

117

it came to changing their ways or learning new things. She and I discussed it quite often. She rather liked my analysis of their problem when I told her their brains were like a coffee cup. You can pour only so much coffee into a cup before it runs over when it reaches the cup's capacity.

I estimated that their brains had reached capacity early in their lives. Since she dared not arrive for Sunday dinner without dessert, Mom griped a lot about the situation while she baked a cake or some pies as the weekend approached.

I first remember visiting Grandma Molly and Grandpa Austin when they lived in a two-story log house in Hopkins Gap near Little North Mountain. The Shoemaker River ran just back of their porch. They rented the house from Bryan and Edith Conley.

Electricity had not come to Hopkins Gap, so Grandma Molly used a springhouse to prevent her food from spoiling. The springhouse was a small log shelter built over one of many cold-water springs that trickled through the rocks on the sides of ridges all over Hopkins Gap. Some remnants of these little log structures remain visible today; but they are no longer used to prevent food from spoiling.

Grandma Molly's springhouse was a fair distance from the house down a narrow path thickly lined with ferns, wild flowers, and weeds. It had a red oak shingle roof. At times when she took me with her, I could see sunlight shining through the roof so I asked her if the roof let rain through and did it get her food wet. That's when I learned about red oak shingles. Grandma explained, "These shingles are made from red oak. When the weather is dry, the shingles shrink up and let in the fresh air from outside, but when it's gonna rain, the shingles swell and keep the rain from coming through them." Every moment with Grandma was an opportunity to learn. I was about six years old when she told me about the shingles. I never forgot a word she said; and when I became a professor of American folk culture, I was able to pass these stories on to my students.

I was about four years old the first time Grandma asked me to go with her to get milk, cream, and butter for Sunday dinner. I had no idea where we were going. She had a dish and spoon in one hand and an empty pitcher in the other. As we walked down the narrow river-stone path, she told me we were going to the spring-house. She warned me to watch for snakes along the way because they might be lurking in the thick foliage. She told me that snakes like to crawl out of the weeds to sun themselves on the rocks in the path and that she had seen them coiled there many times.

Inside the springhouse she had laid a flattened log across a little creek trickling from a pool of water. She walked out on the log and reached into the cold water where she had placed a half dozen crocks filled with milk. There was a large pan setting in the water with chunks of homemade butter wrapped in wax paper.

She skimmed some cream off the top of the milk and put it in the bowl. Then she lifted a crock and poured some milk into the pitcher. She handed me a chunk of butter, and we headed back to the house. Aunt Lena and Mom had Sunday dinner on the table. We had ham, green beans, homemade bread, homemade butter, and cold slaw quickly made with the fresh cream from the springhouse.

I sat on the wooden bench behind the table where the kids always sat. As I watched the grownups enjoying the homemade butter, I felt very much a part of the family because Grandma Molly let me carry the butter to the house. She always included me in whatever she was doing. She said kids needed to feel that they were contributing to the family chores. I guess she let me carry the butter because I couldn't do too much damage if I dropped it along the way, but I was still "helpin' out" as she called it.

Some years later, Grandpa Austin built a house about a quarter of a mile down the road. The house sat next to the Allegheny Mountains at the bottom of a ridge. The cold spring was just a short walk up the ridge, but electricity came through Hopkins Gap before they got the springhouse built. Grandma Molly bought a refrigerator to keep her food from spoiling.

Most of the things they had in the old house were moved to the new house. They took the bench for the kids to use behind the kitchen table. The old wood stove with the warming closet on top went to the new house. Grandma Molly said it cooked the best beans. She took her old poplar and walnut pie safe that smelled like moldy bread and stale pie dough. She stored her homemade bread and leftover beans in the pie safe. She kept leftover meat and fried potatoes in the warming closet above the stove. As I think back to those days, I wonder why we didn't get sick; however, we did have to move the outside toilet real often! In those days, when the toilet hole filled up, another hole was dug and the little building moved to set over the new hole.

My dad often asked Grandpa Austin, Grandma Molly, and Aunt Lena to take a Sunday afternoon car ride or to go to church with him. They sometimes went, but only one person at a time. The reason they gave him was "we can't leave the house by itself."

*Grandma Molly Shifflett in her black cotton stockings,
with her wood kitchen stove and the warming closet
on the day of Grandpa Austin's funeral, 1958*

Grandma or Lena would sometimes go, but somebody stayed at home all the time. Grandpa Austin never left the house until the undertaker took him away.

Their house always smelled the same. There was an old heavy musty smell that made my nose tickle. It was not pleasant, and to this day, when I walk into an antique store, I experience that smell and go back in my memory to fifty years ago. I relive the Sundays at Grandma Molly's house and remember the times I opened her pie safe to see what she had stored in there.

Grandma Molly was a character filled with contradictions, and she was always a bit of a mystery to me. I heard stories about her being somewhat promiscuous, as a younger woman and that possibly some of her children didn't belong to Grandpa Austin. I knew most of them did belong to him because they were the "spittin' image" of him. I simply could not picture Grandma Molly as a sexual being much less a run around. I never witnessed any indication that she and Grandpa Austin were married, in love, or had ever had sexual interest in each other except their ten children, of course. She never called him by name, and he never called her by name. There were no kisses, hugs, handholding, or pats. At the same time, there was no indication that they were mean to each other until Grandpa Austin was on his deathbed. Then they fought each other. When she tried to give him a bath or brought his food to him, he twisted her arms and pinched her until she bled. He threw his food at her, so she started putting his bird-egg beans, bread, and peaches in a tin cup with a handle so she could hang onto it. She often whipped him with a wooden paddle until he gave up and let her care for him, but she and Aunt Lena were determined to care for him at home.

There were no toys at her house for the grandchildren. We had a choice after Sunday dinner of getting out of the house and finding something to fill the time or sitting in the living room with Grandma Molly, Aunt Lena, and Grandpa Austin. Their living room was not the best choice. Each had a rocking chair. There were two or three other rocking chairs for visitors. The chairs faced different directions in the room, and they all rocked at the same time. Crickity crick, crickity crick, crickity crick— was the hypnotizing noise that came from each chair as the rockers rolled over the linoleum floor.

There was a wood stove at one end of the room with a stovepipe going through the ceiling, the upstairs, and out the roof of the house. They kept a fire going in the stove no matter how hot it was outside.

Mom asked them why they kept it so hot in the house, and they said they didn't want the fire to "die down." We laughed about that during the week and wondered who started their first fire and why he or she couldn't start another one.

Grandma Molly and Grandpa Austin dipped snuff so they each had their tin cup for spitting. There was also a large can near the wood stove for company if they dipped or chewed. They did not talk to each other unless a car went up the "BIG" road. Then Grandpa Austin, whose rocking chair sat near the window, would part the curtains with his hand and announce who just went up the road. Then they would all speculate about where the person was going or had been. "That was Clint Ray. I'll bet he's headed into town to bail somebody out of jail," or "I'll bet he's had to go pick up something at the store," Grandpa Austin would say. The only sounds in the room between cars going up the road were the creaking of the three rocking chairs and the squirt-plunk of snuff spit as it left their lips and hit the tin can.

I would sit in the living room with them as long as I could stand the lack of conversation, the snuff spitting, the heat from the stove, and the creaking rocking chairs. Then my brother John and I would go sit in the car and pray for the time to go home. The car sat below the house on the side of the "BIG" road. We could look up through the front yard and have a clear view of the front porch. At times we saw things on the front porch of Grandpa Austin's house that aren't worth mentioning; other times, as you will see later, we were shocked into adulthood.

I remember standing next to Grandma Molly when I was about thirteen years old and noticing that the top of her head came up to the height of my shoulder. I am five feet two inches now, so she could never have claimed extraordinary height. She was quite bowlegged and had a dowager's hump on her back, neither of which got in her way when there was work to be done. She had jet-black hair and sharp black eyes. As she aged, there were a few strands of silver in her hair, but her eyes never dulled.

No matter what season, she wore long underwear under her brown cotton stockings, a homemade dress, and a homemade apron. The only time I saw her change the color of her stockings was on the day of Grandpa Austin's funeral. On that day she wore a brand new pair of black cotton stockings. She never left the house without her homemade bonnet. I never saw her bare legs until just before she died when she was in the hospital. She had a drawer full of dresses, including a new dress she had made to be buried in. She sewed that dress when she was in her thirties. She showed the dress to me one Sunday afternoon as if to insure she would wear it to her grave. She lived another twenty years and then some after showing me that dress; but when she died, she was buried in it.

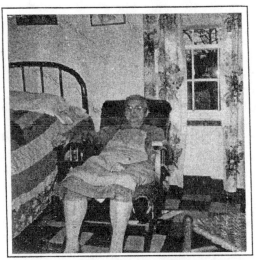

Grandma Molly with her stockings over her long underwear and tied up with strings, sitting in her rocker by the bed in which Grandpa Austin died.

Peggy Ann Shifflett

Grandma Molly was a Granny Woman, a community healer. She claimed her power to be a Granny Woman came from being born after her father drowned in a creek when flooding waters washed his horse and wagon downstream. She talked about her powers as if to legitimize her skills, much the same as modern doctors display diplomas on the walls of their offices. She would say, "Here's how you can get the powers. You can be born the seventh child in the family, you can be born the seventh child of the seventh child, you can be born on Christmas day, or you can be born after the death of your father. That's how I got my powers. I was born after my daddy died."

She was a quiet woman, dwelling mainly within herself until she was addressed. Community members could not conduct any major event such as a butchering, cherry-seeding, apple-butter boiling, or birthing a baby without her presence. I remember hearing many times, "Who's going to pick up Grandma Molly?" That was her community name. She cured numbers of babies with "liver-grown and she measured many children for "undergrowth," including me. She cured warts and mixed sheep manure tea to bring out the measles. She could swipe her hand under a child's chin and move the mumps to both sides of the jaws.

Tobacco, in the form of snuff, was her second drug of choice; and, when her snuff spit was rubbed on a wart, she knew it was going to soon be gone. One day, she said to me, "Let me see your hand." When I held my hand out for her to look, she spit a big glob of snuff on my knuckle where a major wart had been growing. I got so mad, I cried. She laughed and said, "The cure won't work unless you get mad." That statement did not help my humiliation; however, in a few weeks, the wart was gone.

One summer she grabbed my little brother, Warnie, when he wasn't wearing a shirt. She looked at his naked back and said, "Looks to me like you've got the 'tetter'." That was her term for psoriasis. She spit a glob of snuffy saliva in her hand and rubbed it

124

on his back. He was furious, but to this day he credits her with his "tetter" going away in several weeks.

She believed in spending part of her life in an altered state of consciousness with her first drug of choice, moonshine. So she contracted with her son, Uncle James, to leave a pint of moonshine in her mailbox each Friday evening. She would sip at the bottle all weekend until by Sunday dinner she was able to communicate more freely as she lifted her apron to wipe from her lips any telltale signs of alcohol.

One Sunday she disappeared before the noon meal. The grandchildren were told to go find her and make sure she was okay, but not to disturb her. I led the small search party into the woods and pastures until we located her. She was lying in a blackberry patch, sleeping like a baby. Her hands were neatly placed with palms together under her cheek, and her apron was perfectly straight as she lay on her side. All was well as she slept off her altered state. We went back to the house to report that she was fine. There was no further discussion, no condemnation, no shaking heads, so when she walked in later in the afternoon, life went on as usual.

Grandma Molly gave me treatments for undergrowth, warts, and boils; more importantly, she gave me her stoicism, her fatalism, her quiet resolve that all things come to a natural conclusion. In 1971 when she was eighty-six, she stopped eating and told the family she was ready to die. Of course, we didn't listen and put her in a hospital for intravenous feeding. She was constantly trying to escape so she could go home to die. She fell in one of her escape attempts and cracked her hip. One icy night in March I visited her for the last time. When I walked into the room, she got very agitated and asked why we did not let her die. She said she was tired and wanted to go. I acknowledged that she must be tired after eighty-six years of hard work. Perhaps that acknowledgment was the permission she needed. The next morning, she was dead.

Grandpa Austin was a large man. He had a full head of snow-white hair and icy blue eyes. He had bushy eyebrows that sagged over heavy eyelids that seemed to partially block his vision. When I was a child, I thought his eyes looked like that because he was always mad about something. Now, as I have aged, I recognize the heavy eyelids as a Shifflett trait and perhaps Grandpa was not always frowning. It is a shame no one told his grandchildren it was okay to interact with him. We were all scared of him. Some of his habits didn't help his grandfather role. When we arrived at his house, he took out his pocketknife, opened the blade, and pretended to slit our throats. In the summer, if we got close enough to him, he spit on our bare toes. I now think he was playing with us the only way he knew how. I never touched him or sat on his lap.

I inherited Grandpa's white hair and blue eyes. Unfortunately, I also inherited his heavy eyelids. I have considered having my eyelids removed by a plastic surgeon because many times people have asked me if I was in a bad mood when I was really in a good mood.

Grandpa always wore charcoal gray cotton trousers with a tiny herringbone weave held up by suspenders. His shirts were sometimes smooth cotton and sometimes flannel, but always long sleeved no matter what the season. You could tell he had worked hard all his life by the size of his shoulders. He said very little but was definitely the head of his household. He demanded, without saying a word, that his meals be served at six in the morning, at twelve noon, and at four-thirty in the afternoon. He carried a pocket watch, and when eleven o'clock rolled around, he pulled out his watch and walked to the kitchen door.

Grandma Molly and Aunt Lena dropped whatever they were doing and started rattling the pots and pans for the noon meal. The only exception was Sunday when he waited until we arrived after church. If we were late because my daddy found someone to talk about the Bible with, Grandpa would be champing at the bit when we finally arrived.

After I got a little older, I was curious about his eating habits. The fact that he ate bird-egg beans for every meal was enough to peak my curiosity, but he just mixed the rest of his food with his beans. He piled his plate full of crumbled homemade bread, heaped beans on the bread, and then topped it off with home-canned, very sweet, peaches.

I saw Mom watching him all the time, and she finally got enough nerve to ask him why he mixed his food. He never slowed his eating to look up at her from his plate. His response was to the point, "It all goes to the same place." While he ate he said nothing. He ate as if it was his job—big drops of sweat came out on his forehead, he ate so hard. When the weather was warm, Grandpa rested on the front porch after eating Sunday dinner.

My dad, Norman Shifflett and Oscar Crawford
standing in front of Grandpa Austin's house, with Warnie
standing on the porch near the "pecker notch"

After my brother John and I learned we could have more fun sitting in the car rather than in the house, we spent some warm Sunday afternoons watching Grandpa Austin as he sat on the front porch for hours on end. He would occasionally get up, unbutton the fly on his overalls, take out his penis, lay it on the porch rail, and pee out into the yard. We watched him and nearly died laughing as we stuffed our shirts in our mouths. One day we noticed a notch in the porch railing, and we thought he had worn a groove by laying his penis on the railing so many times. We called it the "pecker" notch. The front yard had a very foul odor on hot summer days.

One Sunday our little brother, Warnie, who was just starting to talk, innocently crawled up into Grandpa Austin's lap while he sat on the front porch. John and I expected to see his little body flying high over the porch railing as we watched with mouths agape. Instead, Grandpa, thinking no one was watching, placed his arm around my little brother, who immediately started asking questions. "Why do you have those big knots on your eyes?" At about that time a motorcycle went zooming up the road, and my little brother asked, "Are you going to ride a motorcycle when you get them knots off your eyes?" Grandpa smiled at him--the only smile I ever remember seeing on his face.

Grandpa's mean persona provided material for little poems that my brother and I made up about him. "Austin, Austin, sitting on a pole; pull back, pull back, shoot him in the hole. Austin, Austin, ran out of gas; hurry up, hurry up, shoot him in the ass."

My brother, John, and I adopted Grandpa Austin's mean persona to cope with our world for many years. Eventually I recognized I was covering for my fear of the world, and in my discovery I recognized how scared Grandpa Austin was of the world. Grandpa Austin taught me about being connected. He had a white mule that he had bred and raised. Occasionally he would harness the mule and go up on the mountain to get a pole of wood for the stove. One morning during his eighty-second year, he went to the barn to feed his old white mule. The mule was dead. Grandpa came into the house, announced that his mule was dead, stated that he had no reason to live, got into bed, and got up only once again. He lay there for months while Grandma Molly complained that there was no wood stacked on the porch for the winter. One day he got tired of her nagging, got out of bed, and slowly made his way to the woodpile. He picked up his axe and raised it above his head to chop a block of wood. The weight of the axe caused him to lose his balance and fall backwards. He rolled down the hill to the edge of the "BIG" road before he stopped. Grandma Molly and Lena helped him back up the hill and into the house. He returned to his bed. Four years later he died in that same bed.

Grandpa Austin's death was one of the last times that the traditional wake was carried out in Hopkins Gap. It was customary to bring the body home so the family could sit with it for at least two days before the burial. So his body was picked up by the funeral home, processed, and brought back home. He lay in the living room where he had died until his burial.

Grandma Molly and his daughters took turns sitting with him around the clock. While they were sitting there, they swapped stories of occasions they had heard about when a person was not really dead, but in a coma. Occasionally one of them would get up and go over to the casket and look at him for a few minutes. Aunt Vernie watched him carefully. She would walk over to the casket and stare at his chest. "I swear he's breathin'," she said. Then everybody in the room would gather around to watch for signs of life and finally conclude that he was dead after recalling that he had been embalmed. "He ain't got no blood in him," said Aunt Hattie, "They drained it out and put other stuff in his veins. He can't be alive." Then they sat down again and told stories of people being buried alive and about how others were saved from being buried alive by faithful family members who watched over them and caught them breathing or saw them wake up and sit upright in the casket.

Of course, the neighbors and other family members brought in tons of food for the family so they could spend their time grieving. I thought I didn't like Grandpa Austin and was showing my lack of concern for his dying until the funeral director asked me if I would help carry the flowers to the grave after the funeral. I lost it, started crying, became hysterical, and was soon told I didn't have to carry flowers. I realized soon thereafter that I really did like the old man and would miss him.

Pauline Shifflett

Grandpa Austin's daughter, Pauline, was deaf and mute. She had never been educated and couldn't speak in sign. Other deaf children born in the next generation were sent to the Virginia School for the Deaf and Blind about fifty miles from Hopkins Gap.

I was always scared of Aunt Pauline. Her most effective way to communicate was to let out a heart-stopping scream to get people's attention. Then she waved her arms in the air and pointed to different parts of her body. Her behavior scared all the children in the Gap. As I remember her now, I recognize how painful it must have been for her to grow up deaf and mute in a hearing and talking family.

According to my mother, Pauline had suffered when she was very young. She had gotten pregnant as a young teenager. Grandma Molly took her across Little North Mountain to a doctor in Mt. Clinton. He performed an abortion, and Pauline got a very serious infection. Mom told me, "They had to take out all her 'female' parts. She never got pregnant again."

Over the years, Pauline had worked out a language that everyone in the immediate family understood, but it was just a basic language with no place for humor or trivial conversation such as "hello," "goodbye," "I'm sorry," or "how are you?" She lived her life in a pragmatic and no nonsense manner. I discovered this the day of Grandpa Austin's funeral.

It was winter when he died and the remains of a recent snow resulted in the funeral crowd tracking a lot of mud into the house. I watched Aunt Pauline as she looked at the feet of everyone who walked in. I knew she was getting madder and madder. Finally, she let out a high-pitched squall and told Grandma Molly to get the old man out of the house, take him to the graveyard and bury him so she could sweep the floors.

Pauline's character in Hopkins Gap proved to be useful to the locals. When kids cried loud and for a long time, frustrated parents would say, "Stop squalling. You sound like Pauline." I can only speak for myself, but the image that came to mind when I heard that statement stopped my crying immediately.

Aunt Pauline never married, but lived with a man named Rawley Carr for a long time. One day while Rawley was out working, a drunk from the Peak came into his house. Pauline had Rawley's supper on the table so he could eat when he got home. The drunk grabbed the edges of the table, upset it, and the food went all over the floor. Just at that moment Rawley walked into the house. He walked quietly to the bedroom, got his gun, and killed the man from the Peak. Rawley never spent any time in prison because the court decided he had a right to protect his home.

It was about ten years after the incident that Rawley suffered the repercussions of his actions. Early one evening as the sunset blazed red over the Allegheny Mountains to be west, Rawley was in the barn milking his cow. A car drove up to the barn and a man, hidden in the shadows, beckoned him to the driver's window. When Rawley leaned over to speak to the person in the car, it was the brother of the man from the Peak that he had killed years before. The brother shot him in the throat. Rawley died on the spot.

Shirley and Jim Morris

Two of Mom's brothers, Uncle Shirley and Uncle Jim were strong influences in my life. They chose me as the recipient of their portion of Hopkins Gap tradition. They were members of the eighteen children born to my grandparents. Shirley grew up homeless after the age of ten; and, after he married Ethel, who also grew up

131

homeless, they raised their own children and opened their doors to other homeless children who grew up in the Gap.

Uncle Shirley and Uncle Jim gave me the origins of local place names, moonshine stories, stories of male escapades, bonding, and friendship. They shared hunting stories, ghost stories, and tall tales that, to my constant amazement, ultimately went full circle and always connected to something.

Uncle Shirley was a solidly built man with strong shoulders. One of his favorite things to do with his children was have them stand in the palm of his hand. Then he would hold his arm straight out from his shoulder and have a picture taken with the children standing in his hand.

Uncle Shirley playing a tune in front of Uncle Rob
and Aunt Goldie's house with his dogs, Sooner by his knee
and Splinter in the background. circa 1940

As a young man Uncle Shirley had a full head of black hair and brown eyes. He lost his hair while he was very young, and I

132

only remember him as a bald man. He was a very wise man. Many people in the Gap went to him if they had a problem to work out. I often asked his advice on my life questions. When he was given a problem, he would get real quiet and it was as if you could see the cogs turning in his brain. Sometimes it may take an hour for him to give his opinion. You would think he had forgotten the question, but he never forgot and would ultimately give his advice.

Uncle Shirley drove the "Gap" bus from Hopkins Gap across the mountain to Mt. Clinton elementary school. During his spare time, he hauled junked cars to Pennsylvania, sold them, and hauled back loads of coal that he sold locally. Some times he drove south to Georgia and picked up loads of watermelons to sell locally. He had nine children. The ninth child, a girl, went without a name for a full year because he and his wife, Ethel, had run out of names. One day as he drove through Georgia, he passed through a town named Arvona. He named his youngest daughter Arvona.

Uncle Shirley taught me an important lesson about counting my money. I was just about to turn sixteen years old, and I wanted a shotgun of my own to hunt squirrels. Uncle Shirley had a gun he wanted to sell. I asked him the price. He wanted thirty dollars. I counted the money I had earned painting Mrs. John I. Myers' house during the summer. I was so excited about the gun because my daddy had just given me permission to hunt in the fall when squirrel season opened. I now had my own gun and wouldn't have to borrow a gun. I counted out what I thought to be thirty dollars and gave it to Uncle Shirley. He handed over my new sixteen-gauge shotgun. I took the gun home and was very proud that I had purchased it with my own money. A couple of days later, I counted the small amount of money I had left in my savings. I was five dollars short, and I knew immediately that I had given Uncle Shirley thirty-five dollars instead of thirty.

The next time I saw him, I asked him if I had given him too much money. He said in a very business-like tone, "Yes, you gave me thirty-five dollars." "Well," I said in a quaking voice, "I would like to have the extra five dollars to put back in my savings." His answer was, "I'm sorry. I am not going to give your money back. From now on, you will learn to be more careful when you spend your money." That was a hard lesson since I had earned that money by working as a painter at seventy-five cents an hour. But, I learned the lesson very well. To this day, I count my money three times before I hand it over when I buy something.

Uncle Jim favored my mother in appearance. He was short and round with a head of black hair that remained with him throughout his life. He died fairly young; at age sixty-eight, from a diabetes-related stroke. He taught me how to drive in his brand new 1957 ford. The first driving lesson he gave me, I wrecked his new car. A huge feed truck met me on a hill. I overcompensated and scraped the whole side of the car into a big rock. Uncle Jim took it very calmly saying, "It was the truck driver's fault, he should have stopped when he saw you coming." He told everybody the truck ran me off the road. I knew he was covering for me.

Uncle Jim and his three children -- Loretta, Bus, and Christine

Uncle Jim always had an old car or two in his yard that he was "fixin' up" as he called it. I loved to watch him, so I would

134

hang over the fender with my nose stuck right in whatever he was working on. Every once in a while he would cross up some hot wires and grab my arm. I would get a slight electrical shock. "What happened?" he said after he stopped laughing at me, "Did it bite you?" I never stopped watching him even though he shocked me because I liked being around him so much.

Uncle Jim was fifteen when his father, Grandpa John, died. He left Hopkins Gap and lived in Pennsylvania for a year with Uncle Charlie. He returned to Hopkins Gap and became a small-scale moonshiner to make his living. He gradually increased his moonshine production to about one hundred gallons a week. He spent some time in prison for making moonshine, but his wife, Hazel, carried on the family business until he returned.

Not only did he make moonshine for himself most of his life, but also frequently contracted with the Old Order Mennonites around Dayton to make some whiskey for them. They told Uncle Jim that they never sold the moonshine, but they did enjoy keeping it around for medicinal purposes. Uncle Jim laughed when he told stories about spending a day or two in an Old Order Mennonite's basement making gallons of "medicine."

Toward the end of his life he specialized in apple brandy. He ran a little store across the road from his home and stocked some groceries for sale; but his specialty was always apple brandy. He kept a hidden supply of moonshine and applejack for customers who had a thirst. When folks came in to buy a few groceries and asked him for a pint, Uncle Jim would call to his helper, "It's time to water the stork" or if the customer wanted a quart, he'd call out, "It's time to slop the hogs!" One of my fondest memories of him is behind the cash register, with a large drop of brown apple brandy on his chin left over from his last big drink straight from the fruit jar.

One day the sheriff came to Uncle Jim's house to search for moonshine. He opened all the doors of his out buildings and let him search freely. He hid his moonshine under a trap door in the floor of the barn. He said, "The deputy sheriff walked all over top of my stash, but he never found it."

Uncle Jim also hauled junked cars, coal and fruit. He never held a job other than those activities. The state police were relentless in their search for moonshine and stopped Uncle Jim on one of his frequent trips to haul junked cars to Pennsylvania. They told him he had been reported for hauling moonshine hidden in his junk. He invited them to unload his truck and search it.
"I've placed this load on the truck so it won't fall off," he said. "If you unload it, you have to put it back exactly as you find it."

The police sized up the daunting task and decided to just get on top of the load and look around. They walked all over the top of Uncle Jim's junked cars and got down. They told him to drive on. He laughed as he told me, "They walked right over top of fifty gallons of moonshine I was taking to a Jewish man in Philadelphia. All they had to do was lift up one old car hood, and they would have had me."

Uncle Jim frequently expressed the fact that he remained sexually active into his older years. He said, "I can still cut the mustard." "I may not be able to plow as deep, but I can plow just as long;" and, bragging about no loss of virility, he said, "The older the buck, the stiffer the horn."

Goldie Morris Crawford

Aunt Goldie was a sister to Shirley and Jim. She was my window on the world of possibilities for women. She could not read or write; and after I learned to read and write, I became her scribe and her window on the world. This wonderful illiterate woman unknowingly instilled in me a desire to further my education. When I read the letters to her that I had written, she always smiled and said, "That sounds really good."

She was widowed at twenty-eight with four children. Uncle Rob died when he was thirty-six years old, and I was five years old. He went into the hospital with a gall bladder attack and died soon after his surgery.

Rob Crawford and Goldie Morris Crawford (circa 1945)

His dying was my first experience with death. When Uncle Rob died, the hospital called John I. Myers. He mounted his horse and rode to tell Aunt Goldie and the neighbors the sad news. He arrived at our house at four o'clock in the morning. He pecked on the bedroom window and told Mom and Dad that Rob had died. This was an incredibly sad event. I remember Mom and Dad got out of bed and went into the next room where they sobbed for what seemed like hours.

The funeral home brought Uncle Rob's body home for the wake, and Mom lifted me up to look at him and to touch him. It felt so strange to touch his stiff cold face that had been warm and soft when he played with me just a day or so before.

The time for his funeral arrived, and the undertaker came with the hearse to take his body to the church. Mom didn't attend the funeral. She designated herself as the sitter for the smaller children who were not attending. As the pallbearers carried Uncle Rob's casket out the front door of Aunt Goldie's house toward the hearse, Mom was holding the children back out of the way. She was crying. When the men stepped off the porch with the casket, a few raindrops started to fall. Mom looked up at the sky and said through her tears, "Happy is the corpse that the rain falls on."

I visited his grave with Aunt Goldie many times, and I would try to defocus my eyes and see him lying beneath the ground, so close but yet never to be seen again. About two weeks after his death, we kids were playing a game with Mom in the living room of our house. I heard Uncle Rob call my sister's name. She was his favorite of us kids.

Aunt Goldie learned to drive, got a job at a silk mill in Harrisonburg, raised her kids and died forty-five years later having accumulated a small fortune. She was literally the first woman that I saw driving a vehicle--an aqua green pickup truck. She was also the first woman to work outside the community.

Aunt Goldie loved to go to dances after she was widowed. Before she went out to a dance, she dressed in bright colored, stylish dresses with big floppy hats. She broke the traditional role of the mountain woman. As she dressed for the dance, she turned from a working mountain woman to a strikingly beautiful, stylish woman—smiling through her makeup. She wore her hair in a bun or braided around her head. In her apron and work clothes, she looked like a woman who had put her hair up because she didn't want it to interfere with her work. When she was going to dance, she added a stylish, wide, floppy hat, and suddenly her hair looked like a beautiful beau font.

She did exciting things with her widowed sister-in-law, Annie Reedy. They took rides on the newly built Skyline Drive, a part of the Blue Ridge Parkway. They double dated and went on picnics. Aunt Goldie always talked about her high cheekbones and her high breastbone. She claimed she was part Cherokee Indian. I believed it until I was able to figure out her family tree. It was just a generation removed from my own family tree, and I hadn't found any Cherokee in my background. I asked Mom about the Indian blood, and she told me with a snort, "Aw, Goldie's always wanted to be special."

Because Aunt Goldie liked to go to dances and wear big floppy hats, she was often called a "high stepper" or, it was said she was "kicking over the traces." She bore the brunt of other women's jealousy and gossip; but I admired her and spent many hours watching her dress and helping get her stocking seams straight. She let me play with her hats, too.

Aunt Goldie told me the story of my great grandfather, Adam Morris. He was a small man and his wife, Jane, was a large woman. He needed to be in charge of his family, so he bossed Jane around even though she could have snapped him in two pieces with one hand. He told his family that he was going straight to hell when he died so he wanted to make a grand entrance. He wanted a special casket made for him so the devil would know when he arrived. He wanted the meanest man in Hopkins Gap, Luther Kirkpatrick, to build his casket. The sides were to be made of chestnut, the top should be made of hickory, and the bottom should be made of wood from a gum tree. "That way," he said, "I can go through hell a bouncin' and a crackin'." His wish was granted. Luther Kirkpatrick built Ad Morris' casket when he died and carefully followed his instructions.

Aunt Goldie was full of witch stories and knew many remedies and who in the community could heal diseases. Her specialty was herbs, and she informed me about red sassafras and yellow sassafras, where to find them and how to use them. She took me with her many times when she went digging for sassafras roots. She said, "Tea made from yellow sassafras roots is good to thin the blood." She had high blood pressure, and that was the only medicine she used for years. She told me "Tea made from red sassafras roots is good for low blood pressure or anemia."

She owned many of the tools for butchering and canning that she generously loaned to people in the community and sometimes lost because some folks in Hopkins Gap envied her ability to hold on to her farm and survive after Uncle Rob's death.

Peggy Ann Shifflett

Ruby, Joyce, Randy, and George Crawford

Because Aunt Goldie and Uncle Rob raised my mother, their four children, two sons and two daughters, were like my brothers and sisters. They were all older than me. The daughters, Ruby and Joyce, baby sat for Mom nearly every Saturday while she went to Harrisonburg with Aunt Goldie to get groceries. As soon as Aunt Goldie's truck was out of sight, Ruby and Joyce would make us stand in a corner on one foot so they didn't have to deal with us all day. We were supposed to stay on the same foot until Mom came home. They didn't pay much attention after they got us into our corners, so we switched feet when we got tired of standing on one or the other.

Each of Aunt Goldie's four children was special to me. Her son George was a baseball fan and a hard worker. He wanted to be a pitcher in the major leagues. He shared his interest in baseball and his work with me and used me as his catcher. He threw the baseball so hard that I would bounce back against the fence when the ball hit my catcher's mitt. Mom would yell at him, "You're going to kill that kid." She tried to make me stop catching for him, but I loved him so much, I would have died for him.

He tried to build up my arm muscles by having me carry heavy loads of chicken feed. He periodically checked my muscles to see if they were getting bigger, and had me flex them for his buddies when they came to visit. He mounted a basketball goal on the side of the chicken house taught me to shoot the ball and to do left and right hook shots. He was my guard, so I learned to move fast to get around him. In high school, although I was not very tall, I was the top scorer on the girls' basketball team because of my left and right hook shots and my speed.

Aunt Goldie's daughter, Joyce, taught me how to tie a thread around a June bug's head and let it fly around all day at the end of the string. After she finished school and got a job, Joyce took me to my first movie, "Cinderella" and later to my first musical movie, "Oklahoma." She married a young man from Hopkins Gap named Eugene Crawford, so she never changed her last name. They had been married about two years when there was a terrible accident. Joyce, Eugene, and my cousin Tucker Morris were driving by our house one November day. It was deer hunting season, so Eugene had a loaded rifle in the back seat of the car. He asked Tucker to unload the gun. As he ejected the shells from the gun, Joyce stepped out of the car. The gun went off, and she was shot through the right knee.

I heard the car drive up in front of the house and heard Joyce's little girl, Barbara, calling for her momma as she saw Joyce step out of the car; but when the shot rang out, and I heard Joyce scream, for a moment I changed the scene in my head and before my eyes. It was not Joyce who had been shot, but another cousin that I was not as close to and didn't love as much as I did Joyce.

Eugene grabbed Joyce, threw her into the car, and rushed her into Harrisonburg to the hospital. She lost a lot of blood and eventually lost her foot to gangrene and then the rest of her leg had to be amputated above the knee.

After the car rushed off to the hospital, I noticed a puddle of blood, flesh, and fat on the ground where she had been shot. My mother, pregnant with my little brother, was standing on the porch. She was afraid she had "marked" him, so she told me to get a bucket of dirt and cover the puddle. I never forgot how it felt to look at pieces of Joyce lying on the ground as I covered them with dirt. I felt as if I was burying her. I was ten years old. Many hours passed before Eugene returned from the hospital to tell us that Joyce had lived, but that she was in very serious condition.

Joyce developed gangrene in her toes, so her foot had to be removed. The hospital gave the foot to her husband to bring home and bury. When he came home with the foot in a brown paper bag, he asked me to go with him to bury it. We walked down to the edge of the pasture, and he dug a hole. Before he put the foot in its' grave, he told me he wanted to look at it. I said okay. So he took it out of the wrapping, and we stood and looked at Joyce's foot for a while before we buried it. I remember feeling important because the grownups seemed to depend on my strength, but I also felt some anger because they made little effort to protect my young feelings during those emotional times.

Joyce had a lot of pain after her foot was removed. Aunt Goldie told Joyce's husband to go dig the foot up and change the position in which he had buried it. She said, "If the foot is buried settin' up like she is walkin', then turn it over so it is like Joyce is layin' down like she is now." He folllowed Aunt Goldie's instructions and Joyce recently told me, "The pain eased after the foot was reburied."

For six weeks after the injury, Joyce drifted between life and death. The church had special prayer meetings, and the whole community went to pray for her. I kept a prayer in my head for her day after day. Christmas came and went, and Joyce's life kept hanging in the balance. I had a lot of time to ponder what had happened to Joyce and me the day before the shooting accident.

Joyce and Eugene were planning to move into a different house, and I was helping her clean the windows. We were in an upstairs bedroom cleaning a window that had a long crack in one of the panes. Joyce rubbed over the crack and said the window didn't have to be replaced because the crack was smooth. Just at that moment a bright red cardinal flew against the window, fluttered a moment, and started to bleed from its leg. A streak of blood ran down the window in front of Joyce's face. She turned very pale and looked at me. "It's time to stop for today," she said. "Let's go home."

During the long weeks after the accident, I wondered if the cardinal was an omen of the shooting accident. Was there something I could have done to prevent Joyce getting shot? Should both of us have paid more attention to what the cardinal may have been telling us about the future?

When Joyce came home from the hospital months later, she asked if I remembered that bird. Joyce is seventy years old now and has walked with an artificial leg since that day in 1951. Upon occasion, she and I still consider the meaning of the cardinal and speculate about how her life would be different if we had paid attention to the sign of tragic events to come.

Ruby, Joyce's older sister, was married when I was very young, but she nicknamed me "blondie" because of my corn-yellow hair. She still calls me blondie to this day although my hair is silver gray. She married Joyce's husband's older brother, Robert Crawford.

Occasionally, Robert would be late coming home on Friday evening and Ruby was scared he would drink up his paycheck. She used to stop by our house and pick me up to go with her to find him on Friday evenings. We would drive around to his favorite watering holes, and eventually find him. Mostly we found him at Ma Brown's bar in Harrisonburg. Ruby would take me with her to the door of the bar. We would peer in and see Robert sitting with a group of friends. She told me to stand by the door and watch in case one of Robert's friends jumped on her. Ruby then walked into the bar and start yelling at him. If a fight started, I was supposed to intervene and drag the attacker off of Ruby. Luckily, not a single person jumped her, so I never had to get into a brawl in a bar when I wasn't even old enough to be in there in the first place.

Randy, Aunt Goldie's oldest son, had the greatest influence on my childhood. He brought home, from the public library, the first book I ever read. It was Zane Grey's, *The Lone Star Ranger*. As I grew older, he introduced me to Edgar Rice Burroughs's Tarzan books; and once a month, I would find a new Tarzan comic book in the back seat of his car. He was an avid reader, and I caught the love of books and reading from him.

Randy loved to experiment with different kinds of sandwiches, and often used me as a guinea pig to try his various concoctions. His basic ingredient was peanut butter. He made peanut butter with onion, with banana, with mustard, ketchup, butter, and mayonnaise. Banana with peanut butter was my favorite until the day he made me try a sandwich with peanut butter and tomato. Both of us liked that mixture from the first bite, but he was not satisfied until her perfected the peanut butter and tomato sandwich. Both sides of the bread were spread with peanut butter, then a thin layer of butter on top of the peanut butter was followed by a thin layer of mayonnaise. A huge thick slice of homegrown tomato, still warm from the sun, was placed between the two slices of bread. This was, and still is, my favorite sandwich for two reasons: it has a wonderful taste, and it takes me back to those days when Randy and I laughed and joked about the sandwiches he invented and shared with me because I would have done anything for him.

A long time before he brought home my first book, he taught me how to make a sling shot. We walked in the mountains searching for the perfect forked branch on mountain laurel bushes. Randy cut strips from old inner tubes and made a pouch from a piece of leather. I held onto the slingshot stick while he tied the inner tube around it and attached the pouch. We took our slingshots and knocked a beer can from his house to mine and back on long summer evenings. We talked about fishing, hunting and problems he was having with his girlfriends as we slowly shot the beer can along the gravel road. He would place a little rock in front of my bare toe and ask me to hold still while he shot it away with his sling-shot or sometimes a .22 rifle. I stood quite still, totally trusting his aim. He never touched my toe.

Randy always had a set of boxing gloves around the house, and he used me as a sparring partner. Several times I remember waking up on Aunt Goldie's downstairs bed with Randy tapping my face to wake me up. He had hit me a bit too hard and knocked me out cold. Again, I liked him so much, I didn't mind.

One day during my twelfth year we were in Aunt Goldie's washhouse, and he asked me if I knew how to kiss my boyfriend. I told him I didn't have a boyfriend, therefore, I didn't know how to kiss. He asked me to show him how I would hold my lips if a boyfriend ever kissed me. I puckered up like a child would kiss its' mother on the cheek. He said, "No, that's not how you kiss your boyfriend." So he parted his lips and had me to part mine. Then he laid a kiss on me. He said, "Now get out of here and don't say I never taught you anything."

Randy taught me how to make bows and arrows. He told me that a hickory tree branch made the best bow, so off we went to the edge of the pasture where we knew a big hickory tree was growing next to the fence. We found a nice long straight branch and cut it to the length I needed. He took the branch and bent it into the shape of a bow. He wedged it between the tree and the fence post. He said: "Hickory will bend the way you want it when it's green. Let it dry here for a month, and you will have a good bow." A month later, he helped me string the bow with a leather thong. While we were waiting for the hickory stick to become a bow, we carved arrows out of long narrow sticks that came in the boxes when Aunt Goldie ordered baby chickens. The sticks were a soft, clear pine and could be whittled down to round arrow shafts. Sometimes we carved out the arrowhead from the wood and other times we made metal points to slip into the end of the shaft. Randy showed me how to make feather tips for the back end of the arrows. These made great toys as well as weapons to shoot rabbits. The bows were very strong and we could shoot arrows great distances.

When I was a little older, Randy took me hunting with him. Squirrel hunting season didn't start until October, but he liked to hunt them when the leaves were still on the trees, and the squirrels were fat from eating acorns and hickory nuts. He said they had a better flavor from eating green hickory nuts.

One day, early in September, we went squirrel hunting. We walked for miles, stopping to listen every now and then. He showed me how to walk quietly and step at the exact same time he stepped so we would make less noise. He could see a squirrel hiding in a tree better than anyone I knew. He could hear a squirrel slide around a tree as he walked underneath. When this happened, he quietly picked up a rock and threw it on the ground on the other side of the tree. The squirrel would slide around in full view. One shot and the squirrel fell to the ground. On this particular

145

September day, we returned home with twenty-four squirrels hanging from Randy's belt.

He taught me to fish the mountain trout streams and to fish for small mouth bass in the rivers that ran through the farmland. "You can only catch these fish by knowing how to bait them," he said as he searched along the riverbank. "Small mouth bass like hellgrammites, and trout like cheese balls and worms." Hellgrammites were larvae found under rocks at the bottom of streams. They were ugly creatures with several legs with pincers on each side of a jointed body. I was scared of them, so he placed me in the river with a net tied between two poles while he went upstream about fifteen feet and turned over rocks and kicked up mud. The hellgrammites floated downstream and caught in the net. Once we got a dozen or so, we were ready to start fishing. I always asked him to bait my fishhook when we were using hellgrammites.

Randy Crawford with twice his legal limit of trout.

Mavis Shifflett

Another character that was important among my Hopkins Gap kinfolk was Aunt Mavis, my daddy's sister. She was known in Hopkins Gap and my immediate family as the best worker and the ugliest person on earth. She was so ugly that I would forget how ugly she was until I saw her the next time. Then I would catch myself saying, "My God, she's ugly." Aunt Mavis set the bottom line for ugly in Hopkins Gap. It was often said that she was as ugly as homemade soap, homemade sin, or homemade soup. She was as ugly as a mud fence, a scarecrow, a hound, as a can of worms, a plastic bag full of assholes, and sheep shit on a rocky mountain. Aunt Mavis's ugliness could cause unusual changes such as: she was so ugly, she would make a freight train take a dirt road and her ugliness could stop the hiccoughs. Others indicated that she looked like she had been hit by a dump truck full of ugly or beaten with an ugly stick. It was suggested that she must be a twin because one person could not be as ugly as she was. Her ugliness got in the way of her daily living as it was said that she was so ugly she had to sneak up on a tin cup to get a drink of water. Finally, she was never well liked in her family; because she was so ugly the doctor slapped her mother when she was born.

Although Aunt Mavis was ugly, she married a very handsome man. They had one child, and fortunately she got all her features from her daddy.

Since Aunt Mavis was Grandpa Austin and Grandma Molly's daughter, she occasionally visited them on Sunday afternoons. If the weather was nice, she sat on the front porch with Grandpa Austin. John and I were often sitting in the car and had a good view of the porch up through the front yard. We always knew we would see Grandpa Austin pee out in the yard, but sometimes we saw things we weren't expecting. When Aunt Mavis came out on the porch, she pulled her chair over to the porch railing, propped her feet up on the railing, and spread her legs wide open. She did not wear any under pants. John and I looked and compared the view to a groundhog hole we had discovered in the fence row next to the pasture. On some occasions, we compared the same view to a muskrat slide that we had seen when we placed our traps in Muddy Creek to catch a muskrat or two.

Aunt Mavis led a tragic life. As ugly as she was, she seemed to have no problem attracting men and, she was accused of running around on her husband. He drank a lot of moonshine and would come home and accuse her of running around with other men. He threw rocks at her and, on many occasions, he told her to start running. He got his .22 rifle and shot behind her heels until she was out of sight. He laughed as the bullets kicked the dust up behind her.

Tragically, Aunt Mavis's ugliness was used to discipline me, and I suspect, many of the children in Hopkins Gap. When I misbehaved, my mother told me I looked like Aunt Mavis. I was appalled and would have rather had a beating. I recall visiting Uncle Lurty with the family one evening, when suddenly Uncle Lurty turned to me and told me I looked like Aunt Mavis. I looked back at him and said, "Yes, and you are a son-of-a-bitch." I was about five years old, and my dad looked me in the eye and said, "You will pay for that when you get home." Sure enough when we got home he took off his wide belt that in the eyes of a five year old seemed at least ten inches wide, and whipped me all around the front porch swing. He told me I must tell Uncle Lurty I was sorry for calling him a son-of-a-bitch. I had no choice. I apologized, but I never liked Uncle Lurty after that occasion and waited for the moment I could let him know I didn't like him. The moment came when I was sixteen. It was a Sunday morning, and he dropped by our house to visit. He asked me why I wasn't married yet. I responded, "I will never marry because the chances are I would marry a man like you." He just looked at me. That felt so good, and it still thrills me when I think about it. I am still unmarried

Part Three
MAKING A LIVING

Humble living does not diminish. It fills.
Going back to the simpler self, gives wisdom.

Rumi(4)

My childhood bridged the transition from hunting, gathering and living off the land to moonshining as a major way of survival for the people of Hopkins Gap. The moonshine industry was replaced by the poultry industry. The men raised poultry at home, and the women worked in the poultry processing plants or sewing factories in Harrisonburg. Each major method of survival blended into the next method so that until the moonshine industry became the dominant way of making a living, Gap folks continued to hunt and gather. After the poultry industry and factory work became available, some folks continued to hunt and gather and some made moonshine.

One major industry for early Hopkins Gappers was logging. Groups of men would go into the mountains with a steam engine. They cut logs on private land and by contract on the government owned reserves.

I was fortunate to be taught several ways to survive. My family, to some extent, still holds on to survival by subsistence; and to this day, seems to be most content at certain times of the year when they hunt, pick wild berries, and kill the hogs for meat.

I was taught to survive by hunting and gathering around the calendar year. I also witnessed how moonshining caused competition and feuding between families and ultimately destroyed the communal spirit necessary for survival by hunting and gathering. Unfortunately, I was also a witness to the painful loss of autonomy and individualism brought on by factory work and assembly line production. The consequences reverberated throughout the community with major effects on family life and childhood experiences. The people changed by necessity not by free will or a desire to become one with the changing world around them.

149

From left to right: Uncle Gilbert, Uncle Jim, John Morris, Uncle Rob, and Clarence Payne. Leonard Stultz brought two female visitors to the logging camp for the day (circa 1935).

One major industry for early Hopkins Gappers was logging. Groups of men would go into the mountains with a steam engine. They cut logs on private land and by contract on the government owned reserves.

I was fortunate to be taught several ways to survive. My family, to some extent, still holds on to survival by subsistence; and to this day, seems to be most content at certain times of the year when they hunt, pick wild berries, and kill the hogs for meat.

I was taught to survive by hunting and gathering around the calendar year. I also witnessed how moonshining caused competition and feuding between families and ultimately destroyed the communal spirit necessary for survival by hunting and gathering. Unfortunately, I was also a witness to the painful loss of autonomy and individualism brought on by factory work and assembly line production. The consequences reverberated throughout the community with major effects on family life

150

and childhood experiences. The people changed by necessity not by free will or a desire to become one with the changing world around them.

Gathering

During the days of gathering, all types of wild berries were picked during the summer months. I heard stories of how several families would pack enough food and water for two days and ride a horse-drawn wagon deep into the mountains to pick wild huckleberries. They knew exactly where the berries grew because the previous year they had set a fire on a ridge so that wild huckleberries would grow in the burned area. This ancient practice is still used today by mountain people who harvest the berries and sell them for cash.

In the early days of Hopkins Gap, the berries were picked and processed for winter fruit. They were carried home in buckets and baskets woven at night around the campfire. Sections of bark were stripped from hickory trees and bent into a circle for the sides; a bottom of bark was put in and the bucket held together by weaving with slender hickory branches. If there was a good crop of berries, a lot of buckets and baskets were woven.

Part of the fruit was canned with visions of huckleberry pie in the cold winter months ahead. Some berries were made into jams and jellies, sealed with homemade wax and stored. A small portion of the berries was traded at the local store for staples, such as salt and sugar.

These ways to survive flowed into my childhood. Beginning in early June, my mother gathered me and my brothers and sister, and we went to pick wild strawberries. We must have looked like a momma bear and her cubs as we worked our way from the bottom to the top of a hill in an old apple orchard where wild strawberries were abundant. She forbade us to eat any berries while we picked reminding us: "These berries will taste even better this winter when the snow flies."

When we got home at the end of the day, and she had fed us our supper, we gathered around the kitchen table to "cap" the tiny wild berries. I remember complaining about the berries being so small and having Mom remind us that wild strawberries have the best flavor. Besides, they were free for the gathering. This was often following by a warning that God put these wild berries on the hill, and if we let them waste, He wouldn't provide for us in the future. I must admit that first bite of strawberry shortcake the next evening was a memorable end to a mundane supper.

At the end of June, we picked sweet cherries from trees randomly planted by wild birds as they flew over the fields after feasting on cherries. There were red hearts, black hearts, waxed red and waxed yellow cherries as well as red sour cherries. We picked some of each because each had a special use. Red sour cherries made the best pies. The cherries were canned and later frozen when we were able to afford and to run a freezer after electricity came to our community early in my childhood.

Up until her death in 2001, Mom had frozen cherries that Randy had helped pick before he died in 1972. He was only thirty-six years old when he died of aplastic anemia — one of the first cases ever diagnosed. He had been dead a month when she invited his sixteen-year-old son to help us pick cherries. I discovered that the invitation was part of mom's grieving process. She invited him to help so she could tell him stories about his dad helping her pick cherries and how he had loved her sausage gravy so much he came by every morning for breakfast before work. I would see an occasional tear as she talked. Perhaps the tears fell as she realized she could not replace her dead nephew with his son.

Then came July--wild blackberry season. The earliest to ripen were called low blackberries. You had to stoop over to pick those berries — what a pain. I remember one summer I was picking low black berries with my cousin Ruby. She was married with three children and her husband didn't make a lot of money. She expressed the need to pick wild blackberries so her family would have fruit to eat in the cold months ahead.

Ruby was scared of many things. She often talked about being afraid some strange man might break into her house and hurt her. My knowing these things about Ruby did not bode well for my

152

berry-picking endurance. It was very hot and humid, we were stooping over, and the picking was going slowly. Suddenly it dawned on me that we might need a drink of water from her house not too far from the berry patch. So I volunteered to go for water. As I neared the house, I picked up a rock and threw it against the shed door. I yelled, hey Ruby, I just saw a man running from the house!" Ruby turned white and said, I'll bet it was that damned Marvin Roadcap." She abruptly ended the berry picking. To this day I feel guilty about that trick. It was one of the meanest things I ever did. With this writing, I am finally admitting that I stooped to this level so I could stop picking low blackberries.

When we finished picking low blackberries, the high black-berries were ready for harvest. If we had experienced a cold spring rain—called the "sheep rains-- while the high blackberries were blooming, they grew abundantly in the fields and up against the ridges in Hopkins Gap. High blackberries were very large and quickly filled a bucket. I enjoyed picking high blackberries, so I spent many days climbing through the briars to pick for my mother. When she got all she wanted, she let me sell them to the neighbors for a dollar a gallon.

When two of my nieces were old enough to follow me to the blackberry patches, I showed them how they could make a little extra money. They loved the experience of picking berries with Aunt Peg. I kept them laughing with my antics when a blackberry briar would grab the back of my shirt. They learned how to express their pain with humor, and they sold their berries to neighbors for four dollars a gallon.

August was wild huckleberry and wild mushroom month. We never picked wild huckleberries because my mother was scared of rattlesnakes that she claimed lived in wild huckleberry bushes. I think they probably did. However, we did gather wild mushrooms —the early yellow mushrooms and later growing brown mushrooms or "leatherbacks." We ate the first gatherings to satisfy our appetite for fresh mushrooms that had been building since the year before. Toward the end of the season, the mushrooms were canned for use in soups or for frying during the coming winter.

It was mainly the women and children who did the gathering and food processing for the winter, while the men took care of the heavier survival work. Wheat and corn were grown in small fields. When it was time to harvest, the men carried the grain across Little North Mountain to Stultz's Mill on Muddy Creek.

My daddy told me, "In those days the average man could put two and a half bushels of corn or wheat on his back and walk over two mountain ridges to the mill." The trip on foot was so long that it took two days to complete it; the men slept overnight on sacks inside the mill. The wheat was made into flour and the corn into cornmeal. The products were carried back into Hopkins Gap and stored for use in the winter. Dad said, "People didn't have to go out of the Gap after fall set in."

There was also some limited trade with the outside world. The major sources of money were peeling bark, carving railroad ties, and making barrel hoops. Grandpa Austin used his mule to pull a sled up the mountain. He loaded the sled with bark that he stripped from trees. He pulled the loaded sled down the mountain where all the bark the men had peeled in one day was loaded on a horse-drawn wagon and hauled to a central location in Broadway or Harrisonburg then taken by train to the leather tanning industries.

Animals were hunted and trapped for furs that were sold on "court day" in Harrisonburg. My dad told me, "People trapped and hunted skunks, raccoons, foxes, and on court day, the third Monday of the month, they took them to town where the fur buyers met them." One winter Uncle Shirley killed and skinned two hundred and forty-four skunks. He made enough money to feed his family for several months.

*Uncle Shirley posed with 244 skins before he took them to
Joe Kimbal's junk yard to sell. His favorite dogs, are posing with him.*

Some of the younger men walked across Little North
Mountain morning and evening in the summer to help Shenandoah
Valley farmers. Uncle Shirley told me he worked for a farmer for
four dollars a month. In the fall he picked apples for a penny a
bushel. Aunt Ethel told me that Uncle Shirley was a hard worker as
a teenager. Grandpa John Morris had made a living the same way.
He walked across the rugged mountain to work for a farmer until
he worked long enough to pay for a cow that the farmer had to sell.
Mom told me, "Finally one day he came down the side of the
mountain leading the old cow."

Apple Butter Boiling

At various times during mid to late summer, and into the
fall months, apples and peaches became the focus of a community
effort. Again, in the earlier days in Hopkins Gap, wagons were
loaded with buckets, baskets, and children and pulled with mules to
the "high top patches" to pick apples. The "high top patches" were

communal orchards planted by the earliest settlers in Hopkins Gap. They would go to the top of a mountain and clear a piece of land. Fruit trees were planted and tended by the community, and all shared the bounty. Pears and peaches were peeled and canned in sugar syrup. It was not uncommon for Mom to can two hundred quarts of peaches. Grandma Molly and Aunt Lena canned even more because Grandpa Austin ate canned peaches for every meal.

Apples were probably the most important fruit in Hopkins Gap because they played a role far beyond simple nutrition. To most people an apple is a piece of fruit, red, green, or yellow. Most people have heard "an apple a day keeps the doctor away," and beyond that, the apple is no big deal. It was different in Hopkins Gap. Apples were very useful, meaningful, and connected to significant life events. First, apples had uses and meanings based on their color. Red apples were good for frying, for pies, for feeding the pigs, for drying, and for making apple butter and apple brandy. Green or yellow apples, depending on their shape, shade, flavor, and texture were good for applesauce, frying and pies, but never good for apple butter. Although, one can now find a chart in some cookbooks that delineates the uses of apples by their color, the people of Hopkins Gap had this knowledge handed down to them.

In spite of the seriousness of the apple butter boiling for survival during the coming months and the numerous chores involved, the gathering of people had relatively little to do when it wasn't their turn to stir, so they told stories, gossiped, sang and otherwise enjoyed themselves.

Courting couples were identified and called up to do some of the stirring. The couple, one on each side of the seven or eight-foot long stirrer, was carefully instructed to stir continuously or the apples would stick to the bottom of the kettle and burn. Even the slightest burn would damage the taste and flavor of the entire thirty or forty gallons of apple butter. More important, it would bring down the wrath of Grandma Molly who was not happy if the apple butter burned. Many times I saw her pick up a broom and without a word, whack a person stirring too slowly. No one argued with

156

her. She was in charge; as a consequence, I never knew of a burned batch of apple butter.

The most popular stirring technique was to move the paddle twice around the sides of the kettle and then once through the middle. An ancient rhyme was recited to remind the stirrers:

> *"Twice around the sides,*
> *And once through the middle.*
> *That's how you stir*
> *The apple butter kittle."*

Courting couples often stirred the kettle at the same time, and if they bumped the kettle and splashed the butter, they had to kiss each other in front of the crowd. So you might say that apples served to move romances along toward marriages and ultimately to the arrival of future apple pickers and apple butter eaters.

If a single woman was stirring and splashed, it was believed she would make a poor housewife. So the boiling was a time for a woman to advertise her future housewife talents; or, as in my case, to announce that I would make a poor housewife and avoid marriage. I always made sure I splashed the apple butter once or twice.

When the butter was finished, it was dipped into crocks while it was very hot. Once it cooled, a crock was turned upside down. If the butter stayed in the container without dumping out or dripping, it was "quality" apple butter. Another sign that the apple butter was cooked correctly was when, after being stored in open crocks all winter, it had not acquired a crust of mold on the top.

During the months ahead, apple butter would be served with pinto beans and homemade cottage cheese. It was spread on homemade bread and soaked with milk. This was my daddy's favorite bedtime snack. It was made into apple butter rolls when there was extra pie dough. We walked about half of a mile from the school bus in the evenings. Some of my favorite memories go back to when I would be nearly home and smell apple butter rolls, pinto beans, and homemade bread. I always felt secure as those smells filled my nostrils and my mind with memories of Grandma Molly and apple butter boilings. Mom had been very busy on those special days.

Mom is teaching some of my students how to stir apple butter.

Apple butter was an excellent treatment for burns. Mom said, "It takes the fire out of a burn better than anything I know of." She spread it on a clean white cloth and applied it directly to the wound. The cloth was worn for a day or two.

Gardening

Not only were wild fruits and vegetables gathered, but they were also grown and processed for eating in the winter months. We had ways of keeping food all winter. When the cabbage was ready, we would dig a ditch and bury the heads upside down with the roots sticking out. It stayed good until late March. Holes were dug in the ground and lined with straw for storing apples. They kept that way all winter.

All gardening and preserving was done according to the signs of the Zodiac and the phases of the moon. I remember my mother saying: "There is a sign for almost everything, planting, butchering, preserving, pruning, setting hen eggs, cutting hair. Why, I wouldn't think of planting a garden without looking up the signs first; it says so right in the Bible! To everything there is a season and a time to every purpose under the heaven, a time to plant, and a time to pick what you have planted." She had nicknames for the Zodiac signs based on the symbol for each sign. Gemini was the twins or the arms; Leo was the lion or heart; Libra the scales, weights or balance; Sagittarius was the archer or bowman; Aquarius was the water boy or water man; Pisces was the fish; Aries was the ram or buck; Taurus was the bull, Cancer was the crab; Virgo was variously the virgin, flower girl, or posey woman; Scorpio was the lizard or scorpion; and Capricorn was billy, or the goat. These beliefs about the Zodiac signs were certainly not unique to Hopkins Gap; but they did play a major part in all gardening and preserving habits.

The Zodiac signs were matched with the proper phases of the moon. When the moon was waxing or increasing in size, in the first or second quarters of the cycle, it was in the "up" sign. When waning or decreasing, the moon was in the "down" sign. A "new" moon was the growing phase, a "full" moon was the middle, and an "old" moon was in the last quarter of the cycle.

Everybody in Hopkins Gap knew the signs and used them for all activities associated with planting, growing, and processing. "Plant potatoes in the sign of the twins, and they will multiply and give you twice as much as those planted in other signs." If potatoes were planted in the "up" sign, they would come to the top of ground, and the sun would burn them. It was also good to plant potatoes in the "down" sign, so they wouldn't be bothered by bugs. Grandma Molly said, "Never plant cucumbers, squash or anything that comes from a blossom in the sign of the posey woman; you will get plenty of blossoms but no fruit." Peas were planted the day after a new moon in the "up" sign but not during posey woman.

159

Pole beans would not climb the poles if they were planted in the "down" sign.

When it was time to dig sweet potatoes, Mom and Dad checked the almanac to avoid the sign of the water boy. Otherwise, they made sure to not dig them in the "old" moon or the sweet potatoes would rot in storage. Cabbage was processed into sauerkraut in August during the "down" sign of the moon which kept the brine down in the crock and not spilling over the sides. Sauerkraut was never made in the sign of the fish, because it would turn to slime.

The produce from the garden was canned, dried, and, in later years, frozen for use in the winter. Green beans or snap beans and corn were processed in a community effort under the supervision of Grandma Molly. These gatherings were called bean stringings and corn huskings. Some of the beans were canned and some were threaded onto a string then placed in a warm dry place such as the attic. In a month or two they turned into "hay" beans, or dried beans. They had to be boiled long and hard to get them tender, but the flavor was unique and tasted nothing like the original bean flavor.

During the gardening months my sister and I were warned not to go in or near the garden if we were having a period. Also, we could not help with the processing or canning of fruits and vegetables. These warnings came from Mom and were always attached to stories of how gardens were killed and produce spoiled by a menstruating woman walking into the garden or helping with the canning. Mom told us about our neighbor coming to visit while she was picking cucumbers. The neighbor walked into the garden and stood near the cucumber vines. One day later, the cucumber patch was dead.

Stories abounded of women touching houseplants and killing them. When a houseplant died, Mom could always explain it by remembering a visit from so and so, while she was "on the rag."

Naturally, being the cagey liar I had become from my school experiences, I had a lot of periods during the summer months when the garden was growing and being harvested. I used fake periods to get out of work. Mom's belief that women could contaminate and kill living plants when menstruating made no sense to me. I knew that she was canning and in the garden when she was having her period, so I asked her, "Why don't you kill and spoil things." Her answer was interesting. She said, "God made an exception for the woman who was responsible for growing and canning food for her family. At the same time, He made me responsible for making sure other women didn't kill my plants."

It still made no sense to me when I thought about it long and hard. Therefore, I felt no guilt when I used a fake period so I wouldn't have to pull weeds and pick vegetables in the hot summer sun.

After Mom told me about the birds and bees and how the period was a necessary event in having babies, I recognized further contradictions in her story. She always said babies were important, and people should have as many as they could care for; thus, periods were important. So, why would God make such an important event as a monthly period destructive of the very duties women were responsible for doing? Of course, I presented this dilemma to Mom. She explained, "It as God's way of punishing Eve for feeding the apple to Adam." I ended up more frustrated than before because, on several occasions, I had seen my dad refuse to eat what Mom had cooked for him. Men in my family rarely did what women wanted them to do.

Another hazard of the vegetable garden was cutworms. They lived in the ground and particularly enjoyed the succulent stems of cucumber vines and tomato stems. They cut the plants off at the ground while sucking out the moisture. Grandma Molly solved this problem by digging around the plants until she found three cutworms. She took the worms to the nearest white oak tree and said to them, "Now cut this tree." She claimed that in a few days, the cutworms from the entire garden had arrived at the base of the tree. Grandma knew she had successfully cleared all the cutworms away from the garden and that was all she wanted. I heard my daddy ask her, "Mom, did you kill the cutworms after you got them all in one spot?" Her answer was, "No, they respected me enough to listen to me and get out of my garden, so I let them live."

The garden was also the subject of a lot of fun. My uncles often sang this little garden song to me:

> My darling sweet potato; do you carrot all for me?
> My heart beets for you and my love is as soft as a squash.
> I am for you as strong as an onion.
> You are a peach with your raddish hair and turnip nose.
> You are the apple of my eye, so if we cantaloupe,
> Then lettuce be married.
> I know we will make a wonderful pear.

Hunting

Deer, wild turkey, and squirrels were abundant in the mountains surrounding us. These animals were killed at any time of the year as needed for food. My family ate venison and squirrels instead of beef. Dad loved to hunt squirrels, and he handed that love of hunting down to me and my brother, Larry. Every year by the middle of October, Larry has at least eighty squirrels killed, skinned, cleaned and in the freezer as part of his winter meat.

Dad let me go squirrel hunting with him when I was twelve. The squirrel hunting season was a week or two away. We walked across the hill back into Dean's orchard. We knew the land was posted. Dad hunted with a single-shot twenty-two rifle. We spotted a squirrel on a limb eating a hickory nut. I begged him to let me shoot first. "You'll never hit him," he whispered, but he handed me the gun. I leveled the sights on the squirrel's ear and pulled the trigger. Down he came, deader than a door nail. Dad said, "Well now, ain't you somethin'. That was just a lucky shot."

We walked over to get the squirrel. He had fallen at the base of the tree. As we picked him up, I glanced up on the tree trunk and there was a wooden sign with these words plainly carved on it: "No Hunting." A year or two ago, my brother Warnie and I were hunting morels in Dean's orchard in the early spring. I was telling him that I had killed my first squirrel in that orchard. As we walked over toward the spot, I saw the "No Hunting" sign still nailed to the tree. It is now in my collection of childhood memorabilia.

When we got home with a bunch of squirrels, we knew there would soon be a delicious feast. We ate every piece of the squirrel including the brains. Only two of us could stand the thoughts of eating the brains. Larry and I would clean the heads and boil them in a pot of salty water. When they were done, we took the little heads out of the pot, cracked open the skulls and scooped out the brain. It was a delicious treat.

In my dad and uncles' minds, there was no hunting season as planned by the gaming authority today. They knew when the squirrels and deer were fattest and therefore tender enough to eat. They started hunting squirrels in mid-September after they had been eating hickory nuts for a month. They were not only fat then, but their meat had a better flavor. Deer meat was good in the fall because it was fat; however, it was also good in the early summer when they would often kill what he called a "strawberry" buck. This was a deer with new antlers covered in moss. He had been eating the early spring sprouts and shoots of new grass. My brother Larry claims they are very fat, and the meat is really tender.

Dad, my brothers, and uncles trapped and hunted skunks, raccoons, foxes and muskrats in the winter months. They sold the furs for a little extra money. They sold the skins to Joe Kimble who owned a junkyard in Harrisonburg and also dealt with fur traders. Kimble paid from twenty-five cents to three dollars a skin.

The highest priced skunk skin was a number one. A number one was black all over with a white spot in the forehead and a white tip on the end of the tail. The next best skin was a

163

number two with a white spot on the forehead, a white tip on the tail, and a white stripe down the spine. The price went down as the skunk skin had more white on it. Sometimes an all white skunk skin would bring a quarter depending on the time of year he was caught.

Since skunks roamed only at night, the men left the house with their hunting dogs several hours after dark. They hunted until the wee hours of morning. When they got sleepy, they found a barn, crawled into the hay with their dogs and slept until daylight.

My dad told the story of sleeping in a barn where a man had previously hung himself. At about 5:00 a.m., he and Uncle Shirley were awakened by a loud thud. They woke up and figured it was the ghost of the man had made when he hanged himself. Uncle Shirley told me that he often slept in the barn and would hear all kinds of things like horses pulling wagons into the loft and doors opening. My dad and Uncle Shirley said the barn was haunted because of the tragedy of the shooting and suicide by hanging. The rest of the story always followed. The man hung himself because he had just murdered two people at the house that my Aunt Goldie and Uncle Rob bought shortly after the shooting. He shot one man at the front yard gate and shot the second man through the front door glass as he ran up the stairs to hide.

Hunting generated many tall tales. Some of my favorite times with my Uncles Shirley and Jim were story-telling competitions with each other. They went on for hours to see who could tell the biggest tale about their hunting escapades. I learned later that these stories were not original with them, but had been passed down for generations just as they were passing them to me. When I started college in 1966, I taped them telling the stories.

Sometimes they told true stories about actual events, but the ones that had survived through the ages were usually about fantastic feats of hunters and the strength and size of animals. Uncle Jim told one of the best stories and perhaps the tallest tale. Of course, he was the main character: "I was huntin' deer at the foot of a ridge one day when I spied a big buck. I only had two shells, and 'cause I got 'buck fever,' I missed him on the first shot. The buck turned and run around the ridge. I was anxious to have his horns hangin' on my wall, so I put the barrel of my rifle between two saplins' and bent it. When I pulled the trigger, my last bullet went around the ridge and killed the buck on the other side."

Uncle Jim made himself the main character again in this tall tale. "I went coon huntin' and the dogs treed a coon up on a sycamore poplar, out on a dry limb ten feet above the top of the tree. So I tried to shoot the coon. I used all my shells but one, which is the regular thing all hunters do, 'cause they don't know what they will meet on the way home. So I waited 'til daylight, then climbed the tree and went out on the dry limb that was ten feet above the top. I shook the coon off the limb, the limb broke, and I fell. I fell down straddlin' the fence with both legs on one side, flat of my back, face on the ground. I got up, got my gun and my coon and started for home."

Uncle Jim looked at his audience of children for a reaction to his ridiculous tale; but we were still trying to figure out if we had heard what we thought we heard. Then he went on with his story. "As I come down off the ridge I looked up the holler and saw five turkeys on a limb. There I was with only one bullet. I eased around until I was straight out from the end of the limb. I shot right into the end of the limb, the bullet split the limb open, the turkeys' legs dropped down through the crack, and the crack went shut. I cut the tree down and it fell into a nearby creek. I waded into the water to get my turkeys. As I came out of the water with my five turkeys, I found my boots full of fish. All in all it was a good huntin' trip."

In another tall tale, Uncle Jim claimed he went out one day to shoot a wild turkey for supper. He hunted until afternoon without seeing a turkey, so he decided he would lie down behind a log and take a nap. While he was sleeping, a wild turkey flew over and sat down on the log. When Uncle Jim awoke, he saw the turkey, and realizing that he was too close to shoot, he just grabbed the turkey by the legs. The turkey flew and carried Uncle Jim with him. After holding on to the turkey's legs for some time and distance, Uncle Jim's hands became tired, so he let loose of the turkey, spit in each hand, rubbed them together, grabbed the turkey's legs again and continued his ride to the next ridge.

Many of the men in Hopkins Gap loved to hunt for raccoon because the skins brought a good price from fur buyers. Occasionally, if the coon was young, the family ate the meat. Mom fixed it once or twice, but I think I was away from home when they ate it. My sister-in-law, Hilda, baked raccoon many times. She skinned it, cut off its head, packed potatoes, sweet potatoes, carrots, and celery around it, and baked it. It smelled delicious while it baked but I didn't eat any of her raccoon either.

Probably the most important reason for coon hunting was the battle of wits between man, dog, and the raccoon. It was a lot of fun to hear the dogs bark as they followed the coon's tracks. After days of being educated about coon hunting, I went with Uncle Shirley and my brothers. By the time I got into the mountains, I knew a lot about raccoon, dogs, and the hunting process. Uncle Shirley, who to this day is considered the authority on coon hunting in Hopkins Gap, told me, "You have to know three things to hunt coons. You have to know the coon's habits, you have to know the kind of weather that he likes for wanderin', and you have to know the areas he runs in. It's no point in huntin' coons in an area that has a lot of underground dens and den trees, because the dogs can't get him out of a den."

A coon will use another animal's den under a pile of rocks or go into a den tree. Uncle Shirley bragged, "In my younger days, I would cut the tree down or set fire to it to chase the coon out. And, if I was really energetic, I would dig the coon out of an underground den."

Of course, this practical information was always interspersed with a good tall tale. One of my favorites was the story about a man who loved to hunt raccoons so much he took his coon hounds out for a chase on a very cold winter night. Uncle Shirley was as serious as a judge as he told the story, "The dogs struck a fresh raccoon track; and, as they run along, the hunter noticed a

166

very strange thing. When the dogs barked, their 'barks' were freezing in front of their mouths. Since the man loved to hunt so much, he immediately had an idea. He took a sack, picked up the dogs' 'barks' and carried them home. He left the "barks" outside that night to stay frozen. The next night he built a big fire in the fireplace and put the sack of 'barks' near the fire to thaw. He lit his pipe, sat down by the fire, and listened to the hounds chase the coon all over the mountain."

The nights that I went along to hunt raccoon were perfect—damp, moonlit, and cool. Uncle Shirley untied the coonhounds; we crossed the Shoemaker River, and started to walk up Ground Squirrel Bridge Hollow. We stayed on the trail with kerosene lanterns to light the way while the dogs ran out into the woods smelling for a fresh coon track. From my lessons in hunting, I knew that a good coonhound ignores all other animal trails—deer, rabbit, fox—and searches only for coons.

We walked along for a while until one of the dogs "struck a track." He let out a series of yelps to let Uncle Shirley know he had found a hot track. Then he began the chase with a constant rhythmic bark. The dog ran up and down the ridges, across hollows and back again in hot pursuit of the smart raccoon. Meanwhile, Uncle Shirley was enjoying the sounds of the chase—symphonies to his ears—as he waited for the hounds to chase the coon up a tree. When the coon ran up a tree, the dogs changed their barks from short rhythmic barks to long barks then long howls. We ran to the tree, and one of the hunters shot the coon. Coon hunters always stood around for a few minutes after a successful kill. When I was with them, they pulled out a pint of whiskey and passed it around. Each man took a snort. When the bottle came to me, they offered me a drink. I said, "No thanks, I don't want any." Their response was, "If you can't drink with us, you can't hunt with us." I reached for the bottle and took a snort myself. The hunters regrouped and we walked on up the hollow. In a little while, I was glad I had taken a drink. It did seem to take the edge off the cold. We got three coons that night. We headed home at about four o'clock in the morning. The moon had come up to help light our way. When we came out of Ground Squirrel Bridge hollow into Uncle Shirley's pasture, a heavy blanket of frost had fallen and made the grass crunch beneath our feet.

Just about everybody in Hopkins Gap knew the qualities of a good coonhound. A good coonhound understands the many tricks of the raccoon. If a family of coons is surprised, the male will lead the dogs away and then lose them by one of several tricks. The coon climbs a tree then jumps out of the tree to the ground as far from the trunk as possible. Most hounds think the coon is still up the tree, but the best coonhounds know they should circle the tree for a trail leading away. If there is water nearby, a raccoon might try another trick to throw off the hounds when they come to the creek. He might swim upstream, get out on the opposite bank, mark a trail, get back in the water, and return exactly where he entered.

Coonhounds were known as either an "open mouth" hunter or a "still mouth" hunter. Uncle Shirley had one of each. Old Buck was a "still mouth" hound. He never barked while he was on a hot trail. He only barked to let Uncle Shirley know when he had finally treed the coon.

Old Jack was an "open mouth" dog and a very refined hunter. When he hit a hot coon track, and was running with other hounds, he would wait until the other dogs had barked for a while, then he would "open" his mouth. The communication between Uncle Shirley and his dog was uncanny.

He bragged that Old Jack had fooled him only twice. "One time, when he was younger he treed a possum and barked like it was a coon. I pulled his ears good, and he never chased another possum. The second time, Old Jack found himself cornered by a skunk. He barked so I would come and kill the skunk to set him free. The skunk had him backed up in a fence corner and was spraying him. I took a stick and whacked the skunk behind the head and knocked it piss windin'. Layton Lam was with me. He grabbed that skunk and had its skin off before it was dead."

Alva Hartman often hunted with Uncle Shirley. He was a strong mountain man and an avid hunter. He called Old Jack the "old professor." One night about a dozen men and their dogs were hunting when the other dogs started barking. The men started to follow the dogs, but Alva told them to wait. He said, "Don't budge an inch until you hear the old professor join in." A couple of minutes later, Old Jack gave out about three barks, and they knew for sure the dogs were onto a raccoon track.

Another time, Alva was hunting with Uncle Shirley and Old Jack. They left the house and before they had gone very far, Old Jack had treed three coons. Alva patted Old Jack on the head and said, "Keep that up, old professor, and you'll get this ham sandwich I have in my pocket."

Hog-Killing Time

In the early days of Hopkins Gap, long before I was born, the families would put their hogs out in the mountain to range. A vast forest-covered area still bears the name of Big Hog Pens and Little Hog Pens because it was perfect for ranging all the hogs raised in Hopkins Gap. Each spring, the sow hogs were bred and then driven back into the rugged mountain area. The sows were kept in crude makeshift hog pens until the pigs were born. After the pigs were born, each owner marked his pigs with a brand—either a hole or a notch in the ear. Then the sows and pigs were turned free to make their own living in the mountains. They foraged for roots and sprouts in the early summer; and in the fall, grew fat on acorns and other nuts that grew in abundance in the forest.

When butchering time came, all the men went to round up their hogs. My dad told me the hogs were so wild after a spring and summer without seeing a human that they sometimes had to be shot in order to get them out of the mountains to be butchered. By the time I was born in the early 1940s, families kept their hogs on their property in a hog pen far away from the house.

Pork, supplemented with venison and squirrel, was the mainstay of my family's diet during the winter months, and at butchering time, little was wasted. Hogs not only provided meat, but they provided grease for cooking. Parts of the hog were used to grease saws and make salve. Other parts were used in plaster and to make brushes. Even the tail was used for a little wholesome fun on hog-killing day.

There was lots of talk about hog-killing time when the weather started to cool in the fall. Dad changed the hogs' feed around the middle of October. All year he had fed them table scraps and wheat bran but now he changed to table scraps and corn meal. He always wanted to butcher fat hogs.

Mom argued with him every year about getting the hogs too fat. She said, "Norman, don't get the hogs too fat. It makes the hams and shoulders too greasy, and I want nice lean sausage this year. I always have too much lard left over anyway."

Dad took great pride in how fat he could make his hogs. He countered Mom's argument, "The meat is sweeter and easier to chew if it has a lot of fat in it. I don't want no tough meat to chew on."

I think he might have been thinking about how much lard Mom needed to fry potatoes. I also think he really enjoyed the butchering helpers commenting on how fat his hogs were. There was always a prideful smile playing around his mouth when he heard them remark about the fat as they cut into the meat on hog-killing day.

November was hog-killing month. It was customary at our house to set aside the Saturday before Thanksgiving for this event, but the weather had to be just right. It could not be too warm. Warmer days and crisp cold night temperatures were needed for the meat the start the curing process.

During the week before hog killing day everybody began making last minute preparations. Mom began to gather the products she had preserved from her summer garden. She went to the cellar and got cans of sauerkraut, corn, pickled beets, green beans, dill pickles, and jars of jelly. Other trips to the cellar yielded sweet potatoes, regular potatoes, and apples. She went to the attic to get "hay" beans. These were green beans that she had threaded onto a string and hung in the attic to dry. In the freezer, she located frozen blackberries, cherries, and peaches she had gathered in the summer. She used the fruit to bake at least sixteen pies on the day before butchering. This same day she also made two three-layer cakes from scratch, usually a banana cake and a prune cake.

Mom rushing around to get ready for butchering day

Mom often said, with some dread in her voice as the day for hog killing drew near, "I'll have to 'put the big pot in the little one'." This statement expressed her knowledge of the hard work ahead the next day. She was going to use every pot she had to cook and maybe have to borrow some extra pots from Aunt Goldie.

While Mom was busy gathering the ingredients for the noon meal on hog-killing day, my dad and brothers gathered the butchering tools. To do this, they had to remember where they butchered the last hogs of the season the year before. During the weekend before the butchering, they would gather around the dining room table. Dad would say, "We'd better be thinkin' about haulin' the butcherin' tools this week. Do y'all know where they are?" My brothers, Larry and John, would look at each other and think for a minute then Larry would answer, "They're at Uncle Jim's house. He was the last one we butchered for last year, ain't that right, John?" John always nodded his head in agreement.

The tools included a .22 rifle, axe, butcher saw, wooden tripod hog hangers, scalding chains or ropes, kettles, kettle rings, scrapers, hooks, large tubs, buckets, pans, meat boards, and a wide variety of sharp knives. It was customary for the last family that used the tools to clean and store them for the next year. I often wondered how the men kept the ownership of the tools straight because while each tool or type of tool was individually owned, the entire community used them. Uncle Shirley and Uncle Jim were always there on butchering day. They provided the sharp knives, while my dad provided the scalding pan and some of the iron kettles. Uncle Jim also provided the lard press and the sausage grinder and stuffer. All of these tools were gathered and set in place the day before the butchering.

Butchering day started early and was a busy one for all members of the household. Dad got up at 3:00 a.m. to fill the kettles and scalding pan with water and make fires under them. An hour later the helpers began to arrive. The same men and women always came to help, and some of them we hadn't seen since hog-killing the year before. After a breakfast of hot coffee, biscuits, gravy, and sausage, they were ready to begin the long, hard day. The men joined Dad at the kettles, and the women, Aunt Ethel and Aunt Hazel, helped Mom carry coffee to the men and get the noon meal started.

When the men joined Dad at the steaming kettles, their first question was, "How many we killin' today, Norman?" He answered, "I've got four to kill. I'm killin' another one to divide with the preacher. Larry has two and Brenda one. That makes eight. They'll weigh between seven and eight hundred pounds each."

One of the helpers would inevitably say, "We'll be here all day with that many big hogs." At that point the competition began.

Each year, they tried to do the same number of hogs in less time than they did them the year before.

As the sun peeped up over the eastern horizon, Dad walked with his .22 rifle to the hog pen and shot the first hog. The hogs were killed one at a time so they didn't have to lie around any time before they were processed. This was a very hard time for me, as I felt sorry for the hogs and for my dad who had fed them twice a day for nearly a year. I tried to stay asleep until the hogs were dead; and, if I was awake, I covered my ears. I once mentioned to my mother that I felt sorry for the hogs, and she told me to stop because it caused them to die harder.

The dead hogs were then dragged by truck to the scalding boards. Ropes or chains were laid on the platform that allowed the workers to roll the hogs and turn them over and over in the scalding pan. The men carefully watched the water temperature. If it got too hot, the hogs' skin came off along with the bristles.

*Halves of hogs hung on tripods until a
young man carried them to the cutting boards.*

Next the hogs were scraped clean of bristles and hung on the wooden tripod hog hangers, hind feet up. When a hog weighed 300 to 700 pounds, it was a difficult task to raise it to the top of the tripod. It often required the efforts of several strong men.

The hogs were now in position for butchering. First, the main butcher took a long sharp knife and removed the heads. Uncle

Jake stood by and grabbed each head as soon as it snapped off. He took them, one by one, to his head-cleaning table that was set up away from the major activities. He cleaned the hogs' heads, cut out the jowls and brains, and prepared the scraps of meat for the pudding. He was the "head" man, a job nobody else wanted.

I remember watching him as he rolled the hogs' heads around and wondering if he got that job because he had a face that looked very much like the one he was trimming. He was fat, too. One time I asked Mom, "Did Uncle Jake get the head-cleaning job because he's fat and looks like a hog?" She smiled and said, "Don't you dare let your daddy hear you say such a thing about his brother." Later when I was alone with Mom, we had a good discussion and a good laugh about how much Uncle Jake favored a hog.

Uncle Jake finished his "head" work fairly early in the day then began playing tricks with the pigs' tails. He would sneak up behind people and pin a tail to their shirt. To have the pig tail hanging from you was the least flattering thing that could happen to you on butchering day; but it was all done for fun and to lighten the workload.

After Uncle Jake took the heads away, the head butcher split the hog down the middle and began to remove the intestines. Grandma Molly stood by with a tub to catch them as they fell out of the hogs. Year after year I heard her warn the butcher, "Don't you dare cut a gut. I won't stuff sausage in guts that have hog shit on them 'cause you can't get that smell off."

Grandma took the intestines so she could trim the fat from the large intestines and remove the small intestines. The fat went into the lard kettle for rendering and the small intestine was scraped clean and cut into long sections. When the sections were cleaned, she would put one end in her mouth and hold the other end shut. She blew into the intestine like a balloon. If it inflated, it was suitable for stuffing sausage. This part made me gag, because I had just watched her scrape out the shit.

Once the intestines were removed, the woman of the house, my mother, was called to wash the hog until it was pure white. She used a brush and warm soapy water and removed every speck of dirt from the hog. After my brother married Hilda, this became her job. When the hog was clean, the head butcher split the carcass along the backbone into halves. The head butcher called for a man to carry each half of the hog to the meat boards where it would be cut up and placed into piles.

Left to right: Uncle Shirley, Preacher Isaac Risser, Mom in the foreground, Susan Martindale, and Winston Rhodes trimming and shaping the hams and shoulders.

My brother, John, is a small man, but like Dad, he is very strong. The butcher yelled at him first, "Hey John, come here and get this hog out of my way."

At this point an interesting ritual began to unfold. A half of one of Dad's hogs weighed close to three hundred pounds, so it was no small feat to carry it to the meat boards. If John had carried the first half the year before, he passed the job on to another young man who wanted to show his strength.

He would say to one of our younger cousins who had not carried a half before, "Come here and carry this hog, I've got a bad back this year." The young man would get in position with the half placed solidly across his shoulder. He planted his legs so he wouldn't collapse when the butcher cut the tendon in the foot that was holding the hog up on the hangers. Everybody got quiet just as if they were watching a weight lifter in the Olympics. All you heard was the water boiling in the kettles and the popping of the fire.

When the young man was in position, the butcher sliced the tendon. The full weight of the hog half fell on him. He carefully walked to the cutting boards, trembling under the weight. When he laid the half onto the boards without dropping it and without help, he had passed one of the tests of mountain manhood.

The same young man might carry another half of a hog during the day, but the job was shared with any young man who wanted to show his strength. I always noticed that John's back was suddenly healed as he also carried at least one half.

Once the hogs were on the meat boards the head butcher, usually Uncle Shirley, and the helpers started cutting and several piles of meat began to take shape. Hams, shoulders, and side meat were cut out first. They were the prime pieces, beautifully trimmed and shaped. My dad took his place in the meat house, and it was my job to carry the prime pieces to him. I later turned this job over to my niece, Angie, when she was old enough. Dad had mixed a bucket of cure—a mixture of brown sugar, salt, and pepper—that he packed on the meat as soon as I got it to him. The hams and shoulders were allowed to cure for a year with the exception of one ham that was cut in May to eat with wild asparagus gathered along the fencerows. After a year, hams and shoulders were sliced and fried or cut into large pieces to boil. The broth from the boiled meat was used to make potpie.

Dad had already put the cure on the jowls that Uncle Jake had taken from the hogs' heads. The jowls were the fat part under the hogs' chins. It had a sweet flavor and made the best bacon. The sides of the hogs were trimmed out into squares of meat about two inches thick. This was cured into bacon. The ribs were chopped into three-inch sections and canned by the women the next day or so.

Usually most of the hogs were killed and cleaned by ten o'clock. It had been a long time since breakfast, so the helpers took turns going to the house for hot coffee and a piece or pie or cake. When they stepped onto the back porch, they were greeted with the smells of the noon meal. This meal, for my family, replaced the traditional Thanksgiving dinner since all the men in my family would be deer hunting during the week of Thanksgiving including Thanksgiving Day.

Mom, Aunt Ethel and Aunt Hazel were in their element. All the men bragged on Mom's pies and sniffed the delicious smells coming from the kitchen. They would say things like, "I'm not gonna eat too much pie now, because I want to save room for dinner."

Aunt Ethel would be busy on the porch frying platters of meat, and the men would stop and say things like, "I'm glad to see you fixin' the meat. I remember how good it was last year." The head butcher never left the kettles. It was expected that Mom would carry hot coffee and pie to him throughout the morning.

Aunt Hazel, Aunt Ethel, and Mom
having a good time preparing butchering day dinner

Back at the meat boards, other piles of meat were taking shape. There was a pile of fat to be cut into squares for rendering and turned into lard. Each hog had large slabs of fat on them. At this point even children were included in the butchering process. They were responsible for cutting the fat for rendering. The head butcher loved to give young, naïve children the "gut" fat to cut into small pieces. It was almost impossible to cut because it was warm, and the knife blade just rolled it around instead of cutting it. Older children got the easier fat to cut and passed the "gut" fat to unsuspecting younger brothers and sisters.

The fat chunks were thrown into an iron kettle and fried a long time to release the grease. When the pieces were turning crisp and brown on the edges, they were dipped into a lard press. They were squeezed in the press until every drop of grease was removed.

Hilda stirring the lard kettle

The lard press shaped the crisp chunks of fat into what we called "cracklin' cakes" about eight inches in diameter and two inches thick. These made great snacks and many children ended hog-killing day with sick stomachs from eating too many "cracklins." "Cracklins" were used later to make "cracklin' bread. The lard was stored in five-gallon tanks and kept in a cool cellar. It was used for cooking throughout the winter, and the next summer, whatever lard was left over was used to make lye soap.

A second pile of meat on the meat boards consisted of the lean trimmings from the hams and shoulders and would be ground into sausage. When it was time to grind the lean, the head butcher called my dad to come and season the meat. He sprinkled the meat with salt, pepper, and sage then added his secret ingredient. Uncle Jim pushed his arm into the tub of meat and stirred in the seasonings.

By now it is one-o'clock and time to eat dinner. The men go into the house in shifts. Mom went out to the meat house and told Dad that dinner was ready. He stopped curing the meat and walked to the head butcher, told him dinner was ready, and they went to the table first. Dad sat at the head of the table with the butcher seated to his right.

Mom, Aunt Ethel, and Aunt Hazel had taken the ingredients Mom had gathered during the week and converted them into an unbelievable feast. There was fried potatoes, sauerkraut and dumplings, pinto beans, candied sweet potatoes, mashed potatoes, fried apples, canned peaches, boiled "hay" beans, regular green beans, pickled beets, several kinds of pickles—bread and butter, dill, and sweet pickles, homemade bread and rolls, and, of course, gravy. The meat for this "Thanksgiving" meal was fried liver and fried tenderloin from the hogs that were killed that morning.

Once Dad and the butcher were seated, the table filled up with other helpers. The women served the men first, then the children, and finally, when everyone else was fed, they sat down to eat. Dad was in charge of his household on hog-killing day. Sometimes he got a little carried away and started ordering Mom around. She clamped her jaw down as only she could do, walked into the kitchen, and whispered to Aunt Ethel, "He'll be sorry for that when everybody leaves here today."

Left to right: Uncle Shirley, the back of Bob Crawford's head, Dad, my brother John, and Uncle Jim all enjoying the delicious butchering day dinner with conversation.

The conversation at the table was filled with bragging about how much they had gotten done so far, about who carried the biggest half of hog and about how good the sausage meat looked. Bets were made about how many tanks of lard we would get.

Dad would say, "Well, we got four tanks out of that one kittle. We probably got three more kittles to go. I'll bet we'll get a dozen tanks easy."

One of the helpers would chime in between bites and say, "Maybe not that many, 'cause those last two hogs didn't seem as fat as the others."

Everybody ate a little of everything, and those with the capacity to do so had seconds. This was before Mom sliced her banana and prune cakes.

When the first round of helpers finished eating, they returned to the kettles and meat boards and let the other workers come in to eat. Uncle Jim had been among the first to eat, so he began preparing to grind the lean meat into sausage.

In the early days of my childhood, a hand-cranked sausage grinder was used. Later, Uncle Jim rigged up a small motor so that sausage grinding became less of an effort for him. He watched the grinder while I carefully dropped in the pieces of lean meat. He cautioned me all the time, "Now don't put too much in at a time." Occasionally I would get the grinder too full and the meat would push back out of the top. Uncle Jim would patiently remove some of the chunks and pretend to slap my hand.

Once the big tubs of sausage were ground, Uncle Jim sat up the lard press. It had an attachment for stuffing sausage. Grandma Molly had the sparkling clean intestines ready to use, so she stepped in to help. Her job was to pack the press full of the loose sausage and put the lid on and slip an intestine on the stuffing tube. She sat next to the sausage press and held the end of the intestine shut until at least a foot of the gut was full of sausage. Then she dropped the end into the tub and just supervised the process.

At this point when I was old enough and strong enough, I was called in to turn the crank on the sausage press. It had to be turned very smoothly and slowly as the intestines filled and slithered into a washing tub. If the sausage broke a hole in an intestine, the meat started pouring out. I had to watch carefully and crank the handle backwards to stop the flow. Grandma would take the broken intestine, give it a twist to seal the hole, and we would continue to stuff the gut. When we finished we had enough long ropes of sausage to fill several washing tubs. It sat in the meat house to cool overnight. On Monday, it was cut into three-inch links and canned.

Peggy Ann Shifflett

After Grandma Molly died, Uncle Jim stuffed the sausage
into a hog intestine. I am turning the crank on the sausage press.

Meanwhile, another kettle of meat had been boiling slowly most of the day. This kettle was filled with mainly fat scraps and small bits of lean. The hogs' tongues were also in the pile, and Mom always put at least one liver in to help the flavor. Once tender, the meat was ground, seasoned, and put into crocks for cooling and storage. This mixture was called puddin' meat. In the coldest of winter months, Mom opened a can of puddin', fried it with onions, and served it with pinto beans.

During the winter of 1962, we had a snowstorm that set records for the century. It snowed nonstop for two days leaving a total of forty-two inches. As is typical after a strong nor'easter, the wind blew for two more days.

We had drifts of thirteen feet that started at the front porch and covered the road and the fences. No one left our house except on foot atop the drifts for seven days. Mom was so proud that all she had to do to feed us was go into the cellar and get canned puddin' meat and cornmeal. We ate like royalty for those seven days consuming puddin' fried with onions, pinto beans, fried potatoes, and corn cakes. She reminded me of that week until she died. It was one of her finer moments.

Mom and Uncle Shirley grinding sausage

Toward the end of hog-killing day, the final chore for the men was making the panhaus. This job was always performed by the head butcher, either Uncle Shirley or Uncle Jim. Panhaus was made by boiling the broth from the pudding meat, and mixing in cornmeal, flour, salt and pepper. It was stirred very fast until it thickened. Then the butcher dipped it into small pans and sat it on the meat boards to cool. It jelled into a delicious treat when sliced, fried, and eaten with apple butter in the days to come.

The remainder of the meat—the tenderloin, the stuffed sausage, and the ribs, was turned over to the women. The meat was allowed to cool all day on Sunday. It was believed that meat canned with the warmth of the hog still in it, would spoil. Besides that, everybody was very tired and needed Sunday to rest.

The hooves of the hogs were made into pickled pig's feet. The reproductive organ of the hogs were hung in the woodshed and used for greasing the bucksaw. Hogs' bristles were set aside and sold for use in plastering and making brushes. Sometimes the gall bladders were used to make a salve for treating frostbite. The few scraps left over at the end of the day were fed to the dogs and cats. My dad often made the comment, "We put every part of the hog to good use except the squeal."

Most of the hard work of butchering is over. The men stand around the kettles talking about the upcoming hunting season. L-R: Skip Crawford, John Shifflett, Jennings Shifflett, Bob Crawford, Jim Morris, Preacher Isaac Risser.

Once the men finished their hog-killing work and had bragged to each other about how many hogs they processed in a shorter time than last year, their minds wandered to the upcoming deer-hunting season that always began on the Monday after butchering. They brought out their high-powered rifles and set up targets to practice and align their sights. They also brought out a bottle of whiskey to pass around the circle. They would take turns peppering the targets with bullets, sipping at the bottle, and telling hunting stories from the year before.

Toward the end of the day, they thought their sights were aligned and they knew the bottle was empty. The chill in the evening air drove them into the cellar where they continued their hunting stories around the cider barrel. I remember the hunting stories getting taller and taller as the evening wore on. Few men left the butchering in a sober condition, but they seemed happy.

Peggy Ann Shifflett

Part Four

MOONSHINE

Run from what's profitable and comfortable.
If you drink those liqueurs,
you'll spill the springwater of your real life.
Rumi (5)

If one universal characteristic of the Appalachian people had to be pointed out, it would be the practice of moonshining. The practice was carried from Europe, but was revived by the mountaineer in order to make his dull, harsh, dangerous life more bearable. When the mountaineer realized there was money to made in whiskey, moonshining took on a whole new significance. The practice of moonshining ingrained in him a habit so deeply rooted that generations of revenue officers have been unable to stamp it out. (6)

Moonshining was so popular and widespread that stories of narrow escapes from the authorities and premonitions of death were part of everyday conversations, and even songs. One song I remember my daddy and Uncle Shirley singing goes like this:

> *"My brother Bill has a still on the hill*
> *Where he turns out a gallon or two.*
> *The birds in the sky*
> *Get so drunk they can't fly*
> *Off that good old mountain dew.*
>
> *Chorus:*
>
> *Oh, they call it that good ole mountain dew*
> *And them that refuse it are very few.*

187

I'll shut my mug
If you'll fill up my jug,
With that good ole mountain dew.

My auntie June had some high class perfume,
Well, it gave out a powerful pew.
Was she surprised
When they had it analyzed
It was that good ole mountain dew.
(Repeat chorus)

My second cousin Jeb had a fool for a wife
But she made a fine squirrel stew.
When we ate at her house
We got as drunk as a louse
For she seasoned with that ole mountain dew.
(Repeat chorus) (14)

Moonshine did not catch on in Hopkins Gap until after the passage of the National Prohibition Act in 1919. Better known as The Volstead Act, this legislation was passed and enacted by Congress to ensure the proper enforcement of Prohibition. Uncle Shirley told me, "Most people bought all their 'drinking' liquor at saloons in Harrisonburg and just made enough moonshine for ailments before the prohibition law was passed. Then after the Volstead Act, there was a big demand for illegal liquor, and we saw it as a way to make money."

Moonshine became very important to the people in Hopkins Gap. During the depression years of the 1930s until the mid-1950s, it was the major source of income for every family in Hopkins Gap family except one. I remember Dad telling me that out of twenty-one families all but two made moonshine. One of the two families who didn't make it was bootlegging it for other moonshiners.

Some of my fondest memories are of the times I had Dad and Uncle Shirley in the same room and in the mood to talk about their moonshining days. These times usually came after a big

Sunday dinner of fried chicken and all the trimmings. After eating, they would retire to the living room and lean back in their chairs to digest. I followed them and sometimes got them started with a question. I always asked Dad first because whether he talked or not depended on his mood. If he wouldn't talk, Uncle Shirley changed the subject to deer hunting or something else. If Dad answered my first question, then I knew I would be with them for a long time because Uncle Shirley always liked to talk and tell stories. I usually started with a question such as, "Dad, tell me how you all learned to make moonshine."

Dad thought for a minute as he chewed on his toothpick, then he said, "Well Pop [Grandpa Austin] taught me. That's how we made our livin' after the tannery closed in Harrisonburg. Before that Pop trimmed bark and hauled it to tannery."

"What was the tannery?" I asked him.

He explained, "It was a big factory there on Water St. in Harrisonburg. It's now a parking lot, but we still call it the Tannery Lot. The factory needed tree bark to tan leather. Then the leather was used in shoe factories. Before I went to the army, I worked in the shoe factory, and we used some of the leather tanned in that factory to make shoes. So, when the tannery closed, Pop was out of work. He had no choice but to grow some corn and make moonshine."

"It was a thing that kinda grew on ya," Uncle Shirley added. "You grew up with it. I learned by goin' to the still and watchin.' Before my parents died I had to sneak to the still, but after both passed away it was a means of livelihood for me. When I first started, I worked with a first cousin. I got seven and one-half cents an hour and my board and a place to sleep. My cousin, he boarded himself, and he got fifteen cents an hour. We had it set up so that we worked six days a week. We would have one still set up at a location and maybe a mile away we'd have another location. We kept three stills goin' this way."

Although I had heard the story many times, I would ask them again, "Will you all tell me how to make moonshine? Their

189

description was long and detailed with Dad and Uncle Shirley contributing parts of the story and filling in what the other one left out. By the time I asked them several times and asked Uncle Jim, Aunt Goldie, and Mom the same question, I got a pretty clear picture of the process of moonshining in Hopkins Gap.

Let's Make Some Moonshine

According to my dad, the process of moonshining began with setting the mash. Mash was whiskey before it fermented. The recipe included one-half bushel of rye, ten pounds of cracked corn, fifty pounds of sugar, and one cake of yeast, and warm water about the temperature of dishwater—about one hundred and twenty degrees."

Sometimes homemade yeast was used. Uncle Shirley told me, "At first we used what we called 'rivels' that was made by takin' and mixin' a light cornmeal batter just as if you was gonna make corn cakes. Then you let that batter ferment or sour then you worked other cornmeal into it to make it thick enough to roll. You made it into rolls, about two inches thick. Then you sliced it off into slices about a half of an inch thick and laid 'em out to dry. One slice in a barrel of mash would start the fermentation. That was before we had the yeast like you can buy today."

My dad went on to explain how to set mash. "We would take fifty-gallon wooden barrels, set two of them real close together, and build a wooden pole pen around them "If it was hot weather when we set our mash, we just camouflaged the pen after we got the mash set in the barrels, but in cold weather we needed to pack insulation around them to hold in the heat for the fermentation process. We used different things—leaves or wet sawdust. I sometimes packed my mash barrels with barnyard manure so the natural heat of the tightly packed manure would make the mash ferment faster." He chucked as he said, "I have made whiskey many

190

times, right in the middle of a manure pile." Each barrel was filled with the ingredients in the recipe.

They used the empty sugar bags to cover the barrels to keep leaves and dirt out of the mash, packed the insulation around the barrels in cold weather, and went home to wait for the mixture to ferment.

One of the daily chores was to check the mash barrels. Dad described the trips he made to check the mash. He said, "The morning after the barrels were set, the mash would be bubblin'. A lot of the grain would come to the top of the water. By the second or third day, the mash would be boilin'. On the fourth day, all the grain would be on top of the liquid. I just put my fingers in the grain and moved it around. If the grain stayed apart, the mash would be ready to run the next day. When the mash was fermented just right, the grain settled to the bottom of the barrel, and all the movement was gone out of the liquid. If we left it for a little while longer, it would get a light skim over the top. Then we knowed we had some good mash."

The length of time needed for fermentation varied according to the amount of grain in the mash. Uncle Shirley told me, "After I got older and started makin' whiskey on my own, with my wife's brother, we set our mash right up here in Ground Squirrel Bridge Holler. We had three barrels settin' up there that we made every other day, but that was because we had about three times as much grain than what was needed. We still put the same amount of sugar in it. As a rule, it takes three to five days for a barrel of mash to ferment."

As I listened to Uncle Shirley and Dad describe the hard work and cost of ingredients, my mind wandered back to my younger days when my brothers, Cousin Herman, and I used to play along the creeks and hollows in search of mash barrels. When we found them, we filled them with river rocks so the mash would run out and waste. It was a great way to have fun because whomever the barrels belonged to could not say a word to our parents because of the chance of getting caught.

We justified our behavior to ourselves by assuming the mash we wasted belonged to Uncle Jake since he made moonshine right up until he went into a nursing home. My mother told me that Jake was a dangerous moonshiner. She said, "He uses whatever way necessary to make a quick batch for sale. He runs his mash through car radiators and mixes his whiskey in zinc washtubs. I don't like him selling moonshine to Grandma Molly because I'm afraid she will die from his brew."

I thought Mom might be proud that we filled Uncle Jake's mash barrels with river rocks, so I told her. I got a serious tongue lashing from her. She asked me, "How do you all know the barrels belong to Jake? They might belong to somebody else and you wasted a lot of money. Let the law take care of your Uncle Jake, and you mind your own business." Fortunately, she never told Dad what we had been doing.

I guess we felt justified in spoiling the mash because when Grandma Molly got her hands on a pint of moonshine, she sipped at it until she was drunk. Mom always fussed about Grandma Molly getting drunk on Sundays when we went to visit her and Grandpa Austin. Mom said, "She gets kinda sloppy with her cookin'. She clams up and won't talk to anybody, and then wanders off somewhere and goes to sleep before it's time for us to leave for home." A lot of times, Mom sent my brothers and me off into the woods to find Grandma and make sure she was all right before we left Hopkins Gap for home.

While my mind was wandering, Uncle Shirley and Dad continued to describe the moonshining process. "After the mash was ready to 'run" [distill], we got up early in the morning. At about two or three o'clock we got out of bed to make the dough to see the cap onto the still. Uncle Shirley stopped to explain the dough, "The cap dough was made from flour and water, and had to be made sticky so it would seal the cap on the still."

Mom was well known for the dough she made to seal the still cap. She bragged to me many times, "The dough had to be fresh, so the men got me out of bed, even as a teenager, at two-o'clock in the morning to make dough when they were getting' ready for an early morning run of moonshine. They'd tell me how good my dough worked when they got home at night."

Moonshiners wasted no steps. When they left home to go make moonshine, they carried with them the ingredients to reset their mash barrels at the end of their workday. Off they went, before daylight, with heavy bags of sugar and grain on their backs, walking through rugged mountain hollows and up rocky creek beds. The work was strenuous because they had to choose remote locations inaccessible by car, to better hide their operation from the revenuers.

A crude homemade still was used to run the mash. Uncle Shirley described a still to me, "In makin' we used a round copper boiler. Mine was big enough to hold two barrels or one hundred gallons of mash. The boiler had to have a lid or a 'cap' as we called it. We'd build a level fire pit out of river rocks and put the boiler on it so we could build a fire under it. We had to make our moonshine where there was lots of cold water."

He described the still so well, that I could picture it setting there near the creek. "Out of the top of the still we put a connecting pipe than run over into a barrel called the coolin' tub. That barrel was kept full of cold water at all times while we was makin'. Inside the coolin' tub the connectin' pipe was hooked to a tube called the 'worm'. This tube was solid copper, about an inch across, and was coiled like a spring. The 'worm' coiled down through the coolin' tub and came out a hole in the bottom. We set a keg or a jug under the end of the coil where it came out. We put a funnel in the keg."

Uncle Shirley carefully explained, "We lined the funnel with a red flannel rag with charcoal in the bottom. The charcoal had been burned and washed clean. The charcoal and the red flannel rag removed the impurities from the liquid. It was clean enough to drink when it came through the funnel into the jug."

My daddy added, "When we was ready to start, we strained our mash through a clean rag into the boiler, then the 'cap', as we called it, was put on, and all leaks were sealed with dough made fresh that morning. Then we lit the fire under the boiler."

Moonshiners always chose wood that would not make much smoke while burning, because revenuers sometimes found their location by watching for smoke. Dad told me, "The best wood was dry white chestnut."

There was a large supply of dry chestnut wood in the mountains surrounding Hopkins Gap because of the chestnut blight. All the chestnut trees had been accidentally infected by a blight fungus introduced into the United States on Japanese chestnut trees imported at the end of the 1800s. As people bought mail-order Japanese chestnut trees from nurseries, the blight was spread all over the range of native chestnut trees. The chestnut had been the most important and abundant tree in eastern forests. It was used to build log cabins and rail fences. The blight fungus reduced it to insignificance except for firing up the moonshine stills.

I remember seeing hundreds of trees laying along the roads when Dad took us on Sunday drives deep in the Allegheny Mountains. The trees had fallen and piled on top of each other in all directions, stripped of their bark they lay there smooth and shiny. Dad told us they had been killed by the blight as he looked at them longingly. "I wish I had a truck," he said. "I would haul me a bunch of this wood for fence posts. It gets harder the older it gets. It makes the hottest fires of any wood I know of and don't give off much smoke."

Moonshiners had a lot of knowledge about different types of wood, about the workings of a steam system, and the "flour" or glutin content of various grains. But they sometimes disagreed about the finer points of their craft. According to Dad, "Corn yielded less whiskey than rye, and was also less popular in my family. Rye whiskey didn't leave the consumer with painful hangovers. The rye could also be used again to ferment more batches of mash."

Uncle Shirley, on the other hand, had the opposite opinion. "Now everybody has their taste. Drinkin' is about like food, one likes one thing and the other likes somethin' else. I liked corn whiskey for my own drinkin' and manufacturin'. The reason I like to make corn whiskey is because the corn didn't have as much "flour" in it and when you would boil it, you could boil it faster without the still blowin' up. In other words, what would happen if you got too much fire under your still, you would create too much steam—more steam than can go out through your connecting pipe coil and that would cause the lid of your still to raise off which was just sealed on there with a dough mixture of water and flour. You couldn't clamp that lid on or you would create an explosion that would tear up some things almost equal to a stick of dynamite or even more. You had to have this form of release in case of an emergency just the same as a release valve on a steam system. The corn whiskey didn't have as much flour content in the mash. You could get through a little quicker with same amount of whiskey."

He added, "The reason I liked to drink corn whiskey was because of the effect that it had on me. When you take a drink of corn whiskey, you can feel it as soon as it hits your stomach—it warms you up and you can tell you drank something. Now with rye whiskey you can drink it and walk around for ten to fifteen minutes before you start feelin' the effects. Wheat whiskey is nasty for what we call 'sneakin' up on ya.' You take a drink now and you wait maybe a half hour and feel no effects. You take another drink. In about fifteen minutes, still no effects, so you just keep takin' drinks, and all of a sudden it's got ya."

Everybody in the room laughed as Uncle Shirley described the effects of different grains, then he went on with his description of moonshining. "At certain points after the mash was boilin', we tested the strength of the whiskey. The mash could only be boiled to a certain level in the boiler before it got weak. Now, when we thought we might have all of the alcohol out of our mash, we caught a little of the moonshine in a can top or something and threw it in the fire. If it flared up and burned a blue flame, there was still alcohol there. When it just fizzled out kinda like water, it was ready to take off." A barrel of mash would yield anywhere from two and a half to five gallons of whiskey.

It took at least two men to run a moonshine still. One man kept wood on the fire, tested the whiskey for alcohol content, and changed kegs or jugs when they were full. Another man continuously poured cold water in the cooling tub. If the water in the cooling tub was allowed to get warm, the whiskey came out with a cloudy appearance and did not yield as much final product. The man responsible for the fire had to keep the boiling speed consistent throughout the process.

"What we made out of the mash the first time we called singlins' — it was single if it was only boiled once," my daddy told me. "After we had boiled all of our mash once, then we dumped everything out, cleaned up the still. We took it off the rocks and took charcoal or ashes and cleaned it until it looked like a new penny. Then we poured all the singlins' that we made out of the batches before back into the clean boiler. We run that again which we termed as doublins'. We tested it the same way except we didn't have the fire quite as hot. We didn't let it run quite as low in alcohol before we removed it, because if you get too much of a sour water content it gives the moonshine a bad taste."

When we started the doublin', the first that came out was about two-hundred percent {proof} alcohol and that weakened down at the end to about one hundred and fifty percent," explained Uncle Shirley. "We took this and used just pure water to weaken it down to about ninety-five to one hundred percent. That's the way we put it on the market."

Moonshiners displayed a special skill when they tested the alcohol content of the "doublings." Their only instrument was the "bead" of the whiskey. The "bead" was a small bubble that settled to the top of the whiskey. Dad explained this process to me, "We would pour some whiskey into a clear glass container usually a fruit jar and put a tight lid on it. Then we shook the jar and watched how the 'bead' settled around the top of the moonshine."

Dad and Uncle Shirley had different opinions about where they wanted the "bead" to settle. My dad said he always wanted about three-fourths of the "bead" to hang above the top of the liquid. If the bead was lower, the moonshine was too weak. It was poured back into the mixing tub, and more pure doublings were added. If three-fourths of the "bead" was over the top of the liquid, the moonshine was one hundred proof or fifty percent alcohol.

Uncle Shirley preferred the bead to be half above and half below the top of the moonshine after shaking the jar. "I liked to put my whiskey on the market at about ninety to ninety-five proof."

I asked Dad and Uncle Shirley, "What all did you use to make moonshine? Did you always just use grain?"

They both answered my question. Uncle Shirley jumped right in with his answer. "We made a combination of whiskey and brandy depending on what was available. For instance, if the women had canned a lot of fruit and it spoiled, we would take that, put in into a barrel, add sugar and yeast, and let it ferment into a wine that would be similar to apple cider. We distilled this wine into a brandy. Like I say, I've made it out of peaches and grapes. We used to gather wild grapes. There used to be a lot of them. What we made depended on what was available at the least cost."

My daddy added, "When I was a boy there was an awful lot of peach brandy made because the older people in the community had small peach orchards around over the mountain tops. I can stand here on the porch and show you the sites of at least four orchards. We didn't have the bugs and beetles we have now. You could grow beautiful peaches. Right up the hill here Martin Conley had a peach orchard and grew some of the most beautiful peaches I ever saw. He never had to spray."

Uncle Shirley joined in, "A lot of people just liked brandy. Now when we sold brandy we had to charge more than we charged for whiskey. We sold our brandy a little higher than we did our grain whiskey because it was harder to make and you didn't get as much return for your sugar. The ingredients took longer to ferment and it just cost us more. So, we had to charge a little more for it."

197

I asked Uncle Shirley if whiskey was good for other uses besides drinking. He said, "Oh yeah, it was used a lot for medication and as a stimulant for livestock. If you had a cow or other animal that wasn't eatin' just right, you'd pour a pint of whiskey into her and use it as a stimulant."

"That much for one cow," I asked?

"Oh yeah, that's not much for one cow," he answered. Just like cow doctors today will recommend real strong coffee as a stimulant. I've seen my mom and dad use moonshine as a stimulant for livestock. We also used it as a disinfectant for cleaning wounds and a lot of people used it to lose weight—just like cigarettes. When they get hungry, they just take a shot of moonshine. They say it quenches their hunger. Of course, it works just the opposite with me—if I start drinkin', I want to eat."

I remembered that earlier in their description of moonshining, Uncle Shirley indicated that at one time, he had worked as a laborer for a moonshiner, so I asked him, "How many different kinds of operations went on in the moonshine business?" As usual, the explanation was long and detailed.

Moonshiners Ain't All Alike

Three types of people were involved in the business of moonshining in Hopkins Gap. There were the small-scale moonshiners, the large-scale moonshiners, and the bootleggers.

The small-scale moonshiner joined up with one other man and they worked for themselves. They were typically good citizens by most accounts, except through the eyes of the revenue officers. And the feelings of disrespect ran both ways. Most small-scale moonshiners learned their trade as laborers for large-scale moonshiners.

Uncle Shirley and Uncle Jim struck out on their own as small-scale moonshiners after they learned the trade as laborers. Although they were criminals according to the law, they were firmly convinced that the law was unjust and they were only exercising their natural rights. They, like other small-scale moonshiners, worked with only the crudest equipment and produced a meager output directly related to the amount of time they were willing to work and the risks they were willing to take.

The small-scale moonshiner's major advantage was his physical strength and endurance and his ability to devise new ways to improve the quality of his production and work with his customers. It took a strong man, even with another man helping, to handle fifty-gallon barrels of mash and carry one hundred pound bags of sugar to his still on his back. His hard work kept him in good physical condition to outrun the revenuers, too.

These moonshiners kept their overhead low by devising ways to get the most moonshine out of the products available in the community. Uncle Shirley told me, "At first we used to changed our grain every time we set mash. Later we found that we could get more moonshine from our sugar if we just left the old grain in the barrel. We could use the same grain probably four or five times. The grain was hard and you didn't get the full benefit the first time."

Uncle Shirley told me that later, the moonshiners learned that if they put a small amount of cracked corn with their rye, they got a better turn out from the first run. They sometimes used wheat if rye and corn were not available. "You can make whiskey from anything that has an acid—any berry or fruit. The only fruit that won't make is blueberries, because they don't have no acid, and they will not ferment. You can make it out of potatoes, sweet potatoes, parsnips, tomatoes, but anything you make with a fruit is classed as a brandy."

Small-scale moonshiners made their talents available for special orders from their customers. Uncle Shirley told me, "One time there was a guy who run a building supply company in Harrisonburg. He had come onto a recipe whereby he took a pint of sliced peaches to a half pint of moonshine, and a half pint of sugar. He canned this mixture in quart jars. I don't know what his idea was but what happened is he ended up with practically a quart of sugar because, over time, this had turned to sugar just as preserves or honey will. Well, this man came to me after I was workin' for myself and asked me if I couldn't take this stuff, put it in a barrel and dilute it, and make him peach brandy out of it—which I did. Of course, he paid well. He furnished all the ingredients and paid us good for makin' for him."

Uncle Jim told me that people who drank moonshine preferred to buy from the small-scale moonshiner. "We mostly made for our own consumption, so we kept our whiskey clean and ended up with the best drinkin' whiskey in Hopkins Gap. It didn't take long for customers to figure this out, so they started buying their drinkin' whiskey straight from the man who made it."

When the demand increased for whiskey made by the small-scale moonshiner, he just expanded his operation. Uncle Shirley explained, "Me and my partner set up still sites at three different locations so that if the revenue men would find one of the sites, they wouldn't completely put us out of business." He bragged, "We'd make at one place today, use our sugar and grain and set our mash back at that location. The next day, we would move to the next still site, and we would make the cycle. We did all the work ourselves."

The large-scale moonshiners never involved themselves in the production process. Instead they hired young men in the community to do the work. Several circumstances contributed to the abundance of potential laborers for large-scale moonshiners, according to Uncle Shirley. "There were no jobs available in the community and transportation was such that we couldn't get out where there was jobs. In those early days, we rode horses or walked where we had to go."

He added, "Folks often died young in those days and left young children who were on their own for survival. My mother died when I was ten, then my father died when I was thirteen. I had to live, so I stayed with my brother. Me and my cousin worked together for hourly wages. I got paid seven and a half cents an hour and my room and board. My cousin had a place to stay, so he got paid fifteen cents an hour."

Uncle Shirley described his job as a laborer, "Me and my cousin worked together six days a week for three years, and we made an average of twenty to twenty-two gallons of moonshine a day. That's the average finished product you'd get from two hundred pounds of sugar and two hundred gallons of mash after it was distilled. Of course, that was after running it the second time to make 'doublins'." He added, "Now that sounds like a lot of moonshine, which it was, but at that time the owner was only getting' $1.75 to $2.00 a gallon for it, so it didn't amount to a lot of money after he paid us, even at that."

Uncle Jim was also young when Grandma Mary and Grandpa John died. He was only fourteen years old, and he survived by becoming a helper at his older brother, Uncle Charlie's, moonshine still. He said, "I'd been helpin' with moonshine since I was twelve. So I fell right into it with Charlie. Later, I hired folks to make for me. I produced about one hundred gallons a week."

There was an unwritten agreement between the owner and the workers. If a moonshine still was discovered and raided by government agents, the workers would take the consequences without revealing the name of the owner. The agreement between owner and laborer was so strong that even today, I have never heard Uncle Jim, Uncle Shirley, or my daddy mention the names of the large-scale moonshiners for whom they worked.

This system allowed the owner to reap all the profits, yet be immune to potential punishment. My dad worked for a large-scale female bootlegger and ended up getting caught twice. It wasn't real common for a female to be a large-scale moonshiner, but the boys who worked for her were just as loyal to her as if she had been a man.

The first time he got caught, Dad served four months in prison. He got out of prison and went to work for the same woman and two weeks later was caught again. The second time he served eight months.

Uncle Rob, Aunt Goldie's husband, started out as a small-scale moonshiner but rapidly expanded his business so he had to hire helpers. He was successful because he came up with creative ways to make his moonshine more attractive to his customers. Mom told me, "Rob stored his moonshine in wooden kegs. Before using a new keg he poured in a little moonshine, soaked the inside of the keg, then set it on fire. This charred the inside of the keg. He left the whiskey in the keg for several weeks."

Mom explained, "The charred keg turned the whiskey a golden color; and after ten days, you could drink it straight without makin' a face. Rob was clean with his whiskey, and he was well known for makin' the best moonshine. He didn't drink a drop himself. That was how he got away from the law so many years. He never got drunk and let his guard down."

Aunt Goldie told me how she used to help Uncle Rob gather wild grapes for making wine. She also helped make peach brandy from peach peelings and applejack from apple cider. They experimented by adding dried fruit, such as peaches, pears, and apples, to the moonshine to give it amber color and a fruity flavor. Uncle Rob supplied many bootleggers, and also had a booming business working right out of his home.

My mother, who was raised by Aunt Goldie and Uncle Rob stayed at home many days to sell moonshine for him. One Sunday while Uncle Rob and Aunt Goldie were at church, Mom sold $270.00 worth of moonshine by mid-afternoon. It was 1936 and that was a great deal of money. "I got so scared having that much money that I locked the house and ran up on the ridge to hide until Rob and Goldie came home from church." As she told me this story, she said, "I wonder how much money I could have made that day. I'll bet I missed a lot of customers."

*Uncle Rob in his pickup with Ruby, Joyce, and Randy,
three of his four children, on the back. He had just
bought this new pickup. He built a secret compartment in
the back for hauling moonshine. He later lost this truck to the revenuers.*

Uncle Rob devised ways to haul his moonshine in secret chambers in his car or truck for his weekly deliveries to his friends on the police force and local judges. He bought a new truck from all his profits and the first thing he did was to construct a hidden chamber beneath the bed of the truck. Moonshine was hidden in every conceivable nook and cranny of his cars, trucks, and property. Ten years after his death, his sons found a stash under a pile of rocks as they cleaned a fence line on the farm.

John I. Myers, and friend and neighbor of Uncle Rob, told me a funny story about my uncle. Uncle Rob was on his way to deliver a big lot of moonshine when the revenue agents stopped him. "Rob told the revenuers, 'Let me deliver this batch, and then I will go peacefully to jail with you.' The revenuers followed him. He drove up to the rear door of the local judge's house. When he stopped there to deliver his product, the revenue agents drove on by without stopping."

Revenue agents finally did catch Uncle Rob. The sheriff called John I. Myers' house, since he had the only telephone in the community, and asked him to deliver the message to Aunt Goldie that Uncle Rob was in jail. Mr. Myers mounted his horse and rode several miles the deliver the sad news. The revenuers confiscated Uncle Rob's brand new truck and never returned it.

The third type of person involved in moonshining in Hopkins Gap was the bootlegger. Bootlegging carried a high risk of getting caught and put in jail, but it was an easy job and potentially very profitable.

The large-scale moonshiner that Uncle Shirley and his cousin worked for sold his product to bootleggers for $1.75 to $2.00 a gallon. The bootlegger, in turn, converted the gallons to pints and sold them for $2.00. He was the middleman who made the greatest profit off the hard work of laborers such as Uncle Shirley who worked for a few cents an hour.

Uncle Shirley told me that bootleggers preyed on Hopkins Gap moonshiners, "They often had the local sheriff's hands in their pockets." When the pressure from the law got real bad on us, the bootleggers quit paying us as much for our whiskey. They knew we couldn't make it and also sell it, so they drove into Hopkins Gap and bought it from our houses."

My daddy added, "Nobody liked the bootleggers. As times changed, they became a necessary evil. We had to sell to them because the law was watchin' us too close."

Sympathetic Revenuers?

My dad told me that some people would have starved during the depression if they didn't make moonshine. He believed the revenue agents had sympathy for people during the depression. "I know of times when they got reports of mash barrels at a certain place," he said. "They would go in and bust up barrels that were reported purposely and walk by mash that hadn't been reported. They had to bust up what was reported to save face."

The government began to put pressure on the moonshiners around 1933. This new attitude toward moonshiners coincided with the passage of The Emergency Conservation Work Act establishing the Civilian Conservation Corp (CCC). The CCC employed young men between seventeen and twenty-three years of age in work camps where they were assigned to various conservation projects. The men were paid thirty dollars a month, twenty-five of which was sent home to their families. The CCC was part of President Roosevelt's program to end the Great Depression.

"President Franklin Roosevelt was elected in 1932; and by 1935, his administration was providing jobs for the people in the CCC camps," Dad told me. "It was at this time that the government forced the revenuers to crack down on us."

The government crackdown tended to slow production because the moonshiner had to be more cautious. The safest time for distillation was just before dawn. The moonshiners came up with creative methods of detecting the revenue agents when they came down into the Gap. The moonshiners placed guards on the high ridges overlooking the road at both ends of the Gap.

On days when a father knew he was going to make moonshine, he told his children to watch the road from the schoolhouse window. If strange cars were spotted, the children were to run from school to warn the moonshiner.

Mr. Sem Swope was a teacher in Hopkins Gap for a period of years. He lived a very long life, and I was able to talk with him about teaching in the Gap. He recalled stories of children sitting in school watching the road for the revenuers. "I could tell which men were making moonshine on any given day, because the children didn't pay attention to their lessons. They would sit next to the window and stare at the road instead of listening to me. All of a sudden a child would jump through the schoolhouse window with no warning and take off down the road and through the woods."

I asked Mr. Swope, "Did you try to stop him?"

He answered, "I learned it was best for me to just go on teaching and not try to interfere with what the local people were doing."

Mom often bragged about one of my first cousins, Gifford Payne, "He jumped out schoolhouse window when he saw the revenuers drive down the road. They saw him and caught him before he got away. They said, 'Hey boy, could you tell us where we could find some moonshine?' Gifford told 'em, 'I wouldn't tell you where you could find 'shit water'.'"

The revenue officers changed their tactics and began to come into Hopkins Gap as undercover agents. One officer came disguised as a watermelon peddler. He drove a wagon filled with watermelons down the road through Hopkins Gap and traded watermelons for whiskey wherever possible.

Aunt Goldie, Mom's sister, and Aunt Lena, my dad's sister, were caught trading moonshine to the "watermelon man." The year was 1940, because Lena had just given birth to her son, Jennings. Goldie and Lena were taken to jail to await their trial. Aunt Lena was breastfeeding Jennings. The baby's daddy had to drive him to the jail four times a day to get his feeding. Finally, the health department discovered that an infant was going to jail to breastfeed and forced the sheriff to let Aunt Lena go free. For some reason, Aunt Goldie was released at the same time. Neither woman was ever brought to trial.

It was not uncommon for the wives of jailed moonshiners to take over the business while their husbands were away. My daddy's sister, Aunt Vernie and Aunt Hazel, Uncle Jim's wife, hired some local boys to help with the heavy work and managed to maintain the family income until their husbands returned from jail.

Once the revenue agent lost his cover as a watermelon man, other agents devised new tactics to catch the moonshiners. No matter what disguise they tried, they were always referred to as the "watermelon man." People still use the term today when they talk

206

about moonshining days. When I asked who caught so and so, they still answer, "He was caught by the watermelon man."

Moonshiners were proud people and ashamed when they were caught. But there were different ways to be caught. It was one thing to be chased down on foot by a revenuer, but it was a disgrace to be caught by the "watermelon man" and thrown in jail for making money for the family. "Uncle Jim expressed the feeling best, "When a man ended up in jail by being tricked by a revenuer, it caused a great deal of resentment."

My daddy and Uncle Shirley both narrowly escaped the revenue agents on foot and both loved to tell the stories. Dad laughed as he told how he was making moonshine with Richard Carr when they were surprised by the revenuers. They both took off running through the woods. Dad said, "I could feel his fingers raking across my back, but I got away from him. Richard made the mistake of wearing bib over alls; the other revenuer caught him by the gallowses. He spent time in Chillicothe, Ohio, one of the prisons where we were sent to spend our prison time. The other prison was Camp Lee, in Georgia. That's where I went both times."

One of Uncle Shirley's favorite stories is about the time he gave a revenue agent a wild dash through the mountains on foot. He and another man had been making moonshine since long before dawn. When the process was well underway, Uncle Shirley left the still to go home to get some dinner for the two of them. He was returning to the still with a stew pot full of ham sandwiches and a hundred pound bag of sugar on his back. He came to a little creek and was looking down to find some rocks to step on as he crossed.

Uncle Shirley still gets excited and laughs every time he tells this story. "I happened to look up and there was a revenuer on the other side of the creek looking down for rocks to make his way across. I dropped the sugar, held onto my dinner bucket, and ran up the ridge. He came after me. I ran until my lungs felt like they were on fire."

The revenuer relentlessly followed him. Uncle Shirley stopped at the top of a ridge to catch his breath and looked back.

The revenuer had stopped too; and when he saw Uncle Shirley, he yelled, "Why are you running." Uncle Shirley answered, "To see if you're dumb enough to try to catch me."

Uncle Shirley said, "It was a good thing that he stopped. I couldn't go any further. I just stepped around the ridge and fell against the bank. I laid there to catch my breath and then sneaked on home. I never saw him anymore. I guess he was tired too. When I got home, my brother in law told me to change my clothes in case the agent started looking for me house to house. I went into the bedroom to change my clothes and my brother came by, found my dinner, and ate it. I lost at every turn that day. I lost my sugar and my dinner, but I did outrun the revenuer."

War Against the Revenuers

Moonshiners trained their dogs to sniff out the revenue agents. A moonshiner's dog would give a low growl, and the hair on its back bristled when it heard or smelled someone approaching. Although they would give a warning, the dogs were well trained not to bark and give away the location of the still.

In addition to training their dogs, moonshiners began posting several guards near the entrance to the hollows where they were making whiskey. Sometimes the guards set a charge of dynamite to explode if they saw the revenuers. They also had a quieter system of warning as well. Several men, posted within decent hearing range of the moonshiners, would relay a warning by using birdcalls. Sometimes the guards pretended to be hunting and fired a number of warning shots if they saw revenue agents coming into the hollow.

My dad was guarding for a moonshiner by pretending to hunt squirrels with a .22 rifle when he was caught the second time. He was sitting on a ridge some distance from the still when he saw one revenuer and fired two warning shots. Another revenuer sneaked up behind him and arrested him. One time a revenue agent was shot and wounded by a moonshiner's guard. The shooter was never caught.

Just days after the revenue agent was shot, my Uncle Rob's brother, Tom, came home and told his mother that his dog started barking at the still that day. Tom said, "I looked up and saw Jesus standing on a rock near where I was working. I stopped making whiskey and came on home."

Later that day he told Uncle Rob what he had seen. Uncle Rob said, "Nobody ever sees Jesus and lives," and he warned Tom, "That's a sign that something bad is going to happen." Tom's mother, Alice Crawford, asked him to stay home for a few days. He refused, telling her his "mash" was ready, and he had to "run" it before it wasted.

The next day Tom didn't return home until well after dark, his mother told later, "He was real quiet while he eat his supper. Just as we was getting' ready to turn in for the night, he told me, 'As I passed by the graveyard, I saw a big white bird rise up and take flight.'" Again Alice warned him to stay home and again he refused.

Two days later, on August 10, 1936, Tom was shot and killed while he worked at his still. Dad and Uncle Shirley told me the story many times. "It was just another moonshine day," began Uncle Shirley. "It all happened in the Hog Pens. Me and another man was making whiskey up Little Hog Pen Run. Your daddy and Clint Ray were making moonshine up Big Hog Pen Run. Tom Crawford and Harold Lam were making moonshine in the main Hog Pen Run.

Rob Crawford was posted at the mouth of Hog Pen Run with a stick of dynamite to explode if he saw the revenuers coming in that direction. We posted Rob Craig at the upper end of the Hog Pens where the revenuers came in. They parked at Clint Ray's house and crossed the mountain," continued Uncle Shirley. "Rob Craig saw them and ran to warn us. He got to me and then went on to tell your daddy and Clint Ray. We poured our whiskey out, cleaned up, and hid our still."

When the revenuers entered the Hog Pens, they came in below where Dad, Clint Ray, and Uncle Shirley were making moonshine. According to Uncle Shirley, "They heard Harold Lam chopping wood for the still, turned right, and walked down through Big Hog Pen Run. They could have just as easy turned left and found us. Tom was scraping dough off the still cap when the revenuer snuck up behind him. Without any warning, the revenuer shot Tom through the back of the neck. He died on the spot. The other revenuer caught Harold as he tried to run away."

Tom Crawford was twenty-three years old when he was shot. He had a wife and two small boys, and his wife was pregnant with his third son.

Dad told me, "The revenuers were so scared they would be killed for shooting Tom that they put his body in the back seat of their car and set it up just like Tom was riding with them. They made Harold Lam set against his body to hold it up as they drove through Hopkins Gap. They hauled his body to Broadway without tellin' anybody," Dad said. "They sent the county sheriff out to tell Rob Crawford his brother was dead. It's a good thing they did it that way because they wouldn't have gotten out of there alive. Rob would have killed them."

At his hearing, the revenue agent who shot Tom claimed that his foot caught on a branch and caused his pistol to accidentally go off and shoot Tom. He was never charged with shooting an unarmed man; but he was transferred to the Blue Ridge Mountains in East Virginia.

Months afterward news spread that he had killed another moonshiner. A year later, he was shot and killed by an unknown assailant. Dad told my brother that a Hopkins Gap man had gone to East Virginia and taken revenge for Tom's death.

As the pressure of the revenue agents increased, the quality of Hopkins Gap moonshine deteriorated. New and dangerous tactics were used to speed up the processing to save the time of running the "singlings" a second time. Some people put mothballs in their liquor to make it hold a "bead." Others used lye for the same purpose.

As late as 1970, Uncle Jim told me he saw red seal lye cans lying around a still. My Uncle Charlie Conley died in 1960 from drinking moonshine mixed with red seal lye. Moonshiners also used zinc tubs to boil their mash, mix, and store their whiskey, even after it was determined that moonshine made in this way was poisonous if consumed in large amounts over a long period of time.

As time passed and more people went into the moonshine business, the competition destroyed the communal spirit that was necessary for survival by subsistence. Each family was involved in the illegal moonshine business resulting in a great deal of tension and suspicion between neighbors who had formerly trusted each other. There was constant competition for prices and customers.

Dad told me that if your next-door neighbor was competing with you, he would report you to the revenue agents. Uncle Shirley told me a story of how bad the competition was among neighbors and kin. "Uncle Joe turned my brother Charlie in to the revenue agents. Even though he was able to avoid going to jail, Uncle Charlie took revenge on him. He laid in the woods outside Uncle Joe's house and waited until he sat down to eat supper. A kerosene lamp sat in the middle of the kitchen table. When Uncle Joe pulled his chair up to the table, Charlie shot through the window and hit the lamp. He was lucky the lamp wasn't lit. Uncle Joe said, 'Deed and by God, a man can't set by his own light anymore unless somebody's shootin' at him.'" Uncle Rob was often reported to revenue agents because of jealousy of the quality of his moonshine and his connections to the local sheriff and judges. The distrust and resentment that developed among families during moonshining days lasted for a long time.

Peggy Ann Shifflett

Part Five

SUPERSTITIONS, MAGIC, AND SNAKES

A belief is not necessarily true because it is useful.
Anonymous

Before the "BIG" road came to Hopkins Gap and during the time of subsistence living, everyday life was uncertain. Survival on a day-to-day basis required treatments for illnesses without access to modern medicine. There were special days when folks could predict the future or do specific rituals designed to control the growth of crops and people's health during the coming year. Good weather was needed for growing food, and folks needed explanations for the unexplainable events—both good and bad-- in their lives. Certain people were designated to manage these basic needs. Granny Women took care of injuries and illnesses with age-old rituals that were handed down to them from Granny Women before them. Old farm men and women passed on the signs of floods and droughts to the younger people stepping into the fields they once cultivated. Certain men and women were designated bad witches and good witches. Bad witches brought evil and meanness into people's lives, and the good witches performed rituals to punish the bad witches.

When I was first born, these methods of managing everyday life, based on homeopathic and sympathetic magic, were still being used, so I was exposed to rituals for illness, weather signs, witch stories, and superstitions during the first half of my life. I was the recipient of some healing rituals, and I watched Grandma Molly, Aunt Goldie, and Mom perform many of these rituals on others. I heard them talk about weather and superstitions related to just about everything.

Of course, the older members of the family tried to make sure the beliefs and customs were at least heard by their children and grandchildren whether they were still practicing them or not. Aunt Goldie, Mom, and Grandma Molly shared their experiences and what they had heard about witches with anyone who would listen, and I was always a willing listener.

Signs, Superstitions, and Warnings for Children

On an everyday basis, all Hopkins Gap people understood the portents or "signs," as they called them, of upcoming tragedies as well as positive events. Some of the signs of tragedy such as an upcoming death were hearing an owl screech near you at night, cows mooing in the night, carrying a garden tool into the house, seeing white figures in graveyards or passing by the window, a crowing hen, a bird crashing into a window while flying, or a picture falling off the wall for no obvious reason. And most Hopkins Gap people were superstitious and knew the simple customs to avoid what would happen if a black cat crossed the road in front of them, for example. Positive signs included having the hem of a single girl's dress turn up on its on. If she kissed the turned-up hem, she would soon meet her future husband.

My earliest experience with a sign occurred when I was about four years old. I was playing on the concrete slab front porch when a catbird crashed into the front window and fell dying to the concrete. Mom heard the noise and came to see what had happened. She stared at the bird as it gasped for its final breaths.

Her face turned white as she said, "Somebody in the family is going to die soon." Of course, the look on her face scared me nearly to death and, sure enough, the next day, Uncle Earl, Dad's sister, Hattie's husband, dropped dead while working on his car. Mom reminded me after she heard the news, "Do you remember what I said about that catbird hittin' the window?" I said, "Yes, I do." It was forever etched in my mind.

214

We always had laying hens running around the yard. They supplied our eggs; and, in the summers, they would steal a nest under the barn and hatch little chickens to replace themselves and provide meat for an occasional Sunday dinner. I remember a time when one of the laying hens started crowing like a rooster. Mom caught her and chopped her head off. I knew the hen was a good egg producer; and she had a name, so the plan was that she was going to stay around a while. I asked Mom why she killed her. She said, "I had to kill her and eat her right away or somebody in the family will die." We had chicken for supper that very evening and it was not a Sunday.

Every time somebody died, stories were shared during the wake about signs observed in the days before the death such as mysterious lights, dreams, strange shapeless white objects, and unusual noises. Various family members would say things like, "I dreamed about muddy water just a few days before so and so died," or "I heard an owl screeching through the night."

These beliefs have stayed with me through the years and automatically come to mind when I least expect it. Three years ago, as I was taking my spring pre-dawn walk, an owl screeched in a tree above my head. I felt a cold chill up my spine and Mom's words rang in my ears, "If you hear an owl screeching or hooting outside your window, somebody you know is going to die." I immediately ran down the list of people that I knew who were sick. I walked on further, and the owl flew to a tree further down the street. When I passed under that tree, it screeched again. Mom was not doing well at the time, so I concluded that the owl was signaling to me that her death was near.

A month later, my Yoga teacher died suddenly of a heart attack. Before I had time to cry my first tear, I remembered the screech owl. It was not Mom who was going to die after all. My Yoga teacher's death was sudden and unexpected. She had not been on the list of sickly people I had run through my mind that dark morning. In the style of Grandma Molly, Mom, and Aunt Goldie, I shared the screech owl story, with friends who would

215

listen, after my teacher died. I chose my listeners well. No one laughed at me.

Aunt Vernie's husband, Uncle Charlie, died quite suddenly from drinking moonshine that had been made in an old car radiator. Grandma Molly told us the day of his funeral, "I saw an inchworm crawling on Charlie the day before he died. You remember, don't you Lena? You saw me knock it off. I told him, 'Charlie, you're bein' measured for a shroud."

Every time somebody died in Hopkins Gap, Mom warned, "You mark my words. There'll be two more funerals before three months is out. Death always comes in threes. Two more deaths will follow within three months." When a willow tree is planted, it was believed that the person who planted it would die when the tree was large enough to cover his or her grave. We used to ride past the Showalter farm where the willow trees along the creek swayed gently in the wind. Mom often said, "I really like willow trees, but I'm afraid to plant one." Then, she would repeat the superstition as she had done every other time we had driven past the trees.

A rise in the dirt over a grave was a sign that another member of that family would die soon. The ancestor buried in the grave was calling another family member home. Before the Gospel Hill church and cemetery existed, my relatives in Hopkins Gap were buried on a steep ridge across the road from Clint Ray's house. The cemetery was started because of the flu epidemic of 1918 and was rapidly filled by deaths that year. Mom's grandparents, Ad and Jane Morris, were buried there. I took Mom with me to that cemetery once when I was looking for family members' headstones. I saw one grave that was sunken. "I wonder who was buried here?" I commented to Mom. She replied, "Oh yeah, I know that story. Some old witch was buried in that grave. People tried for years to keep it full of dirt. They'd come up here and fill it one day, and the very next day it would be sunk again. Somebody told me that witches go straight to hell when they die. I guess as her soul passed deeper into hell, the dirt on her grave sunk lower and lower."

Grandma Molly walked past the same local graveyard during a funeral. She met the spirit of the dead person who was being buried walking toward the cemetery. She came home and shared her perspective on what was happening, "I was walking past the graveyard while they was burying old Mike Lam. I met his soul walking toward the graveyard. It was just like a little white cloud. I watched him join the crowd around his open grave. His soul disappeared then. I guess he wanted to be buried with his body."

As I have said before, Grandpa Austin died in his bed in the living room of his house. When Grandma Molly and Aunt Lena knew his time was near, they called in the family to see him for the last time. Everybody was standing around when he drew his last breath. The first thing Grandma Molly did was walk over to the window and opened the sash about twelve inches. We all looked at each other wondering what she was doing. After all, it was February and there was a blanket of snow still on the ground from a recent storm. I was the first to ask, "What are you doing, Grandma?" "I opened the window so his soul can leave the house," she replied. "I felt a chilly breeze pass over my shoulder when I opened the window. I can close it now because his soul is gone."

Old and young people in Hopkins Gap feared the breaking of the Sabbath Day. No woman would dare sew on Sunday. Mom explained their refusal by quoting the old saying: "Every stitch you sew on Sunday, you'll pick out with your teeth on Monday." The story is often told of a man in Hopkins Gap who burned trash on Sunday. It is believed that his face is now the face of the man in the moon.

There were many ways to control bad behavior of children in the Gap. We were taught by being told the consequences of things that kids might do to irritate older people. I heard from Aunt Goldie, Grandma Molly, and Mom as they told older children or sometimes me what would happen if this or that behavior occurred. It is strange how effective these teachings were, at least on me. Once I heard the warnings, I felt a lot of guilt even if I thought about doing one of them. I heard that if I emptied my bladder in a path

217

where people walked, I would get a sty on my eye. Also, if I knocked my chair over when getting up from eating, I wouldn't get married for seven years. I knocked my chair over on purpose a lot and it obviously worked for me.

Sometimes we would, without thinking, rock an empty rocking chair. I only did it once because Mom caught me. Her eyes opened wide with fear and she screamed, "Stop that! Rockin' a empty rockin' chair brings a death to the family." That was one time when I didn't question her belief. It seemed far too important to her.

While many of these superstitions sound very silly today, they had practical significance in my early life. Sometimes as hog killing day drew to a close, we would take sticks and dig in the embers from the kettle fires. Grandma Molly told us to stop, "Y'all stop pokin' in the fire or you'll piss the bed tonight." This superstition wasn't really about wetting the bed. It was about the danger of children playing in the fire. We were also told if we played with toads we would get warts. I never understood this warning. Most all kids in Hopkins Gap had warts anyway. Perhaps they were warning us that we didn't want to be "cured" for warts.

Not So Modern Medicine

Many of the everyday accidents and illnesses that happen to people everywhere also happened to people in Hopkins Gap. However, some of the ways that these common situations were handled were unique during my early life. Most of these treatments had to be done by a Granny Woman, but some could be done by anyone.

Grandma Molly treated a burn by slowly waving her hand over it and blowing her breath on it three times while reciting a little rhyme:

Two angels coming from the west
One brings fire the other brings frost
Out fire! In frost! In the name of
The Father, the Son, and the Holy Ghost.

For the common cold, Hopkins Gap mothers prepared a poultice. Hog lard, onions, and a block of camphor were fried down real slow in an iron skillet. This was rubbed on a red flannel rag while it was still warm and applied to the afflicted person's chest. To prevent colds, Gap folks often wore a small pouch around their necks with garlic or asafetida in it. Asafetida and garlic both had terrible odors with asafetida smelling much worse than garlic. When I asked how these preventatives worked, I was told by Grandma Molly, "Nobody is going to get close enough to you to share a cold with you if you wear asafetida or garlic. It keeps all kinds of evil away."

Some treatments for a cold made you want to get one. Rattle weed and black berries along with a pound of rock candy were put into a quart of whiskey. After it dissolved, the afflicted person drank a teaspoonful three times a day. Another tasty cure for a cold was made with apple brandy. A saucer was poured full of brandy and set on fire. The longer it burns, the strong it gets. You let it cool and drink it.

Folks in Hopkins Gap heated their homes and cooked with wood from the mountains, so they were often using sharp tools. If they cut themselves with an axe or a hatchet, the axe was greased with hog lard and laid away in a dark dry place to keep the cut from getting sore. For any wound with a sharp metal object, the object was treated because it had come into contact with the wounded person's flesh.

There were many treatments for a fever. Mom would peel and split a potato, salt it down heavy, and put it on our foreheads when we had a fever and complained of a headache. She also greased us for a fever. When she could get bear grease, she greased the bottoms of our feet, the palms of our hands, the back of our head, and the top of our shoulders. Bear grease was rendered from

219

fat deposits scraped from the inside of a fresh bearskin. Goose grease was her absolute favorite but it was hard to find. With goose grease she only had to rub the bottoms of our feet, and the fever left our head, traveled down the trunk, and left our body through our feet.

One very common affliction that I remember seeing in Hopkins Gap was goiter. Alice Crawford had a huge one on her neck all the years that I knew her. Just a short time before she died, she had it surgically removed. Goiter was a swelling of the thyroid gland in compensation for a deficiency of the mineral iodine. This was common in Appalachia due to low iodine content in the mountain water supply. Iodized salt was introduced in the United States in 1924 and significantly reduced the incidence of goiter among mountain people. The condition seemed to affect women more than men.

Annie Riley with Charles Knight at her side. Annie was one of a number of women in Hopkins Gap who had a goiter.

As with other mysterious physical conditions, prior to the introduction of iodized salt, goiter was treated by Granny Women. Grandma Molly cured for goiter. On the first Friday of the old moon, she had the afflicted person look at the moon while she said "the words" and rubbed her hand over the goiter. This was done three months in a row while the moon was decreasing in size. If the afflicted person didn't believe that rubbing the goiter would get rid of it, Grandma Molly recommended that they catch a toad and cook it until the bone near the throat fell clear. The toad bone was carried in the afflicted person's pocket so that the goiter would stop growing.

The cures for ailments that both grown up and children could contract often included different objects in their implementation, but the logic was always the same. Yellow jaundice is a good example. While babies were treated for yellow jaundice by placing yellow corn meal biscuits in their diapers for them to urinate on, adults were asked to urinate into a yellow rutabaga after the insides had been hollowed out. The urine-filled rutabaga was hung next to a chimney in the house. It was believed that when the heat from the chimney had caused the urine to evaporate, the yellow jaundice was cured. Another adult treatment for yellow jaundice required the sick person to wear a small cloth sack around his or her neck. The boiled white of one egg was put into the sack. When the egg white had turned yellow, the jaundice was cured.

Grandma Molly told several stories about treating poisonous snakebites. A copperhead snake bit Ivy Lam's brother, John, while he was chopping wood. Ivy grabbed several onions and sliced them as fast as she could. She placed the slices on the bite; and, before she could get another slice ready, the first slice had turned green. She kept replacing the onion until all the poison was drawn out of the wound. Grandma said, "John's leg swelled some, but he never went to the doctor."

Grandma Molly described another interesting treatment for snakebite, "When a person got a poisonous snakebite, a live chicken was caught and split open. The warm chicken was tied to the snakebite for about an hour. The chicken turned green with poison."

Nearly all the children and most adults in Hopkins Gap had warts, and there were almost as many cures as there were warts.

Some folks tied a string around their warts then removed the string and buried under the eaves of the house roof where it would rot quickly. When the string had rotted, the warts were gone. Other folks used an animal bone, rubbed it over the warts, and threw it over their shoulder into a field. They never looked back after they threw it.

Jesse Craig recommended that a person count all their warts and then get the same number of dry beans and bury them under the eaves of the house roof. When the beans had rotted, the warts would be gone. If that didn't get rid of the warts, Jesse suggested a trip to the graveyard, "Get some dirt from behind a tombstone after dark, mix it with water, and rub it on the warts to get rid of them." Or, a person with warts could kill a skunk and bury it in a graveyard at night. The warts followed the skunk into the hole. When I heard about these cures, I was glad Grandma Molly had spit snuff on my hand to cure my wart.

After Grandma Molly spit snuff on my wart, I found a different way to get rid of some that I got later. I went to Aunt Goldie's house, and cut the corner off her dishwashing cloth. I rubbed the piece on my warts and buried it where the water ran out of the downspout. Grandma Molly had some less offensive treatments. She took a pin and stuck it through a person's clothing and told him or her not to remove it. She said whenever the pin lost out of the clothing, the warts would be gone.

Weather

Since the people in Hopkins Gap survived many years by hunting, gathering, and subsistence farming, there was a lot of discussion about the weather--signs of rain, signs of dry weather, signs of cold winters, and rituals for making rain. Subsistence living connected them closely to their surroundings. Even though their ways of making a living changed during my lifetime, they remained connected to their physical environment. Gap people always watched the weather. Some signs of rain were quoted in the form of little rhymes such as:

Evening red,
Morning gray,
Sends the traveler,
On his way.
Evening gray,
Morning red,
Pours down rain,
On the traveler's head.

This particular rhyme has stayed with me to this day. When I awaken in the morning to a red sky in the East, I hear this rhyme in my head. If it actually rains during the day, I always connect the rain to the red morning sky.

Mom always checked the sky when the sun came up in the morning and when she made a fire in her wood cook stove. Monday was an especially important day to check the weather because that was her washday. She loved to hang her clothes out on the line so they would smell fresh and also so she could brag about how white her clothes were compared to other women. Another sure sign of rain or snow for Mom was when the smoke from her wood stove drifted toward the ground. "Smoke's goin' to the ground. It's gonna rain," she said. She would delay her washday until Tuesday, stay in the house, and make homemade bread.

Because Dad loved growing and eating potatoes, he worried each spring about whether we would have a dry summer. He always planted his potatoes on or as close to March 17, St. Patrick's Day, as he could. By mid-April the little green potato plants would be peeping through the ground, and by mid-May they would be blooming. I often heard him say, "A cool wet May, brings a barn full of hay, and it won't hurt my potatoes either." He explained, "Plants have to have a lot of rain while they are blooming." Based on how cool the month of May was and how much it rained, he predicted how many strawberries and

223

blackberries we could pick. May brought the "sheep rains," other-wise known as "blackberry winter." Sheep rains lasted up to five days and they always fall around my birthday, May 9. I said many times, "I've never had a warm, sunny birthday."

Mom would counter my statement with, "But we need the rain for the blackberries to grow."

By about mid-April, the first thunderstorms drifted over the mountain into the valley where we lived just outside Hopkins Gap. Dad watched the first storm with some anxiety. He showed me many times, "If the first storm comes across Little North Mountain from the west and splits as it crosses the mountain, most of the rain will fall in Hopkins Gap and the rest will drift down the mountain and leave us dry. When they start out that way, the rest of the storms will take the same path all summer, and I can forget havin' a good potato crop."

Other weather signs were noted as each season rolled around. Cold, snowy winters could be predicted by noticing where hornets and yellow jackets built their nests. If they built near the ground, the winter would be mild; high nests indicated deep snows and low temperatures. If an unusual number of spiders crawled into the house in the fall, the winter would be harsh. Counting the number of foggy mornings in August was a good way to predict the number of snows in the upcoming winter. Also, some people judged by the date of the first snow. If it snowed on December 15, there would be fifteen snows that winter.

Christmas day was a time for forecasting the weather. Little rhymes were stated to call attention to the weather that day:

"The hours of sun on Christmas Day,
So many frosts in the month of May."

Some of the older people in Hopkins Gap predicted the weather for the entire year by watching the weather during the twelve days of Christmas. The first day represented January. Each day after that represented a month with the last day, January 6th being December. If the day started cold, warmed up, then at the end of the day started to rain, that was the pattern for the month.

The fifteenth day of July was very important in predicting how much rain would fall during the gardening season. Mom always referred to this day as the day "Mary went over the mountain." The reference was to Virgin Mary's trip to visit her cousin Elizabeth. (Luke, Chapter 1). She explained, "Mary was pregnant with Jesus, and she went to see Elizabeth. The trip took forty days. If it rains the day she leaves, it will rain for forty days, and she will come back dry. This day marks a change in the weather and tells you when to plant and when not to plant."

Witches and Granny Women

Closely related to the superstitions and beliefs in Hopkins Gap are the adamant and widespread belief in witches and granny women or healers. There were bad witches and good witches. The bad witches were just called "witches," and the good witches were called "Granny Women" or "healers." The witches could turn themselves into cats or snakes and get into the house through a keyhole. They could fly and cast evil spells on babies, cows, pigs, and cars. When a witch cast a spell, a granny woman or a healer had to be called in to break the evil.

When Mom told me about witches, I asked her if I could be a witch. She told me the story of a local man who was a witch. "He had an awful time dying. He suffered for days until he confessed that he was a witch and told how he got to be one. He told on his deathbed that he went to where two roads crossed, stood in the middle and said, 'I am here to serve the devil.' Then he said he heard a loud rumbling noise and down one road came six white horses, at full gallop, pulling an empty wagon. The devil spoke to him and said, 'Don't be scared; just let it pass.' Next came a herd of horses. The devil said, 'Don't be scared; just let them pass.' Next came a big blacksnake. The devil said, 'Don't be scared; just open

225

your mouth.' The man said he opened his mouth, and the snake ran down his throat. He said, 'I thought I would choke to death, but I could feel the power of the devil going in me.'" I pictured myself at the crossroads near our house waiting for the devil. I was too scared to try it. I still wonder sometimes if it would have worked for me.

Granny Women or healers not only used their powers to cure illness but they also used them to remove evil "spells" that witches had cast on people, animals, or anything else.

The most talked about witch was Ellie Lam, my great grandmother on my mother's side of the family. Mom told me, "She could turn herself into a cat and come into the house through the rafters to put a spell on a baby. Uncle Jim shared an experience he had with Ellie, "I was sleepin' in the loft with my baby nephew when he started cryin' and wouldn't stop. Mom lit a lamp downstairs and opened the stairway to go to the loft and comfort the baby. When the door opened, the light from the lamp showed a gray cat settin' on the baby's chest. The light scared the cat, and it jumped and run under the eaves of the house."

Ellie Lam, it was believed, could also reduce herself down to a size that allowed her to slip into the house through a keyhole. On many occasions, Mom shared an amazing story about Great-Grandma Ellie's witch skills. She said, "Grandma Ellie went to the store to buy some eggs. A storm blew up while she was at the store, and the Shoemaker River started to flood. She had to cross the river to get back home, so she broke one of her eggs, made a boat out of the shell, and paddled herself across the flooding river. Jesse Craig swore until the day he died that he stood on the riverbank and watched her cross the river." Mom continued, "Jesse said she was her full size when she got out of the river on the other side." She also told me, "Brian and Edith Conley followed her across Little North Mountain during a snowstorm. She got way ahead of them so fast that they started to track her. They said they could only find the tracks of her toes in the snow. Each track was about fifty feet apart. She was flying and just touched down once in a while."

Grandpa Austin made his living hauling bark from the mountains surrounding Hopkins Gap to the leather tanneries in the towns of Broadway and Harrisonburg. Once while he was hauling a wagonload of bark out of the mountains, he couldn't get his mule to go. So he cut a piece of hair from the mule's forelock and using his fingers, he shot the hair back over the mule's head between its ears. The mule got up and walked on down the mountain. On his way home, he passed Ellie Lam's house. She was standing at the gate as he went by, and he noticed a piece of hair on top of her head was missing.

Ellie Lam certainly wasn't the only witch in the Gap and everybody knew it. Upon occasion other people were suspected of practicing evil tricks. In these cases, Gap folks had methods of identifying the guilty parties. They used common farm or household items including a three-pronged pitchfork and a broom. They made the pitchfork red hot and jabbed it through the bottom of a chair then pulled it out. If, at any point in the future, the suspected witch sat on the chair and couldn't get up, then he or she was definitely a witch. The broom was laid across the doorway as if it had fallen there. An innocent person could just step over the broom and walk into the house. A witch couldn't step over a broom so if a person came to the door and picked up the broom before entering the house, that person was a witch.

Jesse Craig bought a cow and a calf from Ellie Lam. She asked him to not sell the calf, but he sold it anyway. As he was leading the calf to the buyer's house, he passed by the witch's house. Ellie was working in her garden and saw Jesse passing by with the calf. She called out, "Jesse, where you agoin' with that calf." Jesse answered, "I'm leading her over to Austin's house. I sold her to him." Ellie yelled back at Jesse, "Mark my words old boy, you'll be sorry for sellin' that calf."

Evening came and Jesse went to the barn to milk the cow Ellie had sold him with the calf. The cow would not give a drop of milk. Jesse took some of the milk he already had and churned it into butter. He put the butter in a frying pan and made it hot. He

227

learned later that Ellie Lam had become very sick and suffered a very high fever. After this experience, Jesse Craig tied a red flannel rag around his cows' necks to keep the Ellie's witch spells away.

Witches often cast spells on milk so it wouldn't churn into butter. Grandma Molly always told Mom, "If butter won't come, the cream has been bewitched. To break the spell, take the cream to the pigpen and pour it into the hog trough. Get yourself a hickory switch and beat the cream as hard as you can, and you will be beating the witch. She'll soon remove her spell." Grandma Molly said you could also heat a piece of iron and put it in the churn to drive the witches out. If you didn't have a piece of iron, you could use a silver dollar.

One summer after vegetable and fruit canning time, one Hopkins Gap woman had a problem with her canned food spoiling. There was no obvious reason, so Jesse Craig was called in to check on the problem. He said a spell had been cast on the food. He took three tablespoons from one jar and threw it on the hot coals along with a note he had written to the witch. He instructed the family to not loan anything to anyone for nine days. The next day a woman in the community came to borrow some lard. The family refused to loan her the lard, but they noticed a burned spot on her neck.

It was commonly believed in Hopkins Gap that witches rode horses at night. The next day the horses were tired and had a hard time pulling heavy wagons. The witches rode the horses without a bridle and barebacked. According to Grandma Molly, "The next morning the horses were tired and caked with mud and sweat. Their manes were knotted and plaited."

Special Days in the Year

When certain days of the year rolled around, everyday objects took on a special meaning or had special powers in healing illnesses and curing in general. Some of these days were good times to predict the weather for the months to come.

228

The second day of February was a very important day. The people in Hopkins Gap recognized this as ground hog day, but they referred to it as Candlemas. It was the day when families checked their food supplies because it was the halfway point in the winter. They checked to see if they would have enough staples such as flour, sugar, salt and lard.

Another important day was Shrove Tuesday better known as Mardi Gras in modern times. Shrove Tuesday, the day before Ash Wednesday, was the only time of the year when Grandma Molly made fat cakes. She used most of the left over staples — flour, sugar, salt, and lards-- to make fat cakes. These were doughnut-like cakes without holes. She mixed the dough, cut the cakes into rectangular shapes, then cut a slit in the middle of each one before dropping them into a large pot of hot lard. The first three cakes were broken into pieces and fed to the hens so they would lay more eggs in the upcoming months. Little chickens hatched from the eggs of hens that had eaten fat cakes would be protected from animals and large birds that preyed upon them.

The height to which Grandma Molly could stack the fat cakes before they fell was how tall the grain would grow the following summer. The family was very proud if the stack of "fat cakes" was high. This meant they had stored more than enough food for the past winter.

The Thursday before Good Friday was also a special day. This day was called "Maundy" Thursday or "Green" Thursday. The day before, the woman of the house went into the fields and gathered "weed" greens. She picked the early shoots of dandelion, lambs quarter, blackberry and strawberry leaves, plantain, polk shoots and many other plants that had started to grow. She parboiled a huge pot of these greens and fried them down in grease. The family ate weed greens on Green Thursday to clean all the winter sludge from their intestinal tracts.

Good Friday and Easter were not only the day that Hopkins Gap folks celebrated the crucifixion and resurrection of Jesus Christ, but they believed that eggs eaten on Easter morning would bring them good health throughout the year. They were not just any eggs. The eggs had to be the ones laid by the chickens on Good Friday. Specifically, by eating Good Friday eggs on Easter morning, a person could avoid getting a hernia. Grandma Molly often told me that she used an egg laid on Good Friday to treat hernias. The egg was rubbed against the hernia and then placed behind the chimney in the fireplace. She also used the same method to treat goiter and to remove birthmarks and warts. If you could get an egg laid by a solid black hen, it was especially powerful in removing blemishes, birthmarks, moles, and other skin cancers. Rubbing a Good Friday egg across a child's mouth prevented the thrush or cured the thrush if the child already had it.

Good Friday eggs were used to protect our house. My daddy always put a Good Friday egg in a tin can and placed it in the rafters of the roof so the house wouldn't be hit by lightning during the stormy spring and summer months ahead.

Ascension Day is another special day for the mountaineers of Hopkins Gap. Ascension Day falls forty days after Easter and marks the day that Jesus ascended into heaven. It was often said that if a person did garden work such as planting or plowing a rainstorm would come and wash the garden away. If a woman sewed on Ascension Day, the lightning would strike her. Men usually went fishing on Ascension Day.

When I was about twelve years old, I had a row of dark brown freckles across my nose like many children do. Other kids made fun of me, and when Dad got mad at me he called me a "speckled face son-of-a-bitch." Mom told me how to get rid of my freckles. "You have to get out of bed before the sun comes up on the first day of May, put your clothes on without talking to anybody, walk down the steps backwards, and go to the field. When you get there you say:

> *Good morning to you, Mrs. May,*
> *I've come out to wash my freckles away."*

I followed her instructions carefully. I rubbed my hands in the grass and made them wet with dew. I washed my face with the dew; and, now that the freckles were on my hands, I put my hands on my upper arms. I did the same ritual three years in a row, and the freckles left my nose. Some of them appeared on my upper arms as time passed.

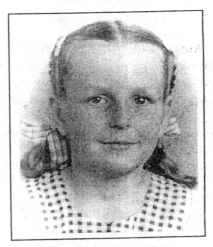

The author with freckles

Rain that fell on the first day of May was good for washing your hair. This resulted in good health all year. People in Hopkins Gap believed if you ran bare headed in the rain on the first day of May, you would not have headaches for the rest of the year. To cure sore eyes, Grandma Molly took May water and placed wheat straws broken up fine in a vessel with the water. Let the concoction stand, pour off the water, and then place the damp straw material over the sore eyes.

If you looked into a well on the first day of May, you could see the image of your future mate. Also, if you spread wet clothing on the grass to dry on the night of April 30, the next day, May first, the wrinkles in the cloth spelled out the initials of the person you

---

would marry. If a woman walked around the garden patch on May first, she would see the man she was going to marry.

May Day was also a time when winter clothing was discarded for summer clothes. It was considered bad luck to change to summer clothes before that date and it was reinforced with a little rhyme:

"Until April is dead,
Change not a thread."

Grandma Molly always told us that "Dog Days" start around the middle of July. This was not a good time for children because one of the things we couldn't do during "Dog Days" was swim. Since these days came during the hottest part of the summer, we didn't like this rule. She claimed that if we went in the water, we would get sores and boils that would never heal. Since I had a couple of boils that did heal, I surely didn't want some that wouldn't heal. Grandma Molly also claimed that snakes were blind and dogs go mad during "Dog Days." She said, "Snakes are mad because they can't see, and they will strike out at anything that gets close; if a dog is going to get rabies, it will be during dog days."

Christmas season was also a magical time. People in Hopkins Gap thought animals could talk on Christmas Eve. Uncle Shirley was a beekeeper and he told me that if you listened to a beehive on Christmas Eve, you could hear them singing. I never tried that trick. Also, cows face in the direction of Bethlehem and kneel in a praying position at midnight on Christmas Eve.

People in Hopkins Gap believed if you changed your clothes between Christmas and New Year, you would get boils. Also, ashes couldn't be taken out of the house because it would bring bad luck for the entire year. If a person wanted to be free of evil spirits and have good luck for the year, they went to a crossroads where they could hear clanking noises of chains. Crossroads were good for acquiring special talents. If you wanted to play the guitar, you took it to a crossroads on Christmas Day. If you got up early and didn't talk to anybody before you got to the crossroads, the ability to play the guitar was yours.

The dew that fell on Christmas Eve could bring good health for the whole year. Grandma Molly told us that Alice Crawford used to bake an apple pie and put it out so the dew would fall on it. The next day the family ate the pie for good health during the next year.

Peggy Ann Shifflett

Part Six

GETTING AND KEEPING BABIES

Nearly all men die of their remedies,
and not of their illnesses.

Moliere (7)

During the early days of survival by subsistence, family planning in Hopkins Gap included the wish for many children who could help with food production as well as provide care for their parents in old age. This tradition of large families lasted through my generation and is exemplified by my ninety-nine first cousins. Most couples had their first child within a year after their marriage. A woman's role of child bearing was crucial and therefore surrounded by many beliefs and practices handed down from generation to generation.

Family Planning the Hopkins Gap Way

It was important for Hopkins Gap families to have a balance of boy and girl babies — boys to help the father with his work and girls to help the mother. Many practices were used to influence the gender of an unborn child. If a woman wanted a boy, she would try to get pregnant during a full moon. If the husband hung his trousers over the bedpost on the right side before going to bed for sex, his next child would be a boy. If a couple were having all girls or all boys and wanted to change the sex of their next child, they simply changed the position of their bed in the bedroom.

Every teenaged girl in Hopkins Gap was given the needle test while she was told that her future husband would want a boy as his firstborn. Older women wanted to know if we were going to give

235

our husbands a son as the first child. When I was about fourteen years old, Mom and Aunt Ethel gathered several of my female cousins who were my age along with me, around the table on a Sunday afternoon. They had a threaded needle that they held between their fingers with the needle hanging just above our wrists. The needle began to swing like a pendulum. When it moved in a circle, it indicated a girl baby and if it swung straight back and forth, it indicated a boy.

Mom held the needle when it came to my turn. It slowly began to move in a circle. "Your husband is gonna be mad at you," she said. The needle stopped and then began to move in a circle again. The faces around the table were watching with concern that I would never have a boy. The third time the needle moved back and forth. Mom said, with a sigh of relief, "Well, he'll have to wait a while for his boy, but he's gonna get one."

The needle stopped when the number of children to be born to each girl was reached. I was supposed to have seven children. I was tested several times. Each time the needle indicated seven children for me with three girls and four boys. Two of the girls were to be born first. By choosing not to marry, I avoided the shame of birthing two girls before I had any boys.

Women often wanted to know how many children they would have in their lifetime. One way to know was to count the number of wrinkles in the forehead of a woman, when her eyebrows were raised. The midwife often counted the lumps in the umbilical cord of a woman's firstborn child. The number of lumps equaled the number of children to be born to that woman in her lifetime.

Infant Death and "Marking" Babies

In the early days, having babies in Hopkins Gap was not always a joyous occasion. There was a very high infant mortality rate. I never met some of my aunts, uncles and cousins because they died in infancy. If a baby was breathing when it was born, or

236

lived only a day or two, it received a name. Grandpa John and Grandma Mary, my mother's parents—had two children who received a name--Vivian who died at age three and Russell David who died before the age of one.

Stillborn babies were not named or given a formal burial. The father or the attending midwife would dig a small grave some distance from the house and bury the tiny body. The graves were never marked. This practice resulted in numerous stories of people passing by one of these burial sites at night and hearing a baby crying. As I said earlier, one location in Hopkins Gap is called "Cry Baby Lane."

The narrow lane leads to an old homestead where it is believed that a woman's many stillborn babies were buried. Uncle Shirley can name several locations where people reported hearing a baby crying late at night. One place was where his mother, Grandma Mary, buried two of her stillborn children.

Every time a woman learned she was pregnant, there was great concern that she deliver a healthy infant, free of disabilities and unwanted birthmarks. The older women warned the expecting mother of the many hazards she might encounter during her pregnancy. They were always worried about the mother "marking" the baby because of the foods she craved while pregnant. "If you crave a certain food, make sure your husband gets it for you," they warned, "or the baby will have a birthmark that looks like whatever you craved." They even gave examples of "true life" stories to illustrate what might happen to an unborn child. Mom told many stories of children born with "strawberry" birthmarks on their faces because their mother craved strawberries and couldn't get them.

I was born with a birthmark on the top of my head. Mom told me, "When I was pregnant with you, I saw a pear in the very top of a tree that looked ripe and delicious. I pointed it out to your daddy, and he threw rocks at the pear to try to knock it down. He couldn't hit the pear, so I never got my craving satisfied. You were born with a pear-shaped birthmark on the top of my head." I've never looked to see my birthmark. I just took Mom's word for it.

Aunt Lena had powerful cravings for beets during one of her pregnancies, but she was unable to get any. She attributed the reddish colored birthmarks on her daughter's arm to this unmet desire. She claimed the marks looked like beets.

Aunt Goldie told me, "One baby was born with a crippled arm that looked like it had a snake wrapped around it because his mother saw a black snake before he was born." When we were picking strawberries, we sometimes found a "twin"--two strawberries that had grown together. Mom would say, "If a pregnant woman eats a 'twin' strawberry, she will have twins."

Reflecting on these beliefs today, it appears that they did serve as a form of prenatal care. They made Hopkins Gap women pay attention to their babies' health during the days of isolation when it was nearly impossible to see a doctor for care during their pregnancies. The beliefs prevented women from stooping and reaching. Many warnings were given which today would translate into encouraging the pregnant woman to avoid stressful situations. "Never look at a corpse. Try to avoid being around a physically handicapped child," the older women said.

It was believed that if a pregnant woman witnessed an accident and touched some part of her body, her child would be marked on that same part of its body unless she remembered to immediately slap another part of her body. When Mom saw my cousin Joyce shot in the hunting rifle accident, the shock caused her to place her hand over her mouth, but she quickly remembered to slap her thigh immediately with the same hand. Mom believes to this day that she prevented my brother, Warnie, from having a large birthmark across his mouth.

An old man who lived at the mouth of Hopkins Gap loved to torture small animals. His wife begged him to stop torturing rabbits by cutting the tendons in their legs and watching them try to hop around the yard. She was pregnant at the time with her little girl. The baby was born with bent and twisted legs and never walked in her life. I remember watching as her older brother pulled her into church every Sunday in a little red wagon. I asked Mom what was wrong with the little girl and she told me what had happened.

If a pregnant woman worked hard up until the birth of her child, the child would be healthy and also be a hard worker. When Uncle Shirley described how hard my daddy worked plowing corn with the mule when he was a small boy, he explained, "Your daddy worked hard because Grandma Molly climbed up on the mountain to High Top Patch. She worked in the potato patch all day, walked down the mountain, started birth pains, and your daddy was born that night."

One Saturday when I was about fourteen years old, I was walking with my mother on a street in Harrisonburg. It happened to be my turn to go with her and Aunt Goldie to get the groceries. Mom looked up the street and saw a woman leaning against the wall of a building. She said to me, "Look at that dirty bitch. She's a queer." I never had heard the word "queer" applied in that way before so I asked her what it meant. She said, "See how she is dressed? She is wearing men's clothes and a man's cap. She has sex with other women." Then I was really curious so I asked more questions including how a person gets to be a queer.

As we walked down the street, Mom answered my questions, "I know how she got that way. Her daddy and mom had sex just before she was born. That causes a baby's sex organs and desires to be in its throat instead of where they should be." I believed that myself for a time. After hearing these tales, suspicions, and beliefs a whole lifetime, it was sometimes hard to separate them from reality.

Midwife Stories

There were two well-known midwives in Hopkins Gap during my childhood — Mary Kirkpatrick and Nettie Conley. Nettie was the midwife who generated the most stories. Aunt Ethel told me that when one of her sister's children was being born, Mary Kirkpatrick was assisting. The baby's arm came out first, and Mary wasn't sure what to do, so she sent for Nettie. She arrived, rolled up her sleeve, took the tiny arm and pushed it back in. She reached in and turned the baby around. Then the little girl was born the right way — with her head entering the world first.

Mom told me about another time that Nettie came to deliver a baby, but she had her arm in a sling. "The baby started to come out backwards with one leg stickin' out. Net took her sore arm out of the sling, dipped her hand in disinfectant, went up inside, and turned the baby around so it would come out right."

Nettie was a carefree and jovial person. According to Mom, "Nothing seemed to scare her. She always laughed and whistled while she worked." My only memory of Nettie is watching her while we were waiting by the bank in front of her house. She was getting into Dad's car to come to our house to help deliver my brother, John. She had a huge grin on her face as she was off to do what she loved best--bring another baby into the world.

While Nettie was at our house helping with John's birth, she entertained us with a story about delivering all of her sister's children. I remember Grandma Molly and Mom laughing so hard they cried. Nettie told us her sister's children were the ugliest children she had ever brought into the world; and "if their father had been a smart man, he wouldn't have to build any fences. He could just place one child on each corner of his land. Neither humans, nor animals would ever dare stray onto his property."

Ordinarily babies were born at home in an upstairs bedroom, and the child was not brought downstairs until it had first been carried to a higher place in the home such as the attic. This ritual assured that the child would "go up in the world." My brother, John, was born in our one-story stucco house. He wasn't even dry from birth when Nettie came from the kitchen with a split-bottom chair. She carefully took him away from Mom's breast as she explained, "I have to make sure this boy goes up in the world." Nettie held him close as she stepped onto the seat of the chair and stood there for a minute or two with John in her arms.

Nettie was sometimes paid with money but most of the time with gifts of food. In return, she not only delivered the baby, but performed other rituals necessary to insure the health of the child and the mother. She made sure the mother stayed in bed for exactly nine days after giving birth. She advised the mother that she must lay quietly on the third and ninth day after the baby was born. On those two days, the womb was moving back into place.

Nettie washed the baby's head in apple brandy to make sure it grew a healthy head of hair. When the umbilical cord came off the baby's naval, Nettie held it in her fingers and made three circles around the baby's head. She then took the cord and placed it in the back of the wood stove or hearth where it would burn slowly. This ritual was to ensure the baby quit wetting the bed in a timely manner.

If the child continued to wet the bed after he or she had been potty trained, the responsibility for a cure fell on the immediate family. Sometimes Grandma Molly was called in and asked to perform a ritual. The ritual consisted of baking a large pan of biscuits. When the biscuits came out of the oven, the bedwetting child was placed on a stool near the family dinner table. Grandma Molly then broke each individual biscuit in two pieces above the head of the child. She placed the broken biscuits on a platter for the immediate family members to eat. The bedwetting child remained on the stool until the family consumed the entire plate of broken biscuits.

I watched this ritual performed for my Cousin Virgil when he was a child. They made him feel very special and it made me wish that I too wet the bed. There were so many kids around most of the time that being the center of attention was a goal for each of us. At times I felt so starved for attention that I just plain asked for it. Other times, I wished for the measles or mumps or that I would get a loose tooth so Mom could pull it. Getting a loose baby tooth was a good way to get attention. Mom tied a string around the tooth, then held your head on her chest, and jerked the tooth out of your mouth.

241

That procedure wasn't a lot of fun either. I got tired of it after she took two or three teeth out that way. One summer while we still lived in the stucco house, I got a loose tooth. Mom noticed and said, "Come here, let me pull that tooth for you. If it falls out in the night, you could choke on it."

"I want to pull it myself this time. You put the string on it and I'll jerk it out," I promised her. She carefully tied the string around my tooth and let me go off to pull it. She laughed, as I walked away, "You won't be able to pull it. "I'll give you 'til supper time. When you come in to eat, that tooth had better be pulled.

I wandered the fields all day. I stopped and tried to talk myself into the gentle jerk it would take to get rid of the tooth. I counted to ten numerous times but couldn't jerk the string when number ten came up. I didn't go home for dinner—just kept wandering around and torturing myself.

Mid afternoon rolled around, and I was getting mighty hungry. I knew when Mom lay down with the baby to take a nap, so I sneaked into the back door to find me something to eat. I opened the cabinet door as quietly as I could and was looking in when I felt a presence behind me. Mom placed her hand gently on my shoulder and turned me around. Of course, the string was hanging out the side of my mouth. She pulled me to her chest, grabbed the string, and the tooth was history. She said, "You ought to be ashamed for torturing yourself all day. That didn't hurt a bit." I was crying from anger and humiliation. I needed to save face so I yelled at her, "That tooth wasn't ready to come out. I've been yanking on it all day. I'll bet my new tooth comes in crooked." She chuckled as she answered, "We'll see."

There were no tooth fairies in Hopkins Gap. The extracted tooth was destroyed. It was either buried or burned so a dog wouldn't find it and eat it. If a dog ate it, the tooth that replaced it would look like a dog's tooth.

Very few babies were born in hospitals--in fact, it was almost unique unless the expectant mother was suffering from a serious ailment or had previous difficulty with childbirth. It was

242

mostly due to isolation. Although there were a few cars in Hopkins Gap in the early 1940's, the road was often not passable. If the weather was good, Dr. Charles Watson was called. His office was in Broadway, a good twenty-five miles from Hopkins Gap.

Mom planned to have me at home. Her labor pains started on a Monday, so she called midwife, Nettie, Grandma Molly, and Dr. Watson. The first thing the midwife did was to go to the wood shed and get an axe. She put it under my mother's bed to cut the sharpness of the labor pains.

Dr. Watson agreed with what Nettie and Grandma Molly's suggested, such as the axe under the bed. However, as the days passed and the end of the week was nearing, Dr. Watson called an ambulance and had Mom taken to the hospital.

I was born Friday evening, May 9, 1941 at 8:30, with the help of Dr. Watson and his forceps. Mom said I had a hole or two in my forehead, a skinned neck, and nasty bruises when she first saw me. She told me many times, "I don't think you wanted to come out," and on days when I wasn't getting along with her, I reminded her, "You told me I didn't want to be born into this family."

Remedies for Babies

Before the roads were passable, midwives and Granny Women turned to the old remedies that had been passed to them by their predecessors. Most of the rituals were based on sympathetic or homeopathic principles. The rituals were used both as preventatives and treatments.

Newborn babies were guarded against any bouncing movement for fear they would become "liver-grown." A baby could get "liver-grown" from riding in a buggy in cold winter weather over a bumpy road. Later it was thought a rough car ride could be just as harmful. To be "liver-grown" was very painful because the bouncing caused the baby's liver to become "attached to the ribs."

When a mother thought her child might be susceptible to "liver-grown," she could use one of several preventatives. She could pass the child around the leg of a table or pass the infant through a horse collar. The collar had to be taken directly from a horse and used while it was still warm. The baby was passed through the collar three times. The practice involving a table leg also was done three times. The child could not touch the floor or the underside of the tabletop while being passed around the table leg.

If the child stopped nursing and was taking only shallow breaths, it was "liver-grown." The treatment had to be done by a granny woman. I watched Grandma Molly and my mother cure "liver-grown" many times. They greased the baby and rubbed its chest and back. Then they placed their hands on its ribs and put their thumbs side by side in the center of the breastbone. They pressed their thumbs into the baby's chest and rubbed them down over the end of the ribs in the upper abdomen. The movement was slow with the thumbs in perfect harmony. They mumbled special words under their breath followed by "in the name of the Father, the Son, and the Holy Ghost." This procedure was repeated three times. The baby always cried from the pressure of the thumbs in its stomach, proving to the healers that "liver-grown" was the problem. After the treatment, the baby began to breathe easier, nursed, and fell asleep.

After the "big" road was built in 1955, it was easier to drive sick babies to the doctor, but it wasn't easy for Hopkins Gap women to trust modern medicine. On many occasions, my cousins would stop at our house for Mom to diagnose their condition before they took the baby on to the doctor. Mom would carefully diagnose the baby and if she thought she could treat the baby she would tell the mother. Most of the time, the mother let Mom do her ritual, then left and went on the doctor.

When this practice first started, Mom got the credit for a cured baby. As time went on, Hopkins Gap mothers began to trust the medical doctors more, and they got the credit for a cured baby.

When it came to me and my brothers and sisters, Mom preferred to care for us at home.

While Dad was in the army, Mom and all three of us kids slept in one big bed in the living room of our house. One of my first memories of Mom was watching her care for my sister, Brenda, when she got pneumonia. She had taken her to Dr. Watson who diagnosed her condition. He wanted to put the baby in the hospital, but Mom said no. She brought Brenda home and treated her for pneumonia with homemade poultices.

She took a red flannel rag and rubbed it with a remedy that every household in Hopkins Gap kept on hand. When the men hunted skunks so they could sell their skins, the women scraped the fat off the inside of the skins. They rendered the fat into a liquid; they let it cool, until it turned into a white salve. Mom rubbed a layer of skunk grease onto a red flannel rag, warmed the rag in the oven of her kitchen stove, and placed it on the baby's chest. The mild odor from the skunk grease acted as a decongestant.

All night for several nights she walked the floor with Brenda in her arms. As Brenda fought to get her breath, Mom patted her and sang lullabies. She also burned a kressoline lamp as a decongestant. She claimed the fumes helped Brenda get her breath. Any time we got a chest cold, she treated us with skunk grease poultices and burned that smelly old lamp.

There was always concern for how young children were growing and developing. Some children were referred to as scrawny or puny and were thought to have "undergrowth." Hopkins Gap granny women used a ritual with a string to determine if a child was suffering from "undergrowth."

Some granny women measured the child by using any kind of string, but Grandma Molly insisted the string had to be red and it had to be made of flax. Grandma Molly performed her ritual for "undergrowth" only on Fridays during the "new" moon.

She described "undergrowth" as "flesh decay" which could be detected by pinching the flesh on the child's upper arm to see if it was separated from the bone. It was Grandma Molly's job as a granny woman to keep an eye on children; so when we got close to her, she would put her fingers around our upper arms, squeeze the flesh, and pull on it to see if it was "loose from the bone."

If she suspected "undergrowth," she told the mother and arranged to treat the child. She often squeezed my upper arms; and, on one occasion she diagnosed my condition as probably "undergrowth." The very next Friday during the "new" moon I found myself standing stark naked in the middle of Grandma Molly's kitchen. Aunt Lena and Mom watched as she carried out the treatment. As a matter of fact, several other members of the family filed through the kitchen and caught a glimpse of my naked body.

A child who was suspected of having "undergrowth" had to be measured. "Measuring" not only gave a firm diagnosis, but the process of "measuring" actually cured the condition if the ritual was done right.

Grandma Molly had her trusty string made of flax and dyed red. She measured my body from the crown of my head to the heel of my foot. She then measured the length of my foot. When she finished measuring, if the distance from my heel to my toe, multiplied by seven, was greater than the length of my body from the crown of my head to my heel I was suffering from "undergrowth." Once Grandma Molly was certain of her earlier diagnosis, she carried out the rest of the ritual. She tied the ends of the red flax string together and laid it down on the table in a circle. She told me to step into the circle. She then took the string and lifted it up over my body in the direction of growth. This was done three times.

When the first measuring was completed, Grandma Molly folded the string and put it in the top drawer of her pie safe. She then marked her calendar for the next two Fridays during the "new" moon and told Mom to bring me back on those days.

When we returned to Grandma's house, she went through the entire ritual again with me naked in the middle of the kitchen table. After the third "measuring," she rolled the string into a ball and buried it under the eaves of the house roof where rainwater dripped. The "undergrowth" left my body as the rain rotted the red flax string. The quicker it rotted, the faster I would start growing again.

Grandma Molly also measured children for asthma. This treatment involved driving a nail into a tree above the head of the afflicted child. The tree had to be a fruit-bearing tree, and the nail had to have some direct relationship with the afflicted child. This meant a nail would be taken from the child's bedpost, or the floor of his bedroom. On the day she drove the nail into the tree just above the child's head, she had to refrain from talking from the time she got out of bed in the morning until the "measuring" was complete. When the child grew above the level of the nail, he or she was cured of asthma.

If a child survived "livergrown," "undergrowth", and asthma, there were still other maladies to endure or face such as thrush, earaches, measles, mumps, and chickenpox. All children went barefoot in the summer resulting in bee stings, "cow itch," and puncture wounds from stepping in nails. Mom or Grandma Molly had a remedy for all these problems.

Grandma Molly and Mom used a variety of things in their curing rituals including urine from the person needing the treatment. When a baby had thrush, its mouth was wiped out with its own, warm wet diaper.

Alice Crawford used a different cure for thrush. I remember watching her treat my little brother, Warnie, for thrush. She took her greasy dishrag from the dishpan and tore three threads off the rag. She said it had to be the main dishrag used to wash the family's dishes. She held the three strings together by the ends and dragged them through his lips three times. She took the strings and hung them on a nail near the stovepipe. She said, "When these strings dry out his thrush will be gone."

When Grandma Molly treated a baby for thrush, she went to the barnyard and pulled three straws out of a manure pile that had been cleaned out of the stables. She brought the three straws to the house and pulled them through the baby's mouth. She immediately took the straws back to the manure pile and put them exactly where she had gotten them. I watched her do this and asked, "Grandma, how does that help?" She answered with confidence and pride, "When I put the straws in the baby's mouth, the thrush got on them. Now when they rot, the thrush will rot with them."

Earache was treated with a few drops of fresh urine from the victim poured into the ear with an eyedropper. On several occasions I watched Mom squeeze fresh, warm urine from a diaper until she got enough urine to drop in my sister, Brenda's, aching ears.

I saw Aunt Goldie treat a sore throat by filling a dirty sock with ashes from the kitchen stove. She placed it in her grandbaby's diaper until it was saturated with urine. Then it was tied around the child's neck and left there until the sore throat was gone.

Mom wouldn't let us start going barefoot until May 10 every spring. This was the day that marked the end of sudden spring frosts. So each spring, we waited patiently for the time to take off our shoes and put them away for the summer. Of course, we often hurt our feet. We would either step on a bee or stub our big toe. While playing around the barn, we often got puncture wounds from stepping on a rusty nail. If we stepped on a bee, Mom told us to go to the outhouse and pee and rub some of our pee on the sting. It worked! Of course, I don't know if it worked because we rubbed the sting with pee or if playing around in our pee took our mind off the pain.

Stepping on a rusty nail was more serious. Mom told us stories about people who had died from "lock jaw" because they stepped on a rusty nail. She said, "When an animal gets "lock jaw," you can shoot it; but, you can't shoot people. They used to just put them in an upstairs room and nail the door shut and wait for them to die. You could hear them trying to get out because they wanted to bite somebody. Foam would run out of their mouth, and they looked wild. It was a hard thing to watch." I asked her if she had ever seen a person dying of lockjaw. She answered, "No, but I sure heard about it."

She told us that horses often carried "lock jaw" germs and if we stepped in a nail around the barn, she wanted to know it right away. She had a special treatment for a nail puncture. She cleaned the wound and wrapped it. But, more important to prevent "lock jaw," she found the nail, put it in a can of kerosene, and put the can up on a shelf. By treating the nail, she was preventing us from getting "lock jaw."

Animal manure from a cow, sheep, rabbit, chicken, and cat was used for teas and poultices. Cow manure seemed to be the most useful in curing a wide variety of childhood maladies. Poison ivy was treated with a direct application of cow manure. Every summer when I started to go barefoot, I would get breaks in the skin on the bottom of my toes. I know now that this was a fungus caused by walking in the damp grass. Mom called it "cow itch." Her term was a good one because it really did itch. In fact, the itch was so bad that I gladly followed her strict regimen for getting rid of the "cow itch." She told me to go to the pasture and follow the cow until she dropped a pile and immediately step my sore toes into the fresh, warm, and gooey manure. In a day or so the "cow itch" was gone.

Sheep manure was used in a number of illnesses, usually in the form of a tea made by boiling the manure in water and adding sugar. Most people called it "mountain tea," or "sheep saffron." The most widespread use was for bringing out the measles. Grandma Molly carried the recipe around in her head ready for dispensing when needed. She said, "You just get some sheep droppin's and boil it in a little water. Then you strain it and reheat the broth. Mix in a little whiskey and you have sheep manure tea." When the child drank a little sheep manure, measles just started popping out everywhere. The last of my cousins to be treated with sheep manure tea was Cousin Joyce. She wasn't told what she was drinking until the measles were gone; but to this day when the subject comes up, she is teased as the last of the "sheep manure drinkers." Sheep manure was also applied as a poultice to treat boils.

While talking about boils, I had a lot of them when I was a child especially on my legs below my knees. I still have the scars. Mom spent a lot of time on my boils, but the best treatment was a milk poultice. She heated some milk to boiling and dipped a piece of homemade bread in the hot milk. She dipped the hot, milk-soaked bread onto a clean cotton bandage and applied it directly to the boil. The bread was boiling hot. As I screamed in pain from the hot poultice, she explained, "This will draw the infection and the "core" to the surface so I can open the boil." I'm not sure the poultice helped because when she "opened" the boil the next morning, the pain was so intense I would often throw up my breakfast.

Rabbit manure was also used to bring out the measles when used as a tea. Chicken manure had limited use—it was only good for stomach cramps. But most potent tea of all was made from cat manure. It served as a last resort after other remedies failed. I heard Grandma Molly say many times, "If it's kill or cure, use cat manure."

Watching for Witches

Many people in the Gap believed that some people were evil by nature and others had chosen to be evil. These people made it their life's purpose to make others' lives miserable. Babies made easy targets for their meanness.

A baby's hair, fingernails, or toenails were not cut during the first year of life. The mother could bite their fingernails and toenails off, but she could not cut their hair. When she bit off the toenails and fingernails, she would carefully dispose of the clippings so they could not fall into the wrong hands. Local witches could cast evil spells if they had an item that had been a part of the baby.

My mother told me about her Grandma Ellie Lam casting a spell on one of Jesse and Nancy Craig's babies. "Ellie never did like Nancy so somehow she stole a dirty diaper off the back porch. Once she got her hands on something that the baby had used, she could put a spell on her. The baby cried for days, and Jesse and Nancy thought she had the colic. Finally, when Jesse couldn't stand the crying anymore, he asked Nancy if Ellie Lam had been to the house to visit. Nancy remembered that she had and that a diaper was missing when she left the house."

Mom continued, "Jesse then knew what he had to do. He told Nancy to catch some of the baby's urine, put it in a bottle, and cork it tight. He took the bottle and drove a sewing needle through the cork. He said, 'Now, we'll wait to see how long it takes that old bitch to ask us to uncork the bottle.' He told his wife the witch wouldn't be able to pee as long as the baby's urine was corked in the bottle, and the needle would give her awful pains in her bladder." My mother said, "Within two days Ellie Lam was hanging on their yard gate begging to borrow an egg. Nancy wouldn't give her anything, so finally she screamed for her to uncork the bottle. Nancy took the cork out, and Grandma Ellie collapsed and pissed all over herself right there in the yard."

After a year, a baby's hair can be cut but the clippings had to be carefully disposed of by burning so that they wouldn't fall into evil hands or so birds wouldn't find them and make a nest. This would cause the child to have severe headaches until the nest was abandoned by the birds, found, and destroyed by fire.

Playful Teaching and Learning

Not all baby care was about treating illnesses and fearing witches. There were also times when my mother comforted me and my brothers and sister with wonderful lullabies and games when we could not fall asleep. Mom played "This little pig went to market" on our toes as we drifted off into an afternoon nap.

At night while rocking us to sleep, she would sing "Rock-a-bye baby," "Bah, bah black sheep," and "Bye baby bunting." She sung these lullabies and acted out each line with gentle rocking gestures and pretending to fall ending with a little tickle. Thus, many of my days ended with laughter and warmth in the arms of my mother or watching her cuddle my brothers and sister as they fell asleep.

Mom also played little games with us to measure the progress of our growth and development. I enjoyed watching her teach my smaller brothers to play "Pat-a-cake." This was the first lesson taught to babies in Hopkins Gap. It was acted out and the baby mocked the hand patting motions, rolling one hand over the other and patting the pretend dough into the pan.

As we grew a little older, the games turned to more serious matters such as whom you would marry. On my first dress with buttons, my mother had me recite the little poem, "Rich, man, poor man" as I touched each button.

The button touched last corresponded to my future husband's occupation. I always ended on Indian chief.

To encourage us to clean the food from our plates or to eat healthy foods like spinach, mom would recite a little rhyme as she shoveled a spoonful into our mouths: "Through the teeth and over the tongue, watch out belly here it comes."

Breastfeeding for Birth Control

During the time that I was growing up, most of the women in Hopkins Gap breastfed their babies. They expressed the belief that breastfeeding would provide natural immunities to colds, measles, and various other childhood diseases. They also believed they could not conceive another child as long as the last child nursed the breast. A few of the children that I grew up with nursed their mother's breast until they were seven and eight years old. This practice spanned at least two generations. My mother told the story of one of her cousins. "I don't know exactly how old he was, but he would stop playing ball with us and go in the house to suck his mama's milk. Once I watched him suck while Aunt Millie was washing dishes. She just took her breast out of her dress, and he stood on the floor and put his head under her arm and sucked her milk. He was the last kid she had."

Not everybody who got pregnant in Hopkins Gap was happy about the situation. Abortions were commonly called "knocking a baby." When a woman didn't want a baby it was usually because she was not married. Nettie Conley, the midwife, was called in to give advice on these occasions. Mom never confirmed that Nettie was the abortionist. Some of the ways of ending an unwanted pregnancy included drinking a mixture of moonshine, quinine pills, and turpentine. Another very painful and dangerous method was also used. Elm bark was stripped from a branch and cut into long narrow pieces. The pieces were boiled so that the outside became very soft and slippery. The end of a piece was sharpened and inserted through the vagina and into the uterus to destroy the fetus.

Mom told me many, many times about a young woman who died from an abortion. She was Nettie Conley's daughter. She was kept at home until she died. While she was dying she said over and over that she heard babies crying—all the babies that she had "knocked" in her short life. She begged Nettie to go between the logs of the house and destroy her quinine and bottles of turpentine so she could rest. When the pills and turpentine were thrown away, she died peacefully.

Peggy Ann Shifflett

Part Seven

CHILDHOOD GAMES AND LESSONS LEARNED

"A quiet child is plotting mischief—or has done it."
Anonymous

As I have grown older and reflect on my childhood, I realize that there were many practical aspects in our daily activities as children. Since there was little or no money for toys, we either made our own from a variety of materials around the farm and woods or used parts of broken toys to rebuild useable ones. We also had to create our own games to pass the free hours after church on Sundays, on long summer evenings, and when we were not in school.

Indians, Turkeys, and Not Thanksgiving

Many summer days were spent building Indian teepees out of saplings we cut from the woods. We tied them at one end and spread the other ends into a circular teepee. We covered the outside of the saplings with feed sacks and old rugs.

We made Indian headdresses using chicken and turkey feathers that we found around the barnyard. If we needed a lot of feathers we visited our neighbor's turkey flock. As we slinked behind the bushes along the fencerow, we pulled along a little cart that we had made from scrap wood and bicycle wheels. We picked up a flat rock or two along the way. When we reached the flock of turkeys, we threw the rocks so they would skip across the turkeys' heads much the way a flat rock skips across a pond of water.

255

As the rock skipped through the air, it clipped one or two turkeys in the head just hard enough to knock them out. The other turkeys moved aside in a predictable manner that we called "the parting of the turkeys." This left the unconscious turkeys in clear view. My brother jumped the fence, picked them up, and tossed them over to me. I put them in our cart and ran for cover in the fencerow. While the turkeys were unconscious, we carefully removed a few of their large tail and wing feathers. By this time, the turkeys were regaining consciousness so we hurriedly returned them to the flock. Our supply of feathers for Indian headdresses had been replenished and the day had been successful. About the third time we replenished our feather supply in this efficient manner, we got caught by the turkey farmer. He paid a visit to Mom and Dad. When they had finished with us, we had lost interest in Indian headbands with perfect feathers.

The First Day I was Glad to Be a Girl

Hunting and gathering was instilled in us at a very young age. So, in the spring, when the creeks were full, my brothers and I went fishing. Around the middle of March, a fairly large fish called white suckers swam up the little creeks to lay their eggs. They were huge fish sometimes reaching two feet in length. They were full of bones but very tasty when rolled in cornmeal and fried.

We caught them with our hands by reaching back under the creek banks. Sometimes we speared them with a sharpened stick. If there were lots of fish in a shallow pool above a small waterfall, I would stand at the edge of the waterfall and tell my brothers to wade in and chase the fish to me. As they crossed the waterfall, I hit them in the head with a long "ugly club." We would find "ugly clubs" on our walks in the woods. They were dead pine limbs with large, heavy knots on the end. These methods of fishing were, of course, against the law; so we always kept one eye on the road to make sure the game warden didn't sneak up on us.

Year after year we patiently waited for our Easter break from school. That time of year was perfect for suckers to swim up the creek to spawn. These occasions were fun, but they were not any more memorable. One day, however, turned out to be locked in my memory forever.

It was a cool, sunny March day with a slight breeze in the air. I was wearing a thin jacket over a tee shirt with the sleeves torn off. I tucked my long blonde hair up under a baseball cap. My brothers and I headed for the creek. We worked our way up the creek stopping at each little waterfall to knock a few fish in the head. We got down on our knees and reached way back under the banks, hooked our fingers into a fish's gills, and threw it out onto the grass.

As the morning hours passed, I got hot in my jacket, took it off, and tied it around my waist. After an hour or so of fishing, I felt the sun burning my shoulders that had not been exposed since the previous summer. Suddenly, we came up on a large pool of fish with a small waterfall just below it. I placed myself at the waterfall with my "ugly club" and told my brothers to wade in and chase the fish to me. I started knocking fish in the head, grabbing them, and tossing them on the creek bank. Including the fish we had already caught, I soon had about two dozen nice-sized suckers.

I was going for more fish when I caught a glimpse of a car turning into the lane that led to the farm where we were fishing. It was the game warden. I yelled to my brothers to grab some fish and run for the mountain. They didn't grab anything. They just took off in several directions as hard as they could run.

The game warden was closing in on me so I jerked my jacket from around my waist, threw the fish in it, and ran for the hills myself. There was no way I was going to leave my fish, but I found it difficult to run with such a heavy load. The game warden pulled his car up beside me. He had a woman in the car with him. She was about his age and next to him like she was his girl friend.

"Boy, where'd you get those fish?" he asked. "Don't you know it's against the law to fish with your hands?" I said, "Yes, I know it's against the law." "Give me those fish," he ordered in a hateful voice. Just then the woman punched him in the ribs with her elbow and said, "That's a girl you're talking to like that." The game warden looked again and asked, "Are you a girl?" I hesitated a moment and said, "Yes." I was thinking it might be a good thing to be a girl in a situation like this.

Sure enough, when I said yes, the game warden said, "Take your fish and go on home, and don't let me catch you fishing with your hands again." I said, "Yes, sir." I didn't go fishing again until the next day.

In late April we hunted for morels, or "toadstools," as we called them. We had our favorite places to hunt these delicious little mushrooms. We found them under the old apple trees that were abundant in the Hopkins Gap area. We always arrived home with our bounty and Mom would cook whatever we brought in for the next meal. Gathering food for the family table was a joyful part of my childhood.

Playing Period

With ninety-nine first cousins, there was never a time when I didn't have anyone to play with. Some of my cousins lived very close to my home, and I could play with them after school and on Saturdays. Other cousins lived four or five miles away across Little North Mountain in Hopkins Gap. Since we went to church in Hopkins Gap, I played with those cousins on Sunday afternoons.

I always preferred playing with the boys because the girls played games about having babies and having periods. I did try to play with them for a while. There was Cousin Suz, Cousin Sis, and several of the tow-headed Conley girls. We were all about ten years old, skinny, and underdeveloped. One Sunday we were all hanging out along the creek when Cousin Suz suggested we all pull our pants down and show each other our private parts. I told them to go first so they all pulled down their pants, and we all took a look from afar. There wasn't a pubic hair in sight. Then they told me to take my pants down, and I refused. That was a dirty trick as I look back on it, but I thought the game was stupid anyway.

I knew I wasn't playing with those girls anymore when they showed up at the creek with a stolen box of kotex and a can of pickled beets. They asked me to join in to play "period" with them. My stomach turned when I thought about wearing a kotex soaked in beet pickle juice between my legs, and when I think about it today, my stomach still turns. I also thought the vinegar in the beet juice would probably burn and God knows what the pickling spices might have done to my private parts. I told them I didn't want to play "period," but I hung out with them while they poured red beet juice on a kotex and put it in their pants for the rest of the day. As I recall, I walked away from that game with no regrets, and I never played with them again. Mom had already told me about periods, and I didn't feel the need to practice.

Cousin Herman in the Bottom

We almost always went to Grandma Molly's house for Sunday dinner. Her house sat on a bank at the bottom of a tall ridge. The "BIG" road ran in front of the house. On the other side of the road was a narrow ledge just wide enough for the outdoor toilet. Aunt Vernie's log cabin was a little farther down on the toilet side of the road.

The bank behind the toilet and Aunt Vernie's house dropped off sharply into a large flat area that we called the "Bottom." It was a wooded area with open spaces of grazing meadows for cows and sheep. The slopes near Grandma Molly's house were covered with old apple orchards with broken and jagged limbs on which a stray apple could be found in the fall. On the opposite side, the Bottom butted up against Little North Mountain. Oscar Crawford's family lived right at the edge of the mountain, and up the main hollow behind Oscar's house was the old Jesse Craig house. The old one room school, White Hall School, stood abandoned a short distance from Oscar's house.

The Shoemaker River ran through the middle of the bottom and was fed by several branches that drained from the surrounding hollows during and after big rains. I used to put on an old belt and stick one of my wooden knives that I had carved out of soft pine in it and pretend that I was Tarzan. I ran and jumped the creek branches stopping occasionally to scoop some water with my cupped hands and drink. I would listen carefully for "elephants" and "lions" and start off running again.

There was one very special place in the Bottom, where the river turned sharply to the right. Over time it had cut into the bank and revealed the roots of a huge red maple tree. The roots curled out over the water and provided me a cozy, private place to sneak off to and spend some quiet time. I sat there for hours daydreaming as the creek flowed beneath me. I fantasized about being the only child and getting all my parents' attention. I wanted to be a hermit when I grew up, build a one-room cabin deep in the Allegheny Mountains, and live like a wild person. I pictured how I would look with long, uncombed, stringy hair. I would never take a bath or brush my teeth. I would live off the land and eat with my hands. I thought about the future and how I wanted to leave my family and live in strange places. I wanted to grow up, get a job to make some money, and work my way across the country. I wanted to speak French and travel around the world. I wanted to become a writer and marry John Mason. He was a very handsome local boy that all the girls wanted to marry. I never let him know that I was interested too, because of my pride. He always vowed that he would never get married. I just played it cool around him. He could draw good pictures, and I fantasized about me being the one to capture his heart and marry him. We would own a large home. I would write books while he painted and we would be rich and happy. John, in fact, did not get married until he was well into his fifties.

The bottom was a great place to spend time with my cousins. We occasionally played ball in the meadows, but most of the time we created our own new games to play.

One of my favorite playmates was Cousin Herman. He was a little round-faced person with green eyes and straight brown, out-of-control hair that tumbled down over his forehead. On school days, he would grease his hair so it would stay in place. One morning on the way to school we heard a loud noise in the back of the school bus. Everybody turned around, and Herman, being who he was, said, "Don't worry that was just my hair falling down."

He was a year or two younger than I was, but I admired him because he refused to follow rules placed on us by our parents, the church, or the community. He embodied the wild child in all of us. Herman was the natural-born, creative leader among our group. He constantly awed us with his brave new ideas for fun.

Herman's hands were covered with large "seed" warts--which is what he called them and occasionally he would take a notion to remove some of them. I remember several Sunday afternoons when we followed him all around to watch him remove his warts.

Herman was very dramatic about everything he did. He told us that he had chosen this day to get rid of his warts. I figured he was going to use one of Grandma Molly's rituals, but I also noticed a far away, stoic look in his eyes as he told us to follow him into a little grove of trees. He sat down on a rock and told us to sit down with him. He reached into his pocket and pulled out a new single-edged razor blade wrapped in its protective cardboard and a can of snuff. I asked him where he got the snuff, and he said, "I stole it from Grandma Molly." There was no sign of fear or remorse. We were all shocked but very proud to be with him.

Herman opened the can of snuff and sat it on the rock beside him. He took the cardboard off the razor blade and paused for effect just before he placed the sharp edge of the razor blade against a large wart on top of his hand. The expression on his face was the same as soldiers going into battle—a determined frown on his brow, tight lips, and flared nostrils. He looked around at all our faces as he very gently but firmly began to slice the wart. Blood flowed profusely and ran off the top of his hand. He became our

261

protector and told us to be careful not to get his blood on us because we would get warts from it. He shook off the excess blood, picked up the can of snuff, and placed a glob on his bleeding wart. The wart was far from being sliced off his hand.

Once he got the bleeding stopped, he asked us to follow him to another location where he repeated the ritual. This drama went on all Sunday afternoon until Herman's biggest warts were gone from his hands. I felt terribly ill as I followed Herman around watching him cut himself and bleed. I knew this was not something Mom would approve of, but I was caught up in the wart-removing event and just couldn't walk away until it was over. I was also sure that Herman wanted some of us to get sick and walk away, so I had to hang in until the finish.

Aunt Lena who lived at Grandpa Austin's house raised chickens. She ordered her baby chicks or, as she called them "peepies," by mail. Once in a while she would order five hundred chicks that came in cardboard boxes with "peepie" straw in the bottom. Cousin Herman, my brothers, and I carried the "peepie" straw into the Bottom along with a skillet and a wooden keg that Herman stole from Aunt Vernie. We were going to make "moonshine."

We built a fireplace with river rocks and filled it with "peepie" straw. We gathered buckets of polk berries, put the skillet on the fireplace, lit the fire and boiled the polk berries until all the juice came out of them. We poured the juice into the keg that we had set in the creek.

We didn't pay attention because we were having so much fun, but when it was time to go back to Grandma Molly's house, we had polk berry juice all over our clothes, on our hands, and in our hair. The whipping we got that Sunday was one for the record books.

Many times Herman challenged me and my brothers, Larry and John, to invent a way to make him cry. As the challenges grew more difficult, our other cousins, Jennings and Tater, joined us. On one occasion, we found some old car tires and told Herman to fold himself up inside the tire. We stood the tire on its tread and rolled it down through the apple orchard with Herman tucked inside. Of course, the tire eventually slammed into an apple tree. Herman gathered himself up from the ground and announced to us, "That didn't hurt."

During the weekdays, Larry, John, and I tried to come up with new ideas and ways to make Herman cry the next Sunday afternoon. We made a sled out of old boards that we found around the barn and chicken house. We just helped ourselves to nails, hammers and saws that were always accessible in the shed. Using a picture from the Sears and Roebuck catalog and a little help from Mom, we built a wooden sled. We greased the runners with "fat back" so they would slide easily.

The following Sunday, we begged Mom and Dad to bring the sled to Grandma's house with us. They had no idea about our plan for the sled. After Sunday dinner, we quickly headed out to the Bottom. Herman was eager to try our new strategy to make him cry. We placed the sled on one side of a large blackberry patch filled with briars, rocks, burdocks and a wide variety of unnamed things that would scratch, puncture, and mar. We took a rope and tied a rock to one end and tied the other end to the sled. Herman stretched out on the sled, laughing like a hyena; and with a white-knuckle grip, he held on. We threw the rock across the briar patch, ran to the other side and pulled the sled through the briars with Herman hanging on for his life. He laughed harder as the briars, burdocks, limbs, rocks and other dangerous protrusions scratched his arms and legs, banged his body, and stuck in his hair and on his clothes. We pulled him a few feet then stopped to see if he was crying. He just laughed harder, so we pulled him some more. When we finally got him to the other side, he was bleeding, his hair was full of burrs, and his clothes were torn; but he was not crying.

Herman lived with his grandmother, Aunt Vernie, so when he got home, she whipped him for the burrs in his hair and his torn clothes. He told her he fell out of a tree and saved the rest of us from a major whipping. Any adult could whip us, so Aunt Vernie would have thrashed the whole pack of kids if she had any idea what we had been doing.

Our desire to make Herman cry was a driving force in our creative little minds. The next effort was to have him climb a walnut tree while we stood on the ground and threw large green walnuts at him. We had recruited a couple of extra boys to help us this time. Cousins Jennings and Tater joined us on this particular Sunday.

A picture I will never forget is Herman shimmying up the tree trunk with green walnuts hitting him so hard on the back of his head that the hulls split into small pieces and went flying through the air. Jennings and Tater were a year or so older and stronger, and they did most of the walnut throwing. Herman laughed harder as the walnuts hit the back of his head, so I suggested we set the tree on fire and smoke him out.

I had a pack of matches with me, because at this time I was sneaking my daddy's cigarettes or buying my own when I had the money. Jennings, Tater, and my two brothers thought a fire would do the trick. Jennings took the matches and lit a fire right under the walnut tree.

The fire, of course, got out of control and burned a rather large patch around the tree and began to spread into the woods.

We started stomping the fire, and Tater's britches caught on fire. We knocked him down and beat his britches with some brush until the fire was out before he was burned. Then we grabbed some tree branches and started beating the fire out before it spread further into the woods. Herman climbed down out of the tree and helped us put the fire out. He still didn't cry.

Finally, one Sunday afternoon we met Herman's challenge. I suggested that he climb a tree and let us chop the tree down with him in it. Jennings and Tater had become even more interested in bringing this challenge to fruition, so they were with us once again. Everybody, including Herman, thought that was a great idea so we went to the woodshed, got an axe, and off to the bottom we went.

We located a small white oak tree about eight inches in diameter at the cutting level. Herman climbed up, and we started chopping.

There were four choppers—Jennings, Tater, my brother, Larry, and me. My brother John was with us but he was too small to handle the axe. The four of us took turns chopping until the tree was just about to fall. Herman was laughing and teasing us the whole time we were chopping—what seemed like hours—until the tree fell. Jennings would swing the axe so many times then turn it over to Tater. When Tater reached his limit, he turned the axe over to me because I was the next oldest. Then Larry took his turn.

We were young and unskilled tree choppers, so we didn't notice a tall pine tree next to the white oak. We didn't know about making a tree fall in a chosen direction by cutting it on one side or the other. So, the white oak fell, slowly and gently, at first, over into the pine. When the dust settled, Herman was pinned at the stomach by the trunk of the white oak crossing a large limb of the pine. He stopped laughing. We all stopped laughing. A heavy silence fell across the bottom.

The situation was suddenly serious. Although Herman was not seriously injured, he was trapped in such a way that he couldn't get his feet placed to get any leverage to escape. His legs were dangling, and I am sure he felt totally out of control of his destiny. Herman sweated; we sweated. Now time went by very fast it seemed, and we were very scared. I climbed the pine tree to try to dislodge Herman. Jennings and Tater climbed the tree to try to help him. Nothing we did helped the situation—now Herman was really crying!!!!!

As I started to climb down out of the pine after my second trip up to help Herman, I looked up the hill and saw Aunt Vernie coming toward us. I could tell by the way she was walking that she was madder than a wet hen. Her bonnet strings were flopping in the breeze indicating the speed she had gathered coming down the hill, and her arms were swinging except when she was shaking her right forefinger at us. She was a woman on a mission. The sight of this furious woman with community permission to give me a whipping scared me so bad I fell out of the tree and landed on my back. I couldn't breathe! The wind had been knocked out of me. At that very moment, Aunt Vernie arrived on the scene. I grabbed her apron with one hand. She saw me pointing to my chest and struggling for my breath. She slapped me up beside the head, and my breath came back immediately.

Aunt Vernie surveyed the situation and walked up the hill to get my dad and Uncle Charlie. I saw her stop in the bushes and break off a switch to use on us. Dad and Uncle Charlie accompanied Vernie back to the fallen tree where Herman was held captive.

They finally got Herman out of the tree after quite a struggle. Once Herman was on the ground and they found no broken bones or bad cuts, they shared Aunt Vernie's switch for a round of whipping. Aunt Vernie whipped Herman, Dad whipped each of us, and Uncle Charlie took care of Jennings and Tater. We all cried, and the challenge to make Herman cry was finally over.

Young Pornographers

My cousins and I shared bawdy little songs taught to us by daring adults or older children. One of my favorites to sing to the younger children was about Lulu.

> *Lulu had a steamboat, steamboat had a bell.*
> *Lulu went to heaven, steamboat went to _____.*
> *Hello, operator, give me number nine.*
> *If you disconnect me, I'll kick you in the _____.*
> *Behind the refrigerator, there was a piece of glass.*
> *Along came Lulu and cut her little _____.*
> *Ask me no more questions, I'll tell you no more lies.*
> *That's what Lulu said, just before she died.*

This was one of the first times I actually talked "dirty." I was probably about five years old when I first heard about Lulu. It

266

was so much fun to sing this song to my younger cousins just beyond the hearing range of adults. They roared with laughter as I reached each blank in the song and moved to the next verse.

Another little song we used to sing was:

> *"The black cat shit in the shavings,*
> *The black cat shit in the shavings,*
> *The black cat shit in the shavings,*
> *And covered it up with his paw.*
>
> *The yellow cat thought it was raisins,*
> *The yellow cat thought it was raisins,*
> *The yellow cat thought it was raisins,*
> *And rammed it back in his jaw.*

Even as a child, I had a good memory for limericks and tongue twisters. These provided entertainment for us before television came to our houses. Some of my favorite limericks were:

> *There was a man from Boston*
> *Who drove a little Austin*
> *He had room for his ass*
> *And a gallon of gas*
> *And his balls hung out*
> *And he lost them.*

> *Went around the mountain*
> *Going ninety miles an hour*
> *When the chain on my bicycle broke*
> *Landed in the grass*
> *With the sprocket up my ass*
> *And my tits were playing Dixie*
> *On the spokes.*

Peggy Ann Shifflett

> Went downtown to see Aunt Lucy,
> Gave her two cents to see her pussy,
> The hair was so black
> I couldn't see her crack
> So, I made Aunt Lucy
> Give my two cents back.

> There was a woman from Alabama
> Who screwed herself with a banana.
> The banana broke,
> Her gut got choked
> I hope she dies, godammer.

Tongue twisters were fun as well as frustrating. We got a lot of laughs from these:

> How much wood could a woodchuck chuck,
> If a woodchuck, could chuck wood?

> Sick sister Sally slit a sheet
> A sheet sister Sally slit
> If sick sister Sally slit a sheet,
> How many sheets did sick sister Sally slit?

> Betty bought some butter,
> But she said, "This butter's bitter."
> If I put this in my batter,
> It will make my batter bitter,

But if I put in some better butter,
It will make my batter better,
So Betty bought some better butter
And made her batter better.

A skunk sat on a stump,
The skunk said the stump stunk
The stump said the skunk stunk
But after the skunk sat on the stump
Both the stump and the skunk stunk.

Spiders and Grasshoppers

Growing up was filled with questions about what one would do in life and whom one would marry. To get answers to the questions we used what we found in our natural environment. To get a glimpse of a future marriage partner, we used a spider known as "granddaddy-long-legs" or "daddy-long-legs." The ritual consisted of slapping the ground next to the spider and then asking, "Granddaddy, granddaddy, where is my true love?" The spider then lifted his right front leg and pointed in the direction of the future true love's house.

The unique talents of the "granddaddy-long-legs" were not confined to revealing the location of future marriage partners. During a Sunday afternoon ball game, granddaddy-long-legs were very helpful. Usually we had only one ball among an entire community of children; and, when an especially strong batter hit the ball into the woods or the brush surrounding the ball field, the game was over until the ball was found.

If, during the hunt for the ball, a granddaddy-long-legs was found, the search was simplified by placing the spider in the palm and asking "Granddaddy, granddaddy, where is the ball?" The spider would raise one of his long legs and point. All the children

269

would run in the direction indicated and, believe it or not, many times the ball would be found in that direction.

The grasshopper was another useful insect when we needed to find a lost ball. We would pick one up and put it in the palm of our hand. Grasshoppers always spit a big drop of what we called "tobacco juice" in our hand. We let him jump away and then took the opposite index finger and hit into the puddle of brown liquid. Someone watched to see the direction of the biggest splash. Then we hunted for the lost ball in that direction. We usually had success finding our ball after we negotiated the "true" direction of the biggest splash.

Not only did I use age-old traditions to determine my future husband and to find a lost ball; but, new life lessons were learned as I interacted with nature in my hobbies. I was always collecting things. I followed the electrical workers as they installed the first electrical line in our part of the county in the early 1950s. They dropped little balls and bits of solder as they installed the lines. I collected these and embedded them into the handles of my homemade slingshots. I pretended they were gold and silver.

I gathered tree fungi that I called "squirrel porches" because I imagined squirrels sitting under them when it rained. I saved these woodsy-smelling artifacts in my half of the bedroom I shared with my sister. We literally had to draw a line down the middle of the room and then down the middle of the bed and dare each other to cross the line. We were so different. She collected movie star pictures and dolls for her side of the bedroom. She hated my collections. She claimed they made the room smell bad.

It was a tragedy that two people, so different, had to share the same bedroom to keep from freezing to death in the winter. Nothing I did was right. I didn't like to get into the cold bed so I would jump in and stand on my hands and knees until the sheets warmed up a little. Brenda got in bed and lay in a fetal position to warm the bed. Then she yelled for Mom and told her I was holding the covers up off of her so she couldn't get warm. Mom tried to explain that I would warm up quicker if I lay down on the bed. I didn't believe her and continued to get in bed my way.

One particularly cold night I was standing on my hands and knees to warm the bed, and Brenda yelled for Mom. She came into our room, madder than a hornet. I saw her look around the room for something to use as a paddle on me.

Her eyes wandered over to the dresser and landed on a book I had been reading. She picked it up, jerked the covers off of me, and gave me about six whacks on the buttocks. "That'll teach you how to get in the bed," she said through clenched teeth. As she turned to put the book back on the dresser, she stopped and looked at the title. She went into hysterics as she read "Bull Dog Drummond Strikes Back." She laughed so hard she fell back on the foot of the bed. I didn't get the joke myself, so I thought she was the cruelest woman on earth to give me a nasty whipping and then laugh like a maniac. I decided right then I would hate her forever.

Dad got out of bed and came in to see what was happening. She showed him the title of the book she had just used to whip me. He didn't get the joke and told all of us to shut up so he could get some sleep. Up until her death, Mom reminds me of the time my "meanness came home to roost" as she puts it. "That was the perfect whipping" she brags, "You needed it, you got it with your own book, and the title was perfect—"Bull Dog Drummond Strikes Back."

Snake Skins and Butterflies

When I was about twelve or thirteen, I decided I wanted to collect butterflies. The inspiration came from the fact that butterflies were beautiful and always in motion. Even when they sat down, their wings stayed in gentle movement, opening and closing, as if they were contemplating their next flight. One day, as I was raiding a junk pile looking for bicycle parts, I found an old picture frame with the glass intact. It was the perfect enclosure for me to preserve and display my butterfly collection.

During the spring and summer months that followed, I devoted many hours to stalking, catching, killing, preserving and framing a variety of butterflies -- the monarch, the viceroy, the painted lady, the mourning cloak, the cabbage, the zebra, and many others. I concentrated most of my free time on completing my collection so that I could fill the empty picture frame. Although there were many more varieties of butterflies than my frame would hold, I wanted a full frame to display to my family and friends. I spent very little time learning about each butterfly that I captured. I knew them only by their colors and size.

As I continued my collection, I saw one butterfly that seemed to be different. It was more elusive; it flew higher and faster, darting to earth only briefly to drink from the creek or sit on a flower. It especially liked to fly around rugged mountain streams and light on mountain laurel blooms. I found a picture of this butterfly and identified it as the tiger swallowtail. It was the catch that would complete my collection, so I saved a space in the center of my frame for that final butterfly that would make my collection complete.

There were very few tiger swallowtails; they seemed to be rare in Hopkins Gap. But, when I spotted one, my heart started racing. I tried to net it in flight. I fell over rocks, slipped into the creek and bruised body parts too numerous to mention. Waiting for it to light, I stalked it, and crept around bushes to capture it. Time after time, the butterfly escaped, and I was never able to capture one by the usual methods.

Then, one day, a tiger swallowtail sat down on the road and a car hit it just enough to stun it. This was the opportunity I needed to complete my collection, so I rushed to pick it up. It was only slightly damaged. I finished killing it, preserved it, and filled the empty center of my frame. I closed the frame and sighed with relief that my collection was complete and that I could look at my butterflies anytime I wanted, at my convenience, in the comfort of my bedroom. I was especially proud of my tiger swallowtail. As time went by, my interests moved to other hobbies, and I did not look at my butterfly collection as often.

Some time later I looked at my butterflies and noticed that the colors on their wings were fading. As more time passed, I noticed that tiny little bugs were eating away at the butterfly bodies. The frame was sealed so the bugs were coming from within the butterflies and consuming them. The bugs were especially busy on the body of the tiger swallowtail. My prized possession, the most difficult to catch, was the first to disappear.

By the following spring, my butterfly collection was unrecognizable, and my sister was pressuring me to get it out of my bedroom. So, I dumped the frame, the remaining butterfly corpses, and the bugs into the garbage.

As the next spring rolled around, my wanderings in the woods led me to my next collection. I discovered a beautiful, fresh snakeskin lying near a rock pile. I learned later that it was a copperhead snakeskin. Snakes' skins are easy to find in the spring and early summer months, so I found blacksnake skins, garter snake skins, and rattlesnake skins. One of my uncles was a truck driver, and he brought me a diamond back rattlesnake skin from Florida. It was my most prized snakeskin.

I preserved the snakes' skins by carefully handling and framing them. I had time between discovering each snakeskin to study the snake that had shed it. I expanded my knowledge of snakes, and to this day, given the opportunity and a captive audience, I can give long and tiresome lectures on many types of snakes.

I shared my collection with my three brothers and my like-minded friends for at least a full year. The skins did not seem to fade, and there were no bugs that lived inside to come out and consume them. The only threat to them was my sister. Eventually, she cleaned our bedroom and hid my snakeskin collection. I assumed she had thrown it away. I cried and screamed at her for several months before forgetting about the skins. Years later she told me she had only hidden them. She did finally throw the snakes' skins away after I forgot about them.

Over the years I came to realize that unlike butterflies, the skin is the part of the snake that is left behind as it lives its life in the woods and meadows of this earth. I didn't have to climb over rocks and creeks and bruise myself to capture snakes' skins. As each snakeskin inspired me to learn about its donor, I acquired several gifts that have remained with me throughout my life. The first gift is the knowledge of snakes that I use to bore friends held captive. The second gift is the knowledge that all creatures that cross my path, human or animal, leave something with which I can enrich my life. The third gift is the knowledge that creatures, human or animal, cannot be collected because the process of collecting and holding kills the very features that make them worthy of collecting in the first place.

Working for Wages

When I was about eleven years old, I decided I had to start making some money if I was going to be anything when I got older. Feeding Aunt Goldie's pig for two years for five dollars and washing her dishes all week for a quarter was not amounting to a lot of money. I asked Mom if I could hire out with the local farmers to shock wheat, barley, and corn, or to help with the threshing. She said I could, so I recruited my younger brothers and off we went to make money. The first job we got was shocking wheat for our neighbor, Lloyd Myers. He paid us twenty-five cents an hour and fed us dinner.

I loved the work and the money, but mainly I loved the dinner. When we went in to eat, I couldn't believe the table. There was roast beef, fried chicken, green beans, mashed potatoes, fresh fruit salad, pies, cakes, and gallons of sweet iced tea. I can still see the sweat running down the outside of my iced tea glass. As soon as I drank it down some, around came Fannie Jane, Lloyd's wife, and filled it up again. I thought I was in hog heaven.

The second job we found was shocking corn. We approached the farmer and asked him if we could shock his corn for pay. He said, "It's a lot of corn. Are you sure you can do it?" We said yes and got started immediately. It took us three days to finish the job. While we worked, we guessed how much money he would give us for such a fine job. I convinced my brothers that we were doing a good job and would make a lot of money. I was sure the farmer would appreciate our efforts and pay us three dollars each.

At the end of the third day we approached him and told him the job was done. He walked through the corn shocks with us and bragged about our work. He reached into his pocket, pulled out three quarters, and laid one in each of our hands. He must have seen the shock on our faces as we held our hands out for more pay. He just turned and walked away.

My brothers never forgave me for misleading them into believing we would make three dollars each. I was furious with the farmer. My brothers and I often talked about that hard job we did for a quarter each, and said to each other, "He'll get what's coming to him someday." Many years later, that farmer contracted cancer and suffered a long hard death. One of my brothers kept up with the news of his condition, and when I would return home for a visit, he reminded me that the man was "gettin' his due."

I learned an important lesson with my second job, and from that day forward, I negotiated the pay scale before I did the work. We continued to work for the farmers around home, and I always told them up front we would work for a quarter an hour. We worked very hard, and between farm jobs, I looked around for more work.

I collected bicycle parts from junk piles and made "new" bicycles that I sold for $7.50 to other children in the community. My cousin Randy helped me with this project. He worked in a tire repair store, so he was able to take my inner tubes and patch them for me. Some of the tubes had more patches than tube when he finished with them. He laughed when he brought home a tube with twenty-three patches, but it held air when I blew it up.

There was an old mill across the hill from our house. It was called Stultz's mill. The miller, Old Mr. Stultz, was bent nearly double and walked with a cane. His favorite thing to do all day was sit on the front porch of his mill and greet people as they drove by. He had a little store in the mill with cigarettes, candy, and other small items. Sometimes my brothers and I would go down there to buy candy or an occasional pack of cigarettes. That's how we spent our earnings from the farm work--so much for me saving for the future.

One day Mr. Stultz was talking about being old, and he told us that there was one thing he wanted to see just once more before he died. I asked what it was, and he said, "I would love to see the water come down muddy creek, fill up my mill race, and make that old wheel turn one more time." I asked, "Mr. Stultz, what would it take to make that happen?" He thought for a minute, then he said, "Well, I would have to clean all the dirt that's settled in the race, so the water could flow through it. Over the years, it's clogged up."

I saw an opportunity to hire myself out right then. I offered my brothers and myself to clean out his millrace for him. He said, "It's a lot of work. I'm not sure you all can do it. But I'll pay each of you ten cents an hour to give it a try." I talked the offer over with my brothers and they agreed it would be a good job.

We started at the point where the millrace branched off from Muddy Creek. We raked and dipped mud out of the bottom of the race and threw it on the bank. The water began to inch its way into the race. We saw progress so we worked harder. The first day we got about one-fourth the distance of the race, about one quarter of a mile, and we each had earned sixty cents. Of course we got thirsty with all that work so we started a drink tab at the mill store. By the end of the day, we had thirty cents left from our wages. We bought a pack of cigarettes and smoked as we walked across the hill toward home. When we reached our fence, we hid

276

our cigarettes in an old stump, broke out a pack of gum to kill the smell, and continued on home.

That night a thunderstorm came up and poured rain on our remaining cigarettes. We were sad we had lost our smokes, but we knew where we could get some more. The next day we went back to work cleaning the millrace. I don't have to tell you, but we repeated the same behavior that day. We were now almost completely done with the cleaning, and the water was creeping into the millrace on its way to turn the grinding wheel.

By the end of that week, we had the water to the wheel but there wasn't enough volume to turn the rusty old wheel. We had drunk a lot of soda, eaten candy bars, and smoked three packs of cigarettes including the ones from the pack that got wet. We had no money to show for our week's work.

Old Mr. Stultz thanked us for our effort. He seemed to enjoy our company as we hung around the store and would tell us unusual stories. He showed us a mark high up on the wall by the doorway with a number written beside it. "See that mark up there beside the door?" he said, "The tallest man in the world came in here one day." We stared at him in disbelief, "How tall was he, Mr. Stultz?" I asked. "Well let me show you," he said, "I got a ladder and marked where his head touched the wall. When I measured it later, it was eight feet and two inches." Long after Mr. Stultz died, and the mill burned to the ground, I read a story about the tallest man in the world. He was eight feet and two inches tall.

Learning the Rules for Living

Many of the rules for living were passed on to us through stories that also filled afternoons, evenings, and weekend hours with entertainment in the days before television. There were many great storytellers in Hopkins Gap. Aunt Goldie and Mom were famous for stories of witches. Uncle Shirley and Uncle Jim were among the greatest storytellers. Fortunately, I took the time to record some of their stories. Uncle Jim told wonderful stories about hunting, and Uncle Shirley was most famous for his stories about buried treasures and restless ghosts. When he told his ghost stories, we sat glued to every word. He acted out various parts and used appropriate facial expressions for the scary moments in the story.

He told us about a house that nobody lived in because it was haunted. One night, two brave young men decided to sleep in the house to see if there really was a ghost as everybody claimed. They hadn't been there long before they heard a noise. They checked around and found the noise was coming from the fireplace. They kept their eyes on the fireplace and saw a man's legs coming down the chimney, followed by his body, and finally his head. The first man came down the chimney followed by a second man, in the same slow way — legs, body, then head.

As soon as the two ghosts saw each other, they started to fight. The two men who had come to the house to sleep were very puzzled by these strange actions, so they said, "In the name of the Father, the Son, and the Holy Ghost, why are you fighting?" The ghosts stopped fighting and answered, "Years ago, before we died, we committed a robbery and buried a fortune beneath the stones of this hearth and now we'll never be able to rest until someone finds the treasure." After the ghosts disappeared, the men moved the rocks in the hearth and found an old iron cook pot filled with gold. They were rich, and the house was no longer haunted. People were able to live there again.

Another tale was about an old maid who lived in a little frame house. Every evening before retiring she lit a kerosene lamp and kept it burning all night. One night, shortly before midnight, she heard someone come up the steps, take the lamp and walk down into the cellar with it. In a short time the intruder came back upstairs, replaced the lamp and left. Each night the ghost reappeared and continued the same activity. After weeks of continuous fear, the old maid decided to follow the intruder and plead with him to leave her alone.

That night she followed him, and he stopped walking at a particular spot in the cellar. She mustered up enough courage to ask it: "In God's name, what do you want?" The ghost told her: "Get a shovel and dig at the spot where I'm standing."

The old maid, fearful and trembling, followed the ghosts' instructions and found several old rusty tins filled with gold coins. The ghost then said, "Now I can rest in peace. Four years ago I lived in this house, and two men came to rob me of my money. I wouldn't give it to them, and they killed me. I cannot get any rest until someone puts this gold to good use." The ghost never returned again.

Grandma Molly often told stories of restless souls who never left this earth because of unfinished business. There was one story she told me many times. "There was a man who moved a big rock that marked the boundary between his and the neighbor's property so he could steal more land. After he died, a headless man carrying a big rock was seen in the area, and he was always mumbling, 'Where shall I put it; where shall I put it?' This went on for many years until one night a drunkard was passing by and heard the ghost. The drunkard, who was braver than usual because of his condition, replied to the ghost: 'You stupid idiot, put it where you found it.' The ghost said, 'I've been restless for years ever since I moved the boundary rock and cheated my neighbor. Now I have the answer, so I'll be able to find peace at last.' "After that the ghost was never seen in the area again."

All these stories were scary, and entertaining; however, they also taught us the awful consequences of stealing. They made me think twice before I pilfered things that didn't belong to me.

Uncle Shirley told me about a place called Mine Hollow. The story was about a man who found a lead mine while he was hunting. He said the lead was streaming from the rocks, but he refused to let anyone help him locate the mine because of his greed. When he went back to the hollow alone, he could never find the mine again; but he hunted for it until he died. Uncle Shirley told me that you could hear strange noises and see strange happenings in

Mine Hollow. One hunter reported seeing a headless man coming toward him. When he shot the man, he just kept coming, and the hunter turned and ran. The hunter thought he had seen the ghost of the man as he continued his endless search for the mine.

Womanhood Arrives at my Door

I reached puberty earlier than my other cousins. In fact, it's hard to believe now at my five foot two inches that at age eleven I was taller than cousins the same age as me. I never suspected that I wouldn't grow anymore after my initial growth spurt. I developed female attributes earlier than all the girls, and lost my childhood with the arrival of menstruation one summer day. What a shock that day was to me.

I had played cowboys and Indians with my brothers and the boys from over the hill. We would jump from the chicken house roof and out of the hayloft into the haystack. I usually wore shorts and an old tee shirt. Later that afternoon I told my mother I had started my period. She immediately told me to put on a dress and stay in the house with her. She said, "You are a woman now, and you can't help the farmers shock corn and wheat, and I am worried about you playing with the boys."

Since my girl cousins were playing "period" games, I had no choice but to hang in the house with the women everywhere we went including Grandma Molly's house and Uncle Shirley's and Aunt Ethel's house.

The Sundays that we didn't go to Grandma Molly's house, we went to Uncle Shirley's house for dinner. I stayed in the house with Mom, Aunt Ethel, and the other women while they cooked Sunday dinner. They gossiped and told stories about giving birth and how much sex they had to give their husbands while they cooked huge platters of fried chicken, pots of green beans, crocks of potato salad, large bowls of creasy greens, fried apples, and fresh homemade bread. Mom never told any stories about Dad and her, maybe because she knew I was listening and perhaps she didn't want to share that part of her life.

My job was to chop fresh fruit for huge quantities of fruit salad that was served over freshly made banana cake. It was during those talks in Aunt Ethel's kitchen that I heard about the pain I caused Mom as she was in labor with me from Monday until Friday. She described how Dr. Watson had to pull me out with forceps. Many times I heard vivid descriptions of her birth pains and the nasty bruises and holes I had gotten in my head from the forceps. No gory detail was spared. I just kept on chopping fruit as these stories were told over and over.

Perhaps the most memorable tales were the stories about who was having sex with whom and who "really" fathered so and so's baby. Mom would end that discussion with "When you run through a blackberry patch, how do you know which briar scratched the deepest." When there was a need to describe an especially promiscuous woman, Mom chimed in, "If she had as many dicks stuck out of her as she had in her, she would look like a porcupine."

Occasionally I would go sit with Uncle Shirley, Dad, and the other men in the living room while they waited for dinner to be served. Sometimes they were listening to a baseball game on the radio, breaking in every once in a while to tell a good story. When they were in the mood, I would get them talking about their days as moonshiners. I was always busy keeping up with all that was going on at both ends of the house.

When dinner was ready, the men were called to the table first. If there were enough men to fill the table, no one else was invited to eat until they were finished. The children were called in next for their dinner. The women served the men and children, going back and forth to the kitchen for more food and drink and washing used plates for the next shift of eaters.

After eating, the men had retired back to the living room where the belching and farting filled the room with "music." The kids went outside to play, and the women sat down to eat their dinner. I ate with the women. I was considered an adult since I had chopped the fruit. Lots of times there wasn't much left by the time we got to the table. I remember many times watching the women gnaw on chicken bones and partially eaten chicken legs left by the kids. They ate whatever was left after their families were fed. There was no complaining. I never understood why I had to leave the dinner table still hungry on these occasions.

When they finished eating what was left on the table, they faithfully washed all the dishes. By the time they finished, it was early evening and time to round up the kids and go home. Seething with anger, I would often mention to Mom that at least the men could help with the dishes. Her answer was always the same. She said, "That's the way it is."

Field Rabbits

Childhood was not easy for some of the kids in my community. They were called "field rabbits" after the little wild rabbits that are born in the fields and turned loose not knowing a family setting or who fathered them. These children were either orphaned at a very young age, abandoned, illegitimate, or victims of domestic violence.

Clusters of the field rabbits had the same father--single men who sewed their wild oats among the females of the community. One of my cousins, who was hearing and speech impaired, never married but had five children by five different men.

Realizing the situation of these children caused me to cry myself to sleep many nights worrying whether they were cold and hungry. I remember being at Aunt Stella's house one evening with Mom and Dad. We were playing upstairs and I saw the comforters on the kids' beds. They were ragged and dirty with the stuffing coming out the holes. Sadness washed over me and I went back downstairs. I was always looking at the way my cousins lived and comparing it to my life. I felt very fortunate to have a home and both parents.

Mom told me who had fathered each of the field rabbits. On Sundays when we all played ball in a field near the "BIG" road, I would see their fathers ride up the road past the ball field and wonder why they didn't wave to their children. I would break into tears for the "field rabbits." They, however, did not seem to notice their fathers driving up the road.

These homeless children didn't have a regular house to go to every day; yet they seemed to be the children of the community. There were several families in the community who provided for them. My two uncles Shirley and Jim were married to two sisters, Ethel and Hazel. Both these families provided most of the care for the field rabbits. Uncle Shirley and Ethel had nine children of their own, but always found room for two or three community children. Uncle Jim and Hazel had two or three extra children at their house in addition to their three children.

I once asked Uncle Shirley why he took care of these children. He told me about being orphaned at twelve years old and that his childhood was spent wandering from house to house. His strategy was to know when each house had meals ready so he could casually drop in to eat.

His wife, Ethel, had grown up the same way after being orphaned. He followed the tradition that had allowed him to survive as a rural homeless child by allowing the "field rabbits" to eat at his table and to share his children's beds in order to survive. Recently he told me that he never locked his door at night because he never knew when some young child would come in, go upstairs, and go to bed. "Ethel knew how much breakfast to make after she saw how many children rolled out of bed in the morning," he said.

The "field rabbits" did not consistently stay at any one house. They moved around according to their needs. When school was about to start, they knew which family would allow them to share school clothing or which family would offer to buy their school supplies.

Words cannot express how these children lived. Their goal was survival, yet they were not thieves or delinquents. They were like little adults taking care of themselves in a community that accepted them and supported them. There seemed to be little or no stigma attached to them. They were not called "field rabbits" to their face. It was simply a benevolent categorical name used to identify the group to whom you were referring. No one in the community made them feel bad. All the children played together and fought together like typical kids. Only once do I remember hurting one of these children. We were fighting about something and she told me my mother was a "fat hog." I was always sensitive about my mother's weight and her comment hurt me. So, armed with my information about her life, I glared at her and said, "At least she stayed at home and took care of her kids." She was devastated, and I learned just how close to the surface these children carried their pain. Never again did I use the information I had about these kids to hurt one of them.

Sometimes drunken husbands threw entire families out of the house into the night. My Aunt Dorothy and her six children were often wandering the roads at night looking for someone to take them in after her husband had beaten her. She slept in people's outbuildings with just a blanket and no bed. When she came to our house, Mom found her a place to sleep and put the kids in bed with us.

I remember many times awakening in the night to a foul odor. I immediately knew it was my cousins, Mildred and Grace, because they always smelled like cigarette smoke, grease, and dirty behinds. I have to admit I resented these intrusions; but after a while, the problem ended when social services started sending a social worker to our community. Her name was Eileen Frye, but everybody called her "Ole Miss Frye." She gathered up some of the field rabbits and all of Aunt Dorothy's six children and took them away. We never saw many of them again. Because when she drove through the gap, children seemed to disappear, she was locally known as the "old fare ye well woman."

Part Eight

SCHOOL DAYS

Who robs a scholar robs the public.
Anonymous

I was excited about my first day of school in September of 1947. Mom dressed me in the latest homemade feed sack dress, over homemade cotton flour-sack underpants and slips and walked me to the school bus door. My dresses were always bright colored, starched, and ironed to perfection. But as hard as she tried, Mom could not get the holes to close where the twine string had held the feed sacks together. The holes stood open and were spotted immediately by schoolmates. They made fun of my dresses causing me a lot of humiliation. I knew how hard my mother worked all day and then sewed our clothes into the night. I didn't want to tell her I was not going to wear feed-sack dresses, but having other kids laugh at me was no fun either.

I remember a dress that she made for me when I was in the seventh grade. It was bright yellow. I had mixed feelings about it when she was sewing it. I loved the color and wanted to wear it, but I knew what was going to happen. I asked Mom, "Would you wash the sacks a couple of times to see if you can get the string holes to go shut?" She washed the sacks several times but the holes were still there. So I asked her, "Is there any way you can sew the dress so the holes won't show." She answered, "I'll try."

When she finished the dress, it was beautiful. She made puffy sleeves and gathered the cloth around the waist. She attached narrow cloth belts to each side of the waist that tied in the back into a nice bow. She expertly put the holes along the seams on the sides of the skirt. I wore the dress to school and within the first hour, the smart alecks had pointed out the string holes along the seams. I was never comfortable in that dress again but I wore it because of the effort Mom had made.

The flour-sack underwear was also a problem for me. We always had a lot of fleas around our house because of the farm animals and dogs. The fleas got into the thick seams of my underwear, went to school with me, and started biting as soon as I got settled in my desk to learn something. I asked to be excused and tried to find the little bastards, but they hid in the seams. Occasionally I would catch one, but most often as soon as I settled into my desk again, out they came to chew on parts I couldn't scratch in public. There were many miserable early fall school days.

Facing Our Being Different

It wasn't long after school started when I discovered how the outside world just across Little North Mountain perceived Hopkins Gap. I was still a "Gapper" through and through, but it made me angry that I was automatically labeled a "Gapper" even though my parents had moved to the "preferred side" of Little North Mountain. Just because the "gap" bus picked me up on the way to school after it had crossed the mountain, I was considered a "Gapper" too. The "preferred side" of the mountain was the Shenandoah Valley between the Blue Ridge Mountains and the Alleghenies.

Living on the "preferred side" I noticed over time that there was drinking, fighting, thievery, and "good for nothing" people, but there appeared to be more forgiveness for these folks. There was another mountain community up the road from Hopkins Gap called the Peak. Those children came to school on the "Peak" bus and were called "Peakers." Even the "Gappers" looked down on the "Peakers," although in later years, I learned they were also my distant relatives.

Some days the "Gapper" children were even easier to identify than we already were by our feed sack clothes. This was

286

because of the way we sometimes appeared when we arrived at school. Even after the red flannel rag incident with Cousin Virgil, on occasion, I innocently arrived at school with a bandage or a poultice that my mother had applied to whatever was wrong with me.

I remember burning myself on the kitchen stove when I was in the fourth grade. Mom put apple butter on the burn and wrapped it with a clean white cloth. The brown apple butter came through the cloth, and I smelled like apples. The teacher asked what the brown stuff was; and, when I told her it was apple butter for my burn, she had a strange look on her face as she said she was worried about me getting an infection.

I learned to anticipate the humiliation I would suffer at school. My first reaction to the hurt was to play sick and stay home from school. That worked for a day after Mom saw me suddenly get well after the school bus passed our house. My next line of defense against humiliation was to resist getting on the school bus. I stood on the cement slab front porch and waved for the bus to go on. Uncle Shirley believed me the first time and drove on without me. I told Mom Uncle Shirley had forgotten to stop for me.

A day or two later, I tried the same tactic. Uncle Shirley had caught on to my trick. He just tooted the horn and Mom came out to see what he wanted. "Do you want that kid to go to school?" he asked, through the side window on the bus. Mom said, "Yes I do." I started to cry and flail my arms and legs. She picked me up, carried me to the bus, Uncle Shirley opened the door, and Mom placed my feet on the steps of the bus. The door closed behind me and there was no escaping.

By the time I reached third grade, I felt such shame about being from Hopkins Gap that I gave myself a different last name. Instead of signing my name as Peggy Shifflett, I wrote Peggy Morris on my homework papers. That worked for me one day since the teacher didn't know who Peggy Morris was when she checked my homework papers. She also never asked me why I was trying to be someone else. I begged Mom to help me change my name. She

287

didn't take me seriously as she was always busy around the house. She finally paid attention one day when I cried and asked her if I could change my name. She asked, "Why do you want to change your name?"

Suddenly I was afraid to tell her, so I said, "I don't like to write my name because the letters fall below the line." I was referring to the g's in Peggy and the f's in Shifflett. "I want a name like Susan Smith so I can write all the letters above the line." "You're being silly," she told me as she went back to getting supper on the table.

Surviving the Ride to School

Not only was my life hard at school but surviving the bus ride to school was no easy feat either. On the one hand I had to deal with the kids who resented me for not living in Hopkins Gap. On the other hand, I felt sorry for my poor cousins who came to school in dirty ragged clothes. My elementary school days were full of conflicted emotions.

As the "Gap" bus driver, Uncle Shirley was very cool and professional toward me so not to show partiality in front of kids on the bus. By the time the "gap" bus arrived at my house, it will filled with a large portion of my ninety-nine first cousins. All the children on the bus were related at least to the point of second cousins.

One of the most difficult things I had to put up with was their jealousy of my clean clothes, shined shoes, and clean hair that my mother curled every night. They used to rub their shoes on my socks so they would be dirty by the time I arrived at school, or rub various substances, including nose boogers, on my dress or coat. Most of the time I didn't know who smeared my dress or coat; however, I knew it was Lloyd Conley rubbing his shoes on my clean socks. We often glared at each other on the school bus.

I once told Uncle Shirley that I was going to start a fight on the bus and asked him what he would do. He said, "I'll whip you as quick as I would Lloyd Conley." I think he knew more about

288

what was happening in the back of the bus than I gave him credit for since he mentioned Lloyd Conley.

I had seen him whip Lloyd for being mean on the bus. He held him in the air by the underarms and knee-kicked his ass all the way up and down the school bus aisle. I pictured myself in that situation and decided to plan a different strategy to get even with Lloyd for putting his feet on my clean socks.

One morning I saw my opportunity. We had arrived at school and the kids in the front of the bus were standing up to get off the bus. Uncle Shirley's view in the rear view mirror was blocked. I had my huge (seemed huge to me then) literature book. Out of the corner of my eye I watched to make sure the rear view mirror was blocked from Uncle Shirley, raised my literature book, and slammed it on Lloyd Conley's head saying, "Don't ever touch my clothes again."

The book landed on his head with a heavy dull thud. I saw his neck bend under the attack. Any normal neck would have snapped. I was hoping to wound him forever. When it was over, he looked up at me with an innocent, "why did you do that" look on his face. I wanted him to cry and beg me never to hit him again. He was not moved to beg for mercy; it seemed from his appearance as if nothing had happened. However, he never rubbed his shoes on my clean socks again. He never sat close to me again. He avoided eye contact. I think he remembers the incident to this day. He still acts as if he doesn't know me. I like it that way.

Some of my cousins who rode the bus with me were very poor. My Aunt Dorothy's kids came to school in rags. Her son, Douglas, often wore bib overalls with holes in the seat and no underpants. It hurt me so bad to see other kids make fun of him as he got off the bus to walk into school. During the day, he walked around school trying to keep his back to the wall. I felt his shame and pain. One day he stopped coming to school and never came again. Shortly after that Old Miss Frye, the "old fare ye well" woman, drove through Hopkins Gap, and Douglas and his five siblings were taken away.

Douglas and his older sister, Genevieve, were in early adolescence so they were sent by the welfare department to the Lynchburg Training School. There they became the victims of the eugenics program carried out in the State of Virginia until 1979. They were sterilized so they could not produce children. Aunt Dorothy's four smaller children were placed in foster care and eventually adopted by various families. We never saw them again until in the last year, my sister made the effort to locate the two youngest. She found them in the state of Virginia not too far from Hopkins Gap.

Douglas and his sister stayed at Lynchburg Training School until they were eighteen years old and then they were sent back home to drift from house to house. In his late twenties, Douglas began to suffer from epileptic seizures. The seizures were so bad that he was constantly hurting himself. They seemed to occur mostly at night. Douglas would get out of bed and run through the fields bumping into barbed wire fences. He was almost constantly scratched and cut all over his face and arms. He couldn't hold a regular job because of his illness. He lived on a small social security supplement, thus he couldn't afford a home.

He loved children, and I could see that he wanted children of his own. He spent a lot of his money buying toys for the children around our house. He often said, "I would love to adopt a little boy or girl, but I will never be able to because I can't afford a place to live."

Douglas at least worked hard to have a sense of home. He saved his money and bought a medium-sized freezer. He asked Aunt Goldie if he could put it in her washhouse. She told him he could, and she and Mom helped him put up some extra garden vegetables that they gave him. He helped the local farmers and they occasionally gave him some meat. He put that in his freezer.

I always felt great sadness for Douglas-- a handsome man with jet-black hair and black eyes. He was a good, strong, hardworking man. He could have gotten married, but he didn't seem interested since he had been robbed of the ability to have children of his own by the laws in Virginia.

Douglas finally settled permanently in Aunt Goldie's washhouse. He had two prized possessions—his freezer and a twelve-gauge shotgun. One Sunday afternoon, in the spring of 1972, he wrote a long note to Aunt Goldie and Mom thanking them for being kind to him. He told Aunt Goldie he wanted Mom to have his freezer and my brother, John, to have his shotgun. He went upstairs in the washhouse, lay down on the bed, and put the gun barrel against his chest. He reached down, pulled the trigger, and ended his sad life.

Genevieve, Douglas' older sister, died just a few months ago. She lived on welfare and food stamps throughout her life. She also expressed great sadness because she could not have children of her own. She was a hard worker and in different circumstances might have been a good mother and a good citizen.

More About Grade School

The kids in my generation who arrived at school on the Hopkins Gap bus were the first to leave the White Hall one-room school that their parents had attended. They had a difficult time adjusting to the large elementary school where they were located in different rooms with different teachers.

My cousin, Sal, was in the same first grade as I was. Everyday she would pee in her desk. I would hear water dripping and look over the see her sitting above a large puddle under her desk. Then she would start crying, and the teacher, Miss Arlene, would yell at her for not asking to go to the bathroom. The teacher was unaware that Sal did not know what a bathroom was because she always used a chamber pot or an outside toilet.

In the first weeks of school, day after day Sal went to the bathroom in her pants while she sat in her desk. Day after day the teacher yelled at her. Finally, Sal stopped peeing in her pants. She survived first and second grades but dropped out in the third grade. I have kept my first, second, and third grade class pictures over the years. One day I was looking at the pictures again and realized that of the children who rode the "Gap" bus, there were only two left in school by third grade. Each one had their own story as to why they quit school at such a young age.

Cousin John's father took him out of school. He was an alcoholic and moonshiner, who wanted his son to ride the roads with him to deliver moonshine. Having his young son with him made him look more legitimate, and the police were less likely to stop him and search his car. This went on for years as John missed out on his education.

Cousin Herman and I were the only "Gap" bus children left in the third grade picture. Herman, as you already know, was a unique character who enjoyed life moment by moment. Somehow he dismissed or ignored all the humiliation from classmates and insensitive teachers until he completed the seventh grade.

There was a period of time, when I was in the third and fourth grades, that the teachers seemed obsessed with head lice, dirty elbows, dirty knees, and decayed teeth. Just about every week, they would line up all the kids and either check their heads for lice or check their teeth to see if they had brushed that day. The kids that came to the school from Dayton and Bridgewater seemed to get less scrutiny than the "Gap" kids or the "Peak" kids.

The fourth grade teacher used a pencil to check for lice on my head. She held the eraser end of the pencil and used the lead end to carefully lift a clump of hair around my ears making sure she never touched my hair as she searched for lice. She had her lips pursed and her nose wrinkled as if she had encountered something stinky. I wondered if she was scared a louse would jump off my head into her mouth.

The kids from Bridgewater and Dayton got a different search. She used her fingers to raise their hair and didn't spend a lot of time looking for lice. She should have checked their heads more carefully because everybody knows that head lice can jump from one head to another. Surely one or two lice jumped off the "Gap" and "Peak" kids heads onto the heads of the kids from the "preferred side of the mountain."

On tooth inspection days, she checked everybody's teeth and usually gave each of us a sample tube of Pepsodent toothpaste. One time she used my teeth to show the other kids why they needed to brush everyday. She had everybody line up and look in my mouth at my dirty teeth. She had no idea how cold my house was on winter mornings. I hated that teacher with her yellow-pencil pointer. I felt she was damned lucky I got all my clothes on in the cold house much less brush my teeth everyday.

The kids from Hopkins Gap probably knew what to do with the toothpaste, but they didn't have toothbrushes at home. So that afternoon on the bus trip home, they ate their tube of toothpaste. I was very ashamed to be riding with them on those days.

A public health nurse visited our school once in a while, and on one of these visits, the same fourth grade teacher took me to meet her in the school gymnasium. The teacher pulled her yellow-pencil pointer out of her hair and carefully lifted the hem of my dress to show the nurse my dirty knees. I felt as if everybody walking through the gym was looking at me.

The nurse just shook her head and said, "Um, Um, Um," as if my knees would never come clean again. I wanted to tell her that Aunt Lena, Dad's sister, was coming to visit us for a few days soon, and that she really knew how to scrub a kid's elbows and knees. She balled a washrag up in a knot and scrubbed. She often said as she added lye soap to her washrag, "That dirt's a comin' off if I have to take yer hide off with it."

Not all of my elementary school teachers had bad attitudes toward Hopkins Gap children. My fifth grade teacher, Mrs. Ralston, would often touch my hair in the morning and tell me how pretty it looked. Mom always washed my head and curled my hair nearly every night. Mrs. Ralston even told me she liked my feed sack dresses. She called me "sunshine" on the days when I wore my bright flowered feed sack dress.   It was these occasional moments that kept me going day to day.

I also had a sixth grade teacher that I really liked. His name was Mr. Morris, the same last name as Mom. He was handsome with black hair and brown eyes. Each day after lunch he read to us. By the end of the year he had read "The Five Little Peppers and How They Grew," "Heidi," "The Little Shepherd of Kingdom Come," "The Wind in the Willows," and many other books. I sat in the front row directly in front of him and facing him. I crossed my arms on my desk and propped my chin on them. I never took my eyes off his mouth. As he read, saliva gathered in the corners of his mouth, and made his voice very smooth and captivating. I imagined myself in the books he was reading. I never missed a word he read, and to this day, I remember those stories.

For several years as a part of our health class, the teachers gave lessons on the appropriate food to have at each meal. They put large charts up in the room showing the ideal breakfast that consisted of one over-easy egg, a slice of toast, two slices of bacon, and a glass of orange juice. Then they placed a chart next to the classroom door that listed all of our names with columns to place check marks if you had eaten the "ideal" breakfast. As you know by now, I had learned to lie to avoid humiliation.   Cousin Virgil's experience in first grade with the red flannel rag loomed ever present in my memory.

The reward for having the ideal breakfast every morning for a week was a gold star in the last column. If you didn't have the ideal breakfast, you got a red star.   Each day when I came in I checked the ideal breakfast while feeling guilty about the country ham, gravy, fried eggs, and oatmeal or various combinations of them that my mother had fed me that morning. However, at the end of each week I got a gold star.

Cousin Herman, on the other hand, never placed a check mark by his name. At the end of the first week of this exercise, one teacher asked Herman in front of the whole class, "Herman, why didn't you check the breakfast chart?" She seemed concerned that he may be hungry. All heads in the room turned toward Herman.

Herman answered, "What I eat for breakfast ain't on the charts so I had no reason to place a check by my name." "Well, Herman, what do you eat for breakfast?" asked the teacher. He innocently answered her, "I eat brown beans, fried potatoes, and canned peaches."

Herman's classmates began to snicker. The teacher seemed to start to get sick to her stomach as she said, "Those things are not breakfast foods." Then the whole class laughed at Herman including the teacher. It was as if that incident was the straw that broke Herman's back. He dropped out of school shortly thereafter.

Following the example of the teachers, the Bridgewater and Dayton kids treated the "Gappers" and the "Peakers" badly. At Christmas we drew names so each child would get a Christmas gift. A girl who sat next to me was from the Peak. She, like me, dressed each morning in a cold house and probably bathed once a week in a large zinc tub. Her face was not always clean when she came to school. Whoever drew her name one Christmas gave her a bar of soap and a washcloth. She opened her gift in front of the whole class. I noticed a few girls who were paying particular attention to her as she opened her gift. She was very hurt by the gift and cried off and on the rest of the day.

Experiencing all this humiliation, I often wondered why we were different from the other kids who went to school with me. However, I didn't stop watching and listening to how my kinfolks in Hopkins Gap lived their lives. Most important, I never hesitated to ask questions about our way of life. Mom, Dad, and my uncles patiently answered each question.

In the fifth and sixth grade, I had invented a new way to survive the humiliation of being a "Gapper." All the humiliating events in the earlier grades had made me a very angry girl. I came out of my shell and borrowed Grandpa Austin's mean persona to survive.

After I began reading Edgar Rice Burroughs books about Tarzan, I started to act like Tarzan. I took a gunnysack, turned it upside down, cut a neck hole and armholes, and wore it as an outfit when I played Tarzan at home. I practiced the Tarzan yell at home until I got it down perfectly, then I gave the yell on the playground at school. It was a blood-curdling scream.

During the summer between the fifth and sixth grades, I planned to become a wild person. I wanted to be like Tarzan and the apes swinging through the trees. I fantasized that the little gravel road between our house and Aunt Goldie's house would become overgrown with trees and vines. I planned to get a dark tan, with weathered skin and tough legs from shimmying up trees and going from tree to tree by swinging on the vines.

So when school was out, I stopped taking baths and combing my hair. This part of my plan didn't last long because Mom started to threaten me on a daily basis. "If you don't take a bath and comb your hair, I am going to do it for you," she promised. I went along for a few days more just to see if she meant what she said. I couldn't imagine her bathing an eleven year old who was starting to develop. Well, I was wrong. Mom captured me one day, sat me on the dining room table, and bathed me in front of my brothers and sister. She combed the "rats," as she called them, out of my hair with more gusto than she would have normally used. She still tells the story when she thinks she can embarrass me. I still daydream about being wild sometimes.

Other things were contributing to my new Tarzan persona. Cousin George was helping me build my muscles. Cousin Randy was teaching me to use a slingshot, shoot a gun, and make bows and arrows. He had also shown me how to carve knives out of wood to carry on my hip. I didn't carry these things to school but they sure made me feel stronger. I became the class bully.

Early in the fall when I was starting fifth grade, a girl who lived just across the hill from our house, called me a "Gapper." I was furious and eagerly invited her to meet me at the top of the hill that afternoon as soon as we got off the school bus. She said she

296

would. I couldn't wait to get home. I jumped off the bus, ran in the house and got one of Mom's peeling knives. Out the door I went to meet the girl at the top of the hill. Fortunately, for my future and probably the other girl's future, Mom came to the door and called me back. I hadn't taken time to change out of my school dress, and Mom got suspicious. She found the knife on me and asked, "What are you doing with this?" "I saw some creasy greens along the road," I lied. "I was just going to cut them for you." She responded, "Yeah, sure. Creasy greens don't come out until February."

By the time I was in the sixth grade I had beaten up all the boys in my class except Wendell Henkel, the milkman's son, and Jimmy Will, one of the smaller boys in class. I got away with all this fighting because I went home on the second bus. In other words, I had to wait at school for a while until my bus returned to get me. During this time, I invited one boy at a time to meet me at the trash bin behind the school. I always asked them in front of other boys, so they couldn't refuse.

The time came for me to invite Jimmy Will to fight. I asked him to meet me behind the trash bin, and we would fight it out. He knew my reputation, so I could see the fear in his eyes as he accepted my invitation. Sure enough, right after school was out, Jimmy and I retired to the trash bins.

We exchanged one or two blows, and one of my blows landed in his left eye. It immediately turned red and started to swell a little. He said he was finished fighting and declared me the winner. The next day he skipped school.

I bragged how he didn't come to school because he had a black eye. The next day he came back to school and sure enough, he had a black eye. Other kids asked where he got it, and he said he ran into a door. I wasn't about to let him tell that lie, so I challenged him again for that evening.

Meantime, Wendell Henkel, the nice son of the milkman, was paying more attention than I had thought. He walked up to me just after I had challenged Jimmy for a second fight and said, "I would like to fight you."

I was a bit shocked, but couldn't turn him down because he had asked me in front of the whole class. "Okay," I said, "I'll see you after school." He said, "No, I want to fight you right now." Class hadn't started yet, and the teacher wasn't in the room. I had no choice but to say yes. The fight was short. Wendell grabbed me, lifted me off the floor, and body slammed me into a desk. Everybody laughed and, in unison, said, "She finally met her match." I went back into my shell.

By the time I reached the seventh grade, I was so ashamed of myself and Hopkins Gap customs that I imagined that other kids laughed at the way I chewed my food. I stopped eating in the cafeteria. Instead I would duck out of the lunch line and stop by the candy store next to the cafeteria. I would buy a dime box of pretzels and a fudge popsicle. When everybody was in the lunch line, I would sneak back up the steps and eat my "lunch" on the back stairs of the school where no one could watch me chew.

This was both a good and a bad habit. It was good because I had fifteen cents left over from my lunch money. I used it to satisfy my obsession with pencils and paper. I would stop by the school supply store the next morning when I got off the school bus and spend, spend, spend. The fudge popsicle and pretzel habit was bad because eventually I started getting sick in class during the afternoon. Finally, school was out for the year, and I got over my shame of chewing by the end of the summer.

In the eighth grade I tried a new strategy to fit in with the Dayton and Bridgewater girls. They started asking me to let them copy my homework. I would arrive early at school, one or two of them met me at the front door, and I let them borrow my homework. One day my civics teacher called me up to his desk. He had just graded my homework paper and he wanted to show me what a good grade I had gotten. He bragged on my work and gave me a C plus.

One of the Dayton girls had copied that paper earlier in the morning. I thought we were going to be in trouble, so I watched to see if he called her up to his desk. Nothing happened. He finished grading and handed the papers back to the class. Later, at recess, I asked the girl from Dayton how she had done on her homework. She said, "I got an A. Thanks for your help."

The Curriculum Included Racism

In elementary school I learned to read, write, and do simple math, but I also learned to be a racist. I had been in close contact with only one black person prior to going to school. My Aunt Goldie and her husband owned a sawmill, and they were part of a program in the 1940's that released young prisoners into the community for rehabilitation. The prisoner would work for a family and, in turn, received room and board.

James Williams, a young black man in his mid teens, had been released from reform school where he was serving time for manslaughter. He had accidentally killed another boy when he was about twelve years old.

James lived with Uncle Rob and Aunt Goldie, worked hard, and shared the household with their four children. I used to watch him shave and wash his face and wonder if the black rubbed off on the washcloth. I asked him and he showed me that it did not rub off. He would cover his whole face with shaving cream and tease me with his black eyes and nose sticking out of the white foam.

We had a good time, and in no way did I learn to judge him as inferior because of his very dark skin color, but I did wonder if he was dirty because I remembered going to Harrisonburg with Mom on Saturdays to buy groceries. She took me to the department stores. Of course, as a little girl I had to go to the bathroom often, and I noticed two women's bathrooms. One sign on the door said "whites only" and the other said "colored." I noticed the "colored" bathroom looked dirty, dingy, and smelled like strong pee.

The water fountain that was marked for the "coloreds" was also dirty and messy looking. So, I asked Mom and she told me, "Well, 'colored' people are dirty and they don't smell good." Of course, I learned many, many years later that "colored" people had been hired to clean the "whites only" bathroom and water fountain, but had not been paid to clean their own bathroom and water fountain.

James grew up and changed from prisoner status to a fine upstanding citizen. He left my Aunt Goldie's house and moved into Harrisonburg. James soon met a girl, got married, and had six children. He became a diesel mechanic and has lived a very successful life. His children all went to college and held professional jobs.

James is still living, and he often came by Mom's house to say hello and buy some hog meat from her. His favorite meat is her canned puddin'. At first, his wife and children always stayed in the car, and Mom never thought to invite them in. Unfortunately, I never got to know them. The last time James came to visit, his great grandchildren tagged along with him into the house.

The "colored" children who came to my elementary school did not fare so well. I remember arriving on the school bus on the first day of school for several years to find a half dozen children standing and sitting on the front lawn of the school. Sometimes they sat on the front steps. I cannot recall how I found out who they were; but I know that some adult at the school told me they were Negro children and could not go to school with us. This was from 1947 to the early 1950's. So, of course, I went home to ask Mom about the situation.

I told her about these children who were not allowed in the school with us. She explained, "They are colored kids from the Ad Shoemaker family. They live in the Peak." "But Mom, I said, they are not colored. Their skin look's the same color as mine." She explained, "Yes, they are colored. You just can't see it. They have colored blood in their veins from their granddaddy, Ad Shoemaker. His grandmother was colored."

Those children were truly just like me. But because the school system in our country was segregated by race at the time, they were not allowed in the school building. They came to school day after day seeking an education, and day after day they were turned away to sit on the front lawn or the front steps of the school until the school bus could take them home in the afternoon. They were persistent. At the beginning of the school year for my first four years in school, they showed up on the first day trying to get an education.

So, it was at my school that I learned there was good skin color and bad skin color, and sometimes the color didn't have to show. I learned that even one drop of "Negro" blood made a person not worthy of learning to read and write even though it did not always show up in their skin. I still think of these children who are now my age. They were denied an education.

The black and white students that I teach now tend to think that racism and its effects are ancient history. I frequently use this story in my classes to illustrate that racism and its effects are still felt, at least by these half dozen people who spent their childhood seeking an equal chance to get an education and were turned away from my elementary school. They are now my age and younger.

Still Fighting Back

All my efforts to fight back at the humiliation of being a "Gapper" failed along the way. By the end of the seventh grade I had discovered the only safe way to express my anger. My cousins and I made the teachers into our scapegoats when we got together on Saturdays and Sundays. We talked about them and recited nasty little poems each of us trying to outdo the other one. Some of these that I remember are:

Teacher, teacher
I declare!
You've got bedbugs
In your hair!

301

Teacher, teacher
Number nine,
Washes her hair
In turpentine.

Teacher, teacher
Number eight,
Will never reach
The pearly gates.

Teacher, teacher number nine
Stuck her head in a bottle of wine.
The bottle broke, and cut her throat,
And that's the end of that old goat.

Teacher, teacher, I declare.
I can see your underwear.

While I was in school the time spent daydreaming was often the same time I was taking a test. If I didn't finish the test in the time allowed, I would very casually write at the bottom of the page:

Roses are red,
Violets are blue.
The test was over,
Before I was through.

I don't think this helped my long-term relationships with the teachers. Toward the end of the school year, we marked each day off on the calendar and recited a little poem:

Hark the herald
Angels shout.
Two more days,
And school is out.

Often the last day of school ended with a brave child writing the following poem on the blackboard for some school authority to find after we were gone for the summer:

No more pencils,
No more books,
No more teachers'
Dirty looks.

When I was about to enter my sophomore year of high school, word came that three schools-- Dayton, Mt. Clinton, and Bridgewater--were consolidating. All the kids in the ninth through the twelfth grade in these three schools were going to a new school—Turner Ashby High School.

I was scared to death. I asked Dad to drive me to Dayton to see the new school. It was huge. I was scared I would get lost in there and never find my way out. I didn't know it then, but Turner Ashby High School was the best thing that ever happened to me.

September came and it was time to go to the new school. I got on Uncle Shirley's bus and rode to the Mt. Clinton School that was now Mt. Clinton Elementary School. I got off the bus there and got on another bus to go to the new school. I didn't know it yet, but I immediately lost my label "Gapper," and I didn't realize it until much later.

When I got to Turner Ashby, I remained in my shell, sat in the back of the room, and did my school work. I thought by doing this I could bide my time until I was sixteen and then legally quit school. I had already made up my mind that I was quitting. The previous year the Mt. Clinton School started to offer a class in typing. Mom told me to sign up so I could get a job as a secretary when I graduated. I was excited about the possibility of not having to work in the sewing factories like my cousins, Ruby and Joyce.

Seventeen girls, including me, signed up for typing class, but the school only had sixteen typewriters. My name was taken off the list. I saw my only hope of getting a secretarial job when I graduated go down the tubes. I made up my mind then that I was going to quit school when I was sixteen. I didn't need a high school diploma to work in a factory and be a wife.

When the first grade reports came out after I started going to Turner Ashby, I was shocked out of my mind. I had three A's and two B's. There was some mistake. The teacher put the wrong grades on the report card. I was on the Honor Roll. One of my teachers had written a comment: "Peggy is an excellent student, but she is withdrawn."

Kids on the Honor Roll got their names put in the school newspaper. After my name appeared in the paper, the other kids started to notice me and, of course, after a period of adjustment and the second report card with A's and B's, I dared to have some confidence in myself because of my grades. My junior year I was elected homeroom president.

The only thing that had changed about me was the school bus that carried me to the schoolhouse door. When I was identified by the school bus as a "Gapper," I earned C's and occasional "B"s. How amazing! I don't actually know when I realized the impact the label "Gapper" had on my grades. My memories of those days in high school are a bit fuzzy. When I go back in my mind all I can remember is a lot of disbelief and distrust about what was changing in my life. I think I recognized what had happened to me years later when I took my first sociology class in college.

Through some standardized testing, the Turner Ashby guidance counselor determined that I was third in my class of one hundred and eight students. I was placed in a "college bound" English class simply because of my test scores. It had never crossed my mind that I could go to college. I had settled into the secretarial training track.

Years later, when I graduated from Texas A&M University with my doctor of philosophy degree, I returned to Mt. Clinton Elementary School. The principal was now an old man in his last year before retirement. I introduced myself as Dr. Peggy Shifflett (one of the few times I have used the title in a nonacademic setting). I asked if he remembered me. He said he did remember me and told me my daddy's name. I related to him some of the things I had experienced in his school many years before. He listened and appeared very sad. He explained that times had changed and this would never happen nowadays. I remembered him as a very kind man who sometimes took the "colored" children home in his own car if the weather was rainy and too cool for them to wait on the front lawn until their bus left in the afternoon. One time he took me home when I was sick. I think he was a good man, but one person's compassion cannot change age-old beliefs about the worth of all human beings.

Peggy Ann Shifflett

Part Nine

GIMME THAT OLD TIME RELIGION

The nearer to church the farther from God.
Anonymous

Organized religion didn't come to Hopkins Gap until 1907. On the second Sunday in April of that year, J. Early Suter and W. M. Heatwole held Sunday school at the White Hall School. Early mission work in Hopkins Gap started in approximately 1886. In May of 1908, permission was granted to build a church at a council meeting held at the Bank Mennonite Church. R. S. and L. K. Switzer donated one acre of land for the church and a cemetery. The first service on the land was held in the open before the church was built.(8)

In the beginning there was no regular minister, but the calendar system was used. Ministers in the district took turns coming across the mountain to hold services. In 1947, J. Early Suter became the regular minister for the church.

Most families in Hopkins Gap worshiped God at Gospel Hill Mennonite Church. It was a little white, framed church building on the hill as you entered the Gap crossing Little North Mountain.

During all of my childhood Reverend Suter was the regular minister. His wife was named Pearl. They brought their children up in our church, and eventually their son Daniel became the minister for a short time.

Devotion to the Church

The people in Hopkins Gap were very devoted to the church and admired Reverend Suter and his family; however, they also viewed religion and the Bible in a very practical everyday manner. In fact, a person was judged by whether he read his Bible every night. Aunt Vernie often said about her husband, Charlie: "He sinned all he wanted during the day, but he always read his Bible at night and prayed his sins away. He never went to bed a sinful man." The Bible was used in many other aspects of life. I often heard folks say, "The Bible says, one unjust penny burns up ten."

My dad told me he was visiting a home when a child developed a nosebleed. Because she couldn't read, the mother brought him the Bible with a verse marked with a string. It was a verse about blood. She asked him to read the verse to stop the flow of blood. He read the verse for her.

An effort was made every Sunday to get as many of the Gap children to church as possible. Clarence Payne had a large truck that he drove up and down the road on Sunday morning to pick up the children. At times, according to Uncle Shirley, the truck would arrive at church with thirty or forty children crammed on the back. After church, the same truck sometimes hauled the kids back into the mountains for a community picnic.

This picnic tradition continued into my childhood. Uncle Shirley became the truck driver. He packed us on the back of his dump truck and drove about twenty miles to Feed Stone Mountain where there were large meadows that had been cleared by John I. Myers for grazing his cattle. All along the dusty mountain road there were low hanging tree limbs. Uncle Shirley would slow down and swerve the truck so the small branches scraped over our heads. We thought that was great fun.

Mom, Aunt Ethel and the other women worked hard all day on Saturday to get tons of food ready for this community event. There was cold fried chicken, potato salad, slaw, baked beans, pies, cakes, and the best treat of all, we thought then, store-bought cookies. The kids played ball, hide-and-seek, tag, and red rover, and some of the adults played with us. After the main part of the picnic, the eating, we would gather around the adults and listen to them swap stories. This after church picnic was a tradition that lasted over two generations in Hopkins Gap.

Clarence Payne is driving his truck to church with more than 34 children on the back. Standing in front second from left is Rob Crawford, the minister, Gilbert Morris, Goldie Crawford with her first baby, Ruby. Mom, Dad and Uncle Shirley are among the children on the truck.

Converting the Heathens

Young Mennonite men and women did their missionary work for two years in Hopkins Gap. This, so far, sounds very good and reassuring; however, not all was as it appeared. There were messages, sometimes subtle and sometimes blatant that the "Hopkins Gappers" were heathen and needed to be changed before they could be saved. The church was constantly proselytizing, and never missed an opportunity to convert a "Gapper." When a family

Peggy Ann Shifflett

was having a crisis, the minister or members of the church would visit the home and prey on the occasion to convert the family. Also when a funeral service was held at the church, the service was not in memory of the deceased, but was an effort to convert the people who attended the funeral and especially the grief-stricken family members.

Many funerals in Hopkins Gap were characterized by hysterical displays of grief by the family of the deceased. I never understood the meaning of these displays until I took anthropology classes and watched displays of grief at the loss of a family member by other cultures. The gnashing of teeth and flailing of bodies in these cultures were simply more extreme examples of how people in the Gap grieved their loved ones. I think grieving the loss of a loved one had to be done quickly so that folks could get back to the business of making sure the living continued to survive.

In Hopkins Gap these hysterical displays became the local gossip in the days immediately following the funeral. The expected behaviors ranged from not crying at all to falling over in a dead faint. Not crying at all was explained as the person did not care about the deceased or he or she was staying in control for the rest of the family. Quiet crying and loud sobbing were considered a sign that the person cared but not a lot. He or she could probably get along okay without the deceased. It was the screaming, fainting, and flailing that the audience spent the most time talking about after the funeral. "Did you see (so and so). I am worried about how (he or she) will get along without (so and so)."

Families in the Gap were expected to put their family members away nicely. So a judgment was made about the style of the casket and whether they put the casket in a vault. People would say, "You know, (so and so) really cared about his momma, she was dressed so nice, and the casket cost a pretty penny. He even buried her in a bronze vault. She was put away nice." I am not saying that folks didn't grieve their loved ones. I am saying that the level of grief and how a family buried their dead had an important role in preventing being talked about in the days to come.

The minister didn't know this routine. He thought he was seeing people at their weakest moment, so he always ended the service with a plea to the family to dedicate their lives over to the church before it was too late and they too would lie dead in sin with no chance for salvation.

Many times this method of conversion was successful even if only temporarily. When the emotional crisis was over, most of the new converts changed their minds about being members of the church. In fact, I remember Grandpa Austin's funeral when the minister tried to convert all of us. I was only in my teens, but I considered accepting Jesus Christ as my savior that day but held off on my commitment. I wasn't going to commit in that church anyway. Aunt Vernie sobbed, screamed, fainted, and threw her self across Grandpa Austin's casket as the pallbearers carried it from the church. When the burial portion of the service was over, she turned to one of the people at the funeral, exchanged a joke unrelated to Grandpa Austin, and laughed all the way to the parking lot. So, in my opinion, the Mennonites didn't know the people to whom they were preaching

Keep to Your Own Kind

A distinction was made between those who were "born Mennonite" and those who were "converted Mennonites." The "Gappers" were the converted Mennonites, so we were told we must work very hard and be extra worthy before we could be saved and enter the kingdom of heaven.

Other messages were given to the "converted" Mennonites. The main Mennonite denomination considered the people of Hopkins Gap as appropriate for a missionary training ground for their young people. Every young Mennonite had to spend two years in missionary service. Some young people went to Africa, some went to Asia, and some went to Hopkins Gap.

A young missionary named Sarah came to Hopkins Gap to do her two years of service. Most of her friends had gone to other countries to do their missionary work. During her two years at Gospel Hill, she met a "converted" local young man named Rolf, and they fell in love.

I watched as their fondness for each other developed into pure devotion. Their feelings were obvious as they glanced at each other across the church isle. Why were they not sitting together? That is another part of this story. As time went by, Rolf asked Sarah to go on a date with him. Sarah asked her parents for permission. The answer was a flat, "No." Sarah was told if she did not forget about Rolf, she would be taken out of her missionary service and disinherited by her family. She explained the situation to Rolf, and his heart was broken.

Sarah finished her two years of service, with her eyes and head cast low. Rolf met a local woman named Ada, married her, and raised a family. Sarah never married.

Now, why did Sarah not sit with Rolf in the early, non-threatening days of their friendship? In the Gospel Hill Mennonite Church, women sat on one side of the church and men sat on the other side of the church. I am not sure this was the custom in other Mennonite Churches at that time because I didn't attend others. The separation of men and women by the church aisle always puzzled me; and in my childish fantasies, I imagined that there was a better view of the preacher and the pulpit from the male side of the church. Here you see the religious institution in Hopkins Gap contributing to my acceptance of a female's subordinate position relative to males. I had already accepted that the men's side of the church was the better side in terms of access to the teachings of the church.

I had to know for myself if the male side of the church was better. Some times when the church service ended and people were not paying any attention to me, I would slip into a pew on the male side and stare at the pulpit to see if males had a better view of the minister. Time and time again, I couldn't see any difference. I asked my mother, and she said, "That's just the way things are done." She was no help with this question. She also told me, "I wish you would just behave yourself and stop asking those kinds of questions."

Getting High on Religion

Once or twice a year Gospel Hill Mennonite Church held a revival. Here is where the "Gappers" were hammered to change their sinful ways. This lasted all week with a long church service every night. If a person in Hopkins Gap never went to church during the year, he or she would be seen, at least one night, at the revival. The service was very fast paced with the preacher saying very little about the love of God and the beauty of holiness. Instead he preached about the sinful lives of the congregation and how they would suffer forever in the fire that never dies.

The sermon was loud; and most of the time I thought the preacher was going to lose his voice from screaming. This behavior had a tremendous effect on the audience. Men and women were crying. Roberta Ray and one of the Conley women jumped out off their bench, ran up to the front of the church, danced in the spirit, spoke in the "unknown tongue", and finally fainted in the spirit. Nobody seemed to notice at the time because they were singing "What a Friend We Have in Jesus," "Jesus Savior Pilot Me," or "Rock of Ages." The next day, however, Roberta and the Conley woman were the talk of the community. I never forgot that experience, because I thought they had bumped their heads and killed themselves when they fell over on the hard floor.

Just when I thought the church was going to cave in with all those people jumping and shouting, the preacher lowered his voice and began to sing the hymn of invitation, "Just As I Am, Without One Plea." He invited people to raise their hands and accept Jesus as their savior. Hands went up everywhere including my mother and dad's hand. The majority of people who accepted Jesus went back to their old ways in the next couple of days.

A different preacher was invited to hold the revival services. The favorite revival preacher was Reverend Lloyd Bridges who could describe hell better than anybody on earth. He told us that hell is located somewhere below the ground and is filled with fire seven times hotter than earthly fire. The devil is in human form and very red from being close to hell's fire as he tosses sinners in with his pitchfork. Rev. Bridges told us that during life, the devil appears in many forms — a bottle of whiskey, a dance hall, a promiscuous woman — to tempt humans to sinful ways that will earn them an eternal life in hell. When they die, he literally pitches them into hell with his pitchfork.

I don't know how other people in Hopkins Gap took that message, but I took it literally until I started to think more about the location of hell. Where was the gate? Why had no one discovered it? Heaven was less vividly described than hell, but we were told it is located somewhere beyond the sky. Airplanes were flying pretty high in those days, and nobody had reported seeing heaven. So I asked Mom. She said, "It says in the Bible that anybody who sees heaven will not live to tell about it."

I thought I might be able to trick God or Jesus into letting me know they lived in heaven. So on several occasions, I went out in the yard and asked God or Jesus to step out on a cloud so I could catch a glimpse of one of them. That didn't work. I asked if they would just do something quick with a cloud like move it real fast or shape it a certain way so that I would know they were there. Since I am not famous today, that didn't work either.

As I grew older, I noticed that the minister directed most of his sermon toward the male side of church. When he asked for audience participation in answering a question, only the men raised their hands. I watched for several Sundays and noted that not a single female participated in the service. Could it be that the women didn't read their Bibles, I wondered? Did the women not know the answers to the minister's questions, and if not, why not? I tried again to ask Mom about the situation, and she again told me, "Stop asking about stuff like that. It's just always been that way."

Shortly after that the church invited Reverend Bridges, to come and hold a revival for a week. On the first night, I noticed that he frequently asked for various comments from the audience. I thought to myself, "Here's my chance. I am going to hold up my hand when the preacher asks for something if I have the answer." I was about eleven years old at this time. The very next night Reverend Bridges asked for someone in the audience to give him his favorite Bible verse. I held my hand really high, the minister noted it with a curious stare, and moved over to acknowledge Richard McDorman's upraised hand. Richard quoted John 3:16 "For God so loved the world, he gave his only begotten son for whosoever should believe in him would have everlasting life." Reverend Bridges complimented Richard for his contribution and went on and on for a long time about that particular verse. Then, Reverend Bridges asked for another verse. My hand went high into the air again. Again the preacher gave me a curious glance and ignored my upraised hand. His eyes rested on the men's side of the church, and another man called out a verse. I cannot recall the second verse because by this time I was focused on getting to say my own verse.

The minister went on and on and finally asked for another verse. This time I just yelled out my favorite Bible verse. "Forgive them, Father, for they know not what they do." My mother jerked my hand down and told me to shut up. Reverend Bridges ignored my verse and went on with his sermon.

The next day Reverend Bridges showed up at our house to visit and pray with us. My mother thought it was wonderful that he had stopped in and wanted to talk with her and us kids. He asked us all how we were doing and said he was glad we were coming to the revival. He looked at me for a long time; then he asked me if I was a sinner. My mother was sitting right there. If I had said no, she would have ratted on me. After what seemed like a whole day, I said, "Yes, I am a sinner." Wow that was not a good answer because the Reverend immediately asked, "What kinds of sins do you commit?" This was a very uncomfortable time in my short life because there were some sins that my mother knew about and some that she didn't know about such as sneaking my daddy's cigarette butts and smoking. I had also dipped some snuff and smoked an occasional cigar.

There were times when I had lusty thoughts run through my head. I had called both Mom and Dad sons-of-bitches behind their backs. I had stolen creamsicles out of Aunt Goldie's freezer and ate them on the way home after school. I had climbed the plum tree in Aunt Goldie's back yard and used my slingshot to shoot green plumbs through the neighbor's newspaper as she walked down the road reading. I had put rocks in mash barrels and wasted gallons of moonshine. There was no end to the hidden sins.

It turned out that this was another occasion when I was glad to be a female. I just started crying and the reverend moved on to another subject. I never forgot what an uncomfortable, sweat-producing situation he put me in with my mother. As I got older, I wondered about his motives for asking a young girl what kinds of sins she was committing. I still detest him to this day.

Confirmation Time for Me

The Mennonites expected young people to join the church at twelve years of age. I was told again and again that up until the time that we joined the church any sins we committed were the sins of our parents. I thought that was a pretty good deal. I could sin all day long and mom and dad would have to pay for it. Responsibility for my own sins was not something I considered important. However, when I turned twelve years old, the pressure was on me to walk to the front of the church and accept Jesus Christ as my savior. Every Sunday at the end of the regular sermon, the minister put out the call for people to be saved by having the audience sing the hymn "Just as I Am." The first verse was:

"Just as I am, without one plea,
But that thy blood was shed for me,
And that Thou'd bid'st me come to Thee"
Oh Lamb of God, I come, I come.

It was a sad song, and they sang it over and over. My mother always cried.   That bothered me and made me want to cry; but I had already vowed I would never cry in front of those "born" Mennonites. I made that pledge while I watched my older cousins go to the front of the church to accept Jesus Christ as their savior. They always sobbed and fell to their knees as if in great pain. I wondered why they cried so hard, because I had been told that you couldn't be totally happy until you accepted Jesus. More than once it crossed my mind that they might be crying because they had to give up their "sins," or as I saw it, they couldn't have fun anymore. It was at these time times that I vowed never to cry in front of the "born" Mennonites.

The end of the summer was near, and I had not walked to the front of the church. I would think every Sunday about going up to the front, but I kept remembering Sarah and the men's side of the church.

Several other things that I had learned at church kept creeping into my mind. I remembered the story of Noah's Ark taught to us in Sunday school. The teacher told us about the first time God had destroyed the world because the people were sinners. He had destroyed it by a big flood. He chose Noah to build an ark big enough to hold his family and two of each kind of animal that existed on earth. She gave us little pictures of Noah building the ark and the animals marching up a plank in pairs. Then the rain came, flooded the world, and killed all the bad people. After forty days the rain stopped, the ark landed on a hillside, and Noah planted vineyards. He used the grapes to make wine.

We were told that one day his son Hamm walked in on his father, Noah, while he was lying drunk and naked on his bed. Because Hamm had stared at his father's naked body, he was cursed by having his skin turn black. We were told that was how black

317

people came to be in the world. There was no mention of Noah getting drunk and lying around with no clothes. This made no sense to me. Why didn't Noah get punished for his behavior? At the time I thought maybe it was because he had followed God's orders to build an ark and save all the animals.

I had also noted how people in Hopkins Gap behaved toward one another on Communion Day. On this day, the men washed each other's feet and then kissed each other on the lips. The women did the same. Then, they ate unleavened bread — the body of Christ — and drank grape juice — the blood of Christ. The preacher always warned them that if they took the body and blood of Christ and were sinners, they condemned their souls to eternal hellfire and damnation. I knew these people. The rest of the year, they were cursing and carrying on all kinds of sinful activities. This really bothered me, and when I got older and joined the United Methodist Church, I had a hard time shaking those rules. The Methodists take communion one Sunday every month. I did not take communion for a long time because of what I had heard the preacher say when I was a child.

Also, I watched my mom and dad take communion, and I knew they were sinners. One Sunday we were getting ready for church, and my dad was sitting in the car waiting for us to get in. I was the first to get in the car, and I slipped and fell into the back seat. The noise scared him because he was listening to a sermon on the radio. He drew back his fist to hit me and called me speckled-faced son-of-a-bitch. He was referring to the thick freckles across my nose that I was planning to remove on the very next May first. We all got in the car and off to church we went. I thought that was a pretty awful thing to say to your own child on the way to church. If that wasn't a sin, I didn't know what else would be. I never forgot that day.

Another time we were on the way to church, and we saw a woman lying in the ditch as we went down the mountain. My dad slowed the car to see who she was. Mom looked out the window and said: "It's that old Lesbian, Lorretta Henry, the dirty bitch," and

318

we drove on to church. Later that day, we were at Grandma Molly's house for Sunday dinner and were told that Loretta had been beaten and raped by several local men. When they finished with her they threw her in the ditch up on Little North Mountain. That's where we saw her.

Another time on the way to church, we saw four of the local men, some of them married, having sex with a woman. She was lying back on the trunk of a car, drunk, and they had all taken their turn with her. My mother called her a dirty bitch. Later that day, the same men were bragging about the things they had done to the woman. Nobody condemned them. I was never comfortable with those situations and silently questioned their putting all the blame on the women.

The men were never arrested or charged with any crime. So, you can see that I had some serious doubts about joining the church and even more serious doubts about religion itself. It was just full of contradictions that were never adequately explained to me; and believe me, I asked questions.

Another major reason I did not want to join the church was that I would have to change the way I dressed. When girls joined up, they had to wear what Mom called "cape" dresses. The dress had a loose piece of cloth across the shoulders and down over the front to the waistline. It was long with the hem falling between the knees and ankles. Then, thick hose had to be worn to cover the ankles.

I asked why we had to wear those clothes and was told that women had to dress to keep men from having sinful thoughts. Whoa, I had to know more! The explanation made little or no sense to me. It seemed that women had to cover the contours of their breasts and their ankles, so that men wouldn't look at them and feel lust and therefore commit sin. I thought to myself, if they don't want to sin, they don't have to look. I did not want to dress up in such garb to protect men from themselves.

It was the same with a woman's hair. Once we joined church, we had to wear a little white gauzy bonnet on the back of our heads. Mom told me that a woman's hair was tempting to men, so we had to cover it. This rule seemed even more stupid to me; I was not wearing a "sin-sifter" on my head for people to laugh at me. The young people called the little hats sin-sifters because we heard the older boys talk about how they couldn't kiss or have sex with a "born" Mennonite girl until they got her to take off her little bonnet. Again, I was very troubled by things that made no sense.

I dragged my feet on joining the church until the last possible Sunday for the confirmation to happen. I remember crying while Mom made me put on a new homemade dress, and pulled my braided hair particularly tight. Off to church we went.

I dreaded the end of the sermon when they started singing that song, "Just as I Am." The time came, the song began, and Mom pushed me to walk to the front of the church. I refused. I sat down and wrapped my feet around the pew in front of me. She pulled and pushed; I would not budge. Finally, after what seemed like a month, the song was over. I figured I would be in deep trouble when we got home.

When we did arrive home, my mother asked me why I refused to go to the front of the church and accept Jesus as my savior. I told her I did not want to wear that little bonnet on my head; why should I accept Jesus as my savior and be only a "converted" Mennonite, and besides I was not allowed to talk in church because I was a female. She listened carefully and didn't say much. Three months later, she stopped going to church and never attended that church again.

Part Ten

HOPKINS GAP MEETS THE WORLD

And when the stream
Which overflowed the soul was passed away,
A consciousness remained that it had left,
Deposited upon the silent shore
Of Memory, images and precious thoughts
That shall not die, and cannot be destroyed.
Wordsworth, *The Excursion* (9)

As with all things, time has changed Hopkins Gap. It all started with the "BIG" road and moonshine. The "BIG" road allowed more and more customers to enter Hopkins Gap to purchase moonshine thus increasing the demand for the illegal whiskey. In turn, the supply of moonshine had to increase. This resulted in most all families getting involved in the production process. Ultimately, families began to compete for customers and the community spirit necessary for subsistence survival rapidly unraveled.

Moonshining, because it resulted in young men being sent to prisons outside the state of Virginia had an additional consequence for Hopkins Gap. For the first time, young men who were sent to prison met all kinds of people from different parts of the country. They were exposed to different foods and libraries filled with books. For those like Dad and Uncle Rob, who loved to read, this was an opportunity to know different ways that people lived.

World War II, the Korean War, and the Vietnam War were other major events that resulted in change for Hopkins Gap. Many of the young men served in World War II including Uncle Jim and

Dad. Some lied about their age and enlisted for the adventure of war. Others saw the army as a way to survive because they had been orphaned. Uncle Jim was sixteen when he falsified his age and enlisted. Another cousin went to the army at age fourteen. He went to Germany and fought in the infantry. All of those who fought in World War II returned to Hopkins Gap. Some carried home physical wounds; but each of them returned with psychological wounds. Some turned to alcohol and domestic violence. Others, like my dad, lived with nightmares for the remainder of their lives.

The men from the Gap were not so fortunate in the Korean War. One young man was killed and another remains missing in action to this day. The first military funeral in Hopkins Gap was for the young man, blown to pieces by heavy artillery fire. Nearly everyone in Hopkins Gap including my family attended that funeral to see the twenty-one-gun salute. The young men who returned from Korea were never the same—some physically wounded and all forever changed.

The Vietnam War was easier to avoid by getting married or going to college. My brother, Larry, married Hilda when he received his draft notice. My brother, John, went to fight in Vietnam. He survived physically but struggled for many years with nightmares and flashbacks.

A major economic opportunity came to Hopkins Gap with the poultry industry. Many of the families built poultry houses to raise chickens for the increasing demand for processed chicken and the growth of processing plants in Harrisonburg. Growing chickens at home in the Gap gave the men the freedom to maintain the tradition of hunting squirrels in October, deer in November, and bears in December and early January. They didn't have to keep regular working hours and leave their familiar way of life.

The poultry industry didn't last but a decade or two for most of the Hopkins Gap families. It was soon taken over by large corporations, and the small independent grower who couldn't update his equipment and expand to meet the corporate needs could not stay in business. A few poultry farmers were able to meet the demands of the corporations and continue to raise chickens and turkeys.

In the 1950s the women of Hopkins Gap began to work in the poultry processing plants located twelve miles away in Harrisonburg, and in the sewing factories that had come from the Northeast to take advantage of the cheaper labor available in the South. Working the poultry and sewing plants became a tradition for Hopkins Gap females. When a young woman finished high school or dropped out of school to go to work, her older cousins had a job waiting for her.

The women working outside the home brought major changes to Hopkins Gap families. Initially there were a few cars, and the women rode together to work. Eventually each woman who worked in Harrisonburg had a car of her own. The income from their work was used to remodel their houses. They put in indoor bathrooms, nice kitchens, and bought new furniture. It is interesting to see some of the old traditional houses since they have been remodeled. The original designs were never intended for indoor bathrooms, so modern additions have been attached to the old houses resulting in some architectural originality.

Grandpa Austin's house in 2003, with additions to both sides and the back.

Pre-packaged and processed foods were introduced to Hopkins Gap families for several reasons. With the woman working away from home, she didn't have time to cook "from scratch" as she always had before. Also, eating processed food was a sign of "coming up in the world" — a sign the family had arrived in the changing world and that they had extra money to spend. Processed food tasted better because of the extra salt and additives used to extend its shelf life and make it sell. I might add here that this change brought with it high blood pressure, obesity, and diabetes. These are the major killers of Hopkins Gap people at the present time. While I have been writing this book, I have lost several of my cousins to strokes and heart attacks. During the past month, several cousins have lost their legs due to uncontrolled diabetes. Hopkins Gap has met the outside world but has not always prepared for the changes that came with the meeting.

Ivy Lam Morris, my step-grandmother, in 1970

The most poignant sign of change came to me with a visit in 1970 to my step grandmother, Ivy Lam Morris. After Grandpa John died and left her a young widow, she had moved back home with her parents, Ed and Cass Lam. They lived at the lower end of Hopkins Gap in an old log cabin that had housed several genera-tions before them. The cabin sat at the mouth of the Hog Pens and the creek, Hog Pen Run, flowed past the cabin. Ivy nursed her parents until their deaths. After that she lived alone and kept company with black snakes that lived in her dresser drawers. She remained there until her death in 1978.

It had been a long time since Mom and I had visited her. In 1970 she still spoke broken English interspersed with Pennsylvania Dutch and wore her traditional apron and bonnet. She planted a vegetable garden each summer and "put up" enough food to last over the winter. She fed her table scraps to a pig or threw them into a nearby creek. For many years, all traces of Ivy's daily living returned to the earth leaving no evidence.

During the 1970 visit, Ivy expressed concern that Hog Pen Run was not flowing as it always had, and that it had a bad smell. She walked to the creek with Mom and me, and the problem was immediately obvious to me. Uncle Shirley and Aunt Ethel had taken over her care as she had aged. They either took her to Harri-sonburg with them to buy her groceries when they bought their own, or they brought her groceries home to her. As she had always done, Ivy was throwing her garbage into the creek, but now there were pieces of plastic wrap, tin cans, and jars that Ivy could not wash and reuse. These items interfered with the natural decaying process of her table scraps.

This simple mountain woman had not changed her habit of disposing of her garbage as the world had changed around her. I felt an overwhelming sadness as she showed us the creek. She did not understand what was happening to the little creek that had always been a part of her world.

With new cars and the "BIG" road, the women gradually stopped taking their babies to the granny women to be cured. This process was slow because in 1970 when I was writing my Masters thesis, one of my cousins stopped to have Mom treat her baby for "livergrown." She left our house and took the baby to a medical doctor. The baby recovered, of course, and in this instance, she gave my mother credit for curing the baby. Gradually, my cousins began giving the medical doctor credit for curing the babies. Eventually they used only the medical doctor for their sick babies.

The way Hopkins Gap children were educated changed abruptly one summer. The school administrators announced that the Hopkins Gap children would now be bussed through the lower end of the gap to a new elementary school—Fulks Run Elementary. This made a big difference in the future lives of Hopkins Gap children, as the school bus was no longer labeled the "Gap" bus. The children who went to Fulks Run Elementary were similar to the "Gap" kids in that they also came out of Allegheny Mountain hollows.

With their income, the women were able to dress their children in the latest fad clothing to go to school. Hopkins Gap kids were no longer different when they arrived at school on the first day—no one wore feed sack dresses with twine string holes and feed sack underwear with thick seams where fleas could hide. By this time, the red flannel rag was no longer used in the fall to prevent colds and sore throats.

More of the young Hopkins Gap folks were changing due to their exposure to education outside the Gap. By the 1970's there were many high school graduates, several college graduates, and a few people who went on to achieve even higher degrees. One of the Conley boys became a medical doctor and, of course, there was my choice of a different path from my female cousins. Today, just about every profession has at least one person whose roots are in Hopkins Gap. Not long before her death I accompanied my mother to the hospital in Harrisonburg. She was treated in the radiology department. A young man who was helping her seemed very familiar to me. I knew he was a Conley. When I asked him, I found that he was the son of one of my Conley cousins that I spent Sunday afternoons with while playing in the "Bottom."

The children in Hopkins Gap today depend on video games, and store-bought toys for their fun. They no longer have to create their own toys and games. The baseball games in the Bottom no longer exist; and if the children played baseball together, the goal of the game would be for one team to defeat the opposing team and loudly acclaim victory. There would be an informal declaration of the most valuable player in the game. Individualism and competition have arrived in Hopkins Gap.

Since the young men and women are going to school outside Hopkins Gap and have access to cars, their courtships are indistinguishable from any other place in the country. They meet at school or at a party, they date, they cohabitate for a period of time, and sometimes they get married. When their affection for each other changes as time goes by, they divorce and get remarried. Divorce is accepted as an ordinary event with little or no stigma attached.

The church changed also with the arrival of a new minister after Reverend Earl Suter retired. His name was Isaac Risser. Reverend Risser never placed himself or his family higher or separate from the Hopkins Gap people. He changed the structure of the church and made sure that Hopkins Gap people filled leadership roles in the church.

He became involved in the community in several ways. He is a big strong man with a talent for butchering. So for many years, Reverend Risser was the head butcher at every family's hog killing in the fall. Not only was he the preacher—a role that carried a lot of respect, he became the head butcher—perhaps the second most important role for a man in Hopkins Gap.

Reverend Risser also started several businesses in order to support his own family. He started an egg processing plant and hired many people from Hopkins Gap to work for him. According to my memory, this was not always an easy task for the Reverend. Some Hopkins Gap folks screamed about conflict of interest, and Reverend Risser had to walk a thin line; but overall he made a significant positive difference with his presence in Hopkins Gap.

After he resigned as the minister of Gospel Hill Mennonite church, the newly established local church leaders were able to shape the church to better meet the needs of the Hopkins Gap community. In recent years, the leaders have remodeled the original clapboard church into a modern facility with a community room, modern kitchen, and modern bathrooms. The funds for this change were collected from present church members and past members. Over the years as I have watched the local people take charge of their church, I forgot my unpleasant childhood experiences in the church. So when they called me for a contribution to the remodeling, I gladly contributed to the project.

The use of homeopathic and sympathetic magic faded with the disappearance of the traditional rituals used in treating illnesses. Now more folks get their vegetables from a can rather than grow them in the garden. The signs of the moon and zodiac no longer matter. In recent years Mom and Dad still watched the signs when they planted certain staple vegetables such as potatoes, green beans, and cucumbers. Until her death she warned my brothers and sister to pay attention to the signs; but they plant when they can conveniently take time from their regular jobs rather than wait until the sign is correct. It is interesting, however, to hear my brother explain the failure of his cucumbers to produce a bountiful crop when all things were in favor of a good crop. "I'll bet I planted them in the sign of the posey woman. They just bloomed a lot, but I got no cucumbers," he says.

One year the hams and shoulders from the hog killing didn't take the cure and eventually spoiled. There was talk about the need for cold nights and warmer days. The conclusion was that the weather was good for curing. The final blame was placed on their ignoring the signs of the moon. The cure didn't go "down" into the meat because the butchering was done in the "up" sign of the moon.

The logic of homeopathic and sympathetic magic was passed to my generation, but it stopped there. My brothers and sister did not pass it to their children. So homeopathic and sympathetic magic practices died with Grandma Molly, Uncle Jim, Uncle Charlie, Aunt Lena, Aunt Vernie, and Mom. We still enjoy telling witch stories and making predictions about the weather, but no one lives day to day by the "signs" of the moon. Nobody hangs a dead snake over the fence to bring rain for the crops. The knowledge of homeopathic and sympathetic logic will die with my generation.

The one tradition that has remained intact over the years is the use of colorful language and expressions. Some of the folks in my generation still use the traditional pronunciations and describe events, people, and the world around them with colorful comparisons. Nobody has forgotten Aunt Mavis. All the young men still love to hunt and love to hear and tell wild hunting stories.

Most of the relatives I have written about are dead. Some have died during the writing of this book. Of the relatives, I have written about, the only ones still living today are Uncle Shirley, Aunt Ethel, cousins Ruby, Joyce, George, Herman, Suz, and Sis.

Mom was exactly eighty-one years old when she died. She had numerous strokes and only had use of her right arm the last five years of her life. She was confined to her chair and required around-the-clock assistance. In her memory, children always took care of their elderly parents, and she demanded that we take care of her in her own home. None of us moved far enough away from Hopkins Gap tradition to defy her wishes. It is with great difficulty that my siblings and I negotiated the demands of our work with her demand that we care for her at home. We all changed our lives to meet her demand.

After she refused to move in with one of us and refused to go to an assisted living facility, my sister gave up her job to stay with her during the day, and my sister-in-law, Hilda, left my brother's bed to stay with Mom at night. My two brothers shared the care-giving duties on the weekends to give the women a break. Every third weekend, I left my job and my home to provide around-the-clock care for Mom and to relieve my siblings. This conflict was not necessarily unique to Hopkins Gap people; however, the resolution was probably more difficult for those of us who grew up in two different cultures. Looking back on the struggle to care for Mom, I would not do anything different. It was a long and difficult five years, however, she certainly earned our care and respect for her wishes.

Uncle Shirley is still living at home with Aunt Ethel. He is not well, but Ethel insists on taking care of him at home. He still enjoys telling stories, especially his hunting stories, and has not lost his capacity to make a group of people laugh although they may have heard the stories a hundred or more times. The stories still come out the same after all the years of telling them.

Most of Uncle Shirley's nine children still live in Hopkins Gap. He has two sons who died early in their adult lives. Two of his daughters live in Arkansas. The other children live just across the Shoemaker River from Uncle Shirley's house or within a mile of his home.

This pattern of living reflects the original Hopkins Gap settlement. The Morris's at the upper end of Hopkins Gap are the offspring of Uncle Jim. The Conleys in the middle of Hopkins Gap are several generations of the offspring of Bryan and Edith Conley. Another cluster of Morrises are the offspring of Uncle Gilbert. The Shiffletts are the offspring of Grandpa Austin and Grandma Molly. Branson Conley's offspring are clustered in between the Shiffletts, and Uncle Shirley's home is surrounded by at least three of his sons. The Crawford's no longer have a distinguishable pattern of settlement in Hopkins Gap. However, the Gap's pattern of settlement has continued with my own family. Mom's home set on top of a hill about a mile from the entrance to Hopkins Gap and a quarter of a mile from where Uncle Rob and Aunt Goldie lived until they died. All my siblings live within a mile of Mom's home.

This past Easter Sunday, April 15, 2003, Uncle Shirley turned eighty-six. There was a large family reunion. I took a picture of five generations beginning with Uncle Shirley, and as I was snapping the camera, he was telling the same old wonderful stories to the younger generations surrounding his chair.

Over time many of the men of Hopkins Gap have ingeniously avoided employment outside the community. Today as I reflect on many of my male cousins, I find that they are mainly self-employed. Some are independent truck drivers, owners of heavy equipment, bricklayers, poultry farmers, and mechanics with their own garages in Hopkins Gap. The spring that ran through Grandma Molly's springhouse and kept her milk and butter cool now supports a trout farm owned by one of the Conley men. He supplies restaurants up and down the east coast with fresh mountain trout while remaining independent of employment outside Hopkins Gap. Those who do work outside Hopkins Gap carefully choose their jobs and negotiate time off during hunting season before they take a new job.

At the present time, several families still raise vegetable gardens, process the food for the winter, make apple butter, and kill hogs in the fall for their meat. My own family has maintained these traditions. Every spring the vegetable garden is started with a huge potato planting around March 17—St. Patrick's Day. Then the onions, peas, and greens are planted next because the spring frosts will not kill them. After May 10 the remainder of the vegetables is planted. July and August are the months for processing. Green beans are canned or processed and frozen; cabbage is shredded and fermented in ten-gallon crocks until it becomes sauerkraut. It is not unusual for Hilda to make seventy-five gallons of sauerkraut in one season. It is eaten all winter with mashed potatoes, pinto beans, and chopped hot dogs. She never has any left over sauerkraut by cabbage harvest time the next summer. My brothers faithfully look forward to hog-killing day each November.

In the past five years I have not attended the hog-killing event. The choice to not attend has not been easy for me, but after Dad died I felt that hog killing was not the same. I have finally, since my mid-fifties felt less guilt for staying at my own home away from the cold, wet, November event. I still call at the end of the day to ask Hilda how the day went and if they finished up early. For the past seven years, Hilda has been the woman of the house on hog-killing day since Mom's disability and death. I also couldn't attend hog-killing when I was finishing my education in Texas, but I always knew when the day was and called Mom several times to see how butchering was going for everybody.

All other family members return for the hog-killing event. Each member has a job to do at the butchering. My job was slicing and frying the fresh liver and tenderloin for the big noon meal. I am afraid to ask who has replaced me, because I feel so guilty for abandoning my duty.

A phone call at the end of the first day of deer hunting season assures my family I haven't forgotten them. They proudly relate how many deer my brothers and nephews brought in from the mountains.

Following the more recent Hopkins Gap tradition, as soon as I graduated from high school, Cousin Ruby found me a job in a factory that sewed women's underwear. I rode to work with Cousin Ruby. We ate lunch together and sat together during breaks. It was nice that she helped me, and it was fun to be with her so much; but the work began to take a toll on my body after only three weeks. My job on the assembly line was cutting tiny pink, yellow, and blue rosebuds from endless rolls of buds. I stood all day and clipped buds with scissors—clip, clip, clip—for eight hours. I had two ten-minute breaks and thirty minutes for lunch. I asked for a stool to sit on while I clipped buds. The supervisor, a man who had moved from the Northeast with the factory, said a flat "No." He gave no explanation. I asked Cousin Ruby why he refused, and she told me not to ask any more questions or I would get fired. At the end of each day, my right hand was blistered from using the scissors. By the end of the third week my ankles were swollen at the end of each day, and I had begun to feel like my brain was dying.

One day I told the supervisor that I would be in late the following morning because I had a dentist appointment. The truth was that I had an appointment for an interview with Dr. Elmer Smith at James Madison University for a job as his secretary. After the appointment, Dr. Smith asked me when I could start working for him. I said, "Immediately." He smiled and said, "I'll be in touch soon." I never went back to work at the factory.

After five years, Dr. Smith told me I was too intelligent to spend my life as a secretary. He insisted that I sign up for a college class. After two years of convincing me I could pass a college class, Dr. Smith escorted me to registration. I signed up for an English composition class. When I read William Faulkner's short story, "The Bear," I became hooked on higher learning. Two years later, I resigned my secretarial position and became a full-time student. This was not an easy choice. I had to live at home for the first year, and the men in my family resented me writing papers on the dining room table and practicing my German pronunciation when they could hear me.

There were many moments during my college classes that led to my understanding of Hopkins Gap tradition. The first time I realized that we had experienced poverty was in my introductory sociology class. The professor pointed out the characteristics of the social classes and the consequences of poverty for people who experienced it. When I wrote a paper on the Hopkins Gap community for one of my classes, I grew to understand my daddy for the first time in my life.

However, one moment in my music appreciation class stands out in my mind as having effectively lifted my right foot out of Hopkins Gap. The professor was playing a symphony by Smetna. The movement was "The Moldau." It was the most beautiful music ever to enter my ears. Tears of sadness and joy rolled down my cheeks as I listened. I realized at that moment that I must follow my left foot into the world outside my tiny Appalachian community, Hopkins Gap. I felt sad about leaving the comfort of my family and my community, but I knew I had to hear more of that beautiful music for the rest of my life.

While I have chosen to live my life in the world outside Hopkins Gap, it is easy for me to return there any time. All I have to do is visit Dad and Mom's grave on Veterans Day, Father's Day, Mother's Day, their birthdays, and at Christmas. In plain view of their tombstone are the graves of the people who lived the lives I have recorded in this writing.

The End

REFERENCES

(1) Walker, Alice. 1997. "While Love is Unfashionable." Pp. 95-96 in *Anything We   Love Can be Saved*. New York: Random House.

(2) Sandburg, Carl. 2003. *The Complete Poems of Carl Sandburg: Revised and Expanded Edition*. New York: Harcourt.

(3) Hughes, Langston. 1959. "My People." Pp. 13 in *Selected Poems of Langston Hughes*. New York: Vintage Press.

(4) Smith, Elmer L. 1972. *Valley Folklore: Ballads and Songs of the Shenandoah Valley*. Unpublished collection. Dr. Smith's collection assisted me with the words to this song that I had never written down as I heard it sung.

(5) Rumi, Jelaluddin. 1991. "A Spider Playing in the House." Pp. 55-57 in *Feeling the Shoulder of the Lion: Poetry and Teaching Stories of Rumi*. Translated by Coleman Barks. Putney, VT: Threshold Books.

(6) Kellner, Esther. 1971. *Moonshine: Its History and Folklore*. New York: Bobbs Merrill.

(7) Moliere, Jean-Baptiste. 1898. *The Dramatic Works of Moliere*, Vol. II. Edited by Charles Heron Wall. London: George Bell & Sons.

(8) Risser, Isaac. 1976. *Gospel Hill Mennonite Church and Community Directory*.

(9) Wordsworth, William. 1888. *The Complete Poetical Works*. London: Macmillan Co.

.

Peggy Ann Shifflett (B.A., M.A. James Madison University, 1969; Ph.D. Texas A&M University, 1980) is Professor of Sociology and Chair of the Department of Sociology and Anthropology at Radford University where she has taught since 1986. Professor Shifflett has studied anthropology and folklore at the University of North Carolina, Chapel Hill. A native of Rockingham County in Virginia's Allegheny Mountains, she has devoted her life to understanding rural America and Appalachia. She has studied the aged in rural Appalachia, Appalachian folklore, sociology of the family, and rural homeless children.

Other publications by Professor Shifflett include *The Fundamentals of Sociology* (2003) (with Dr. Kevin Everett) and *Essential Readings in Sociology* (2004) (edited with Dr. Kevin Everett) and many research publications in the journals of her discipline. Professor Shifflett can be contacted for questions or comments at pshiffle@radford.edu.